Artificial Intelligence-Based System for Gaze-Based Communication

This book focuses on the artificial neural network-based system for gaze-based communication. It covers the feasible and practical collaboration of human–computer interaction (HCI) in which a user can intuitively express tasks using gaze-based communication. It will target the vast applications of gaze-based communication using computer vision, image processing, and artificial intelligence.

Artificial Intelligence-Based System for Gaze-Based Communication introduces a novel method to recognize the implicit intention of users by using nonverbal communication in combination with computer vision technologies. A novel HCI framework is developed to enable implicit and intuitive gaze-based intention communications. This framework allows the users to intuitively express their intention using natural gaze cues. The book also focuses on robot caregiving technology, which can understand the user's intentions using minimal interactions with the user. The authors examine gaze-based tracking applications for the assisted living of elderly people. The book examines detailed applications of eye-gaze communication for real-life problems. It also examines the advantages that most people can handle gaze-based communications because it requires very little effort, and most of the elderly and impaired can retain visual capability.

This book is ideally designed for students, researchers, academicians, and professionals interested in exploring and implementing gaze-based communication strategies and those working in the field of computer vision and image processing.

Artificial Intelligence-Based System for Gaze-Based Communication

B.G.D.A Madhusanka, Sureswaran Ramadass,
Premkumar Rajagopal, and H.M.K.K.M.B. Herath

CRC Press
Taylor & Francis Group
Boca Raton London New York

CRC Press is an imprint of the
Taylor & Francis Group, an **informa** business

Designed cover image: © Shutterstock

First edition published 2024
by CRC Press
2385 NW Executive Center Drive, Suite 320, Boca Raton FL 33431

and by CRC Press
4 Park Square, Milton Park, Abingdon, Oxon, OX14 4RN

CRC Press is an imprint of Taylor & Francis Group, LLC

© 2024 B.G.D.A Madhusanka, Sureswaran Ramadass, Premkumar Rajagopal and
H.M.K.K.M.B. Herath

ISBN: 978-1-032-43823-8 (hbk)
ISBN: 978-1-032-44792-6 (pbk)
ISBN: 978-1-003-37394-0 (ebk)

DOI: 10.1201/9781003373940

Typeset in Times LT Std
by Apex CoVantage, LLC

Contents

Preface

Welcome to Gaze-Based Communication with Artificial Intelligence. This book explores the intersection of artificial intelligence (AI) and gaze-based communication technologies, which is a fascinating topic. One of the most compelling applications of AI is its ability to improve communication for people with varying abilities. Gaze-based communication has emerged as an essential interaction channel for individuals with motor impairments or other conditions that impede conventional communication. Integrating AI into gaze-based communication systems has opened new frontiers, allowing for more natural and efficient ways for individuals to express themselves, interact with technology, and connect with the world.

Step into the world of Gaze-Based Communication with Artificial Intelligence, a captivating exploration of the fusion between AI and gaze-based communication technologies. Delving into this intriguing subject, the book highlights the remarkable application of AI in enhancing communication for people with diverse abilities. Gaze-based communication has emerged as a pivotal avenue for individuals facing motor impairments or other challenges in conventional communication. By integrating AI into these systems, new horizons have unfolded, enabling individuals to express themselves, interact with technology, and connect with the world more naturally and efficiently.

The theoretical underpinnings and practical applications of AI-powered gaze-based communication are examined in this book. This book aims to offer insightful information to all readers, whether they are skilled AI practitioners, researchers in human–computer interaction, clinicians working with patients with communication disorders, or those interested in how AI might improve human communication.

Significant features of this book

- An examination of the fundamentals of gaze-based communication and its relevance in various contexts.
- Extensive explanations of AI techniques and algorithms that enable gaze-based communication systems.
- Case studies and real-world examples demonstrating AI's successful applications in enhancing communication through the gaze.
- Ethical considerations and guidelines for designing user-centric and inclusive AI-powered communication solutions.
- Future trends and opportunities involving AI and gaze-based communication.
- As we embark on this journey, I would like to thank the experts, researchers, and individuals who have contributed to the development of AI and gaze-based communication. Their efforts have paved the way for a more inclusive and interconnected global community.

I hope this book is useful for comprehending, designing, and implementing AI-driven solutions for gaze-based communication. Collectively, let us harness the power of technology to facilitate meaningful and expressive interactions for all.

Dr. (Eng.) B.G.D.A Madhusanka
8 August 2023

Biography of Authors

Dr. B.G.D.A Madhusanka graduated from The Open University of Sri Lanka (OUSL) in 2010 with Bachelor of Technology Honors in Mechatronics Engineering. He also won the gold medal for outstanding performance for Best Student in Mechatronics Engineering. In 2017, he completed his M.Sc. in Industrial Automation at the University of Moratuwa. In 2022, he graduated with his Ph.D. in Informatics from the Malaysian University of Science and Technology. He has been Lecturer in the Department of Mechanical Engineering at OUSL for the last 12 years. Currently, he is working as Senior Lecturer and Head of the Department of Mechatronics Engineering at SLTC Research University. Dr. Achintha Madhusanka has focused on service robotics, the Internet of Things, human–computer interaction, computer vision, and artificial intelligence. Also, his Soft Robotics research team was the runner-up in the high school soft robotics design competition at Harvard University in 2016. He holds professional membership at the Institution of Engineers Sri Lanka, the Engineering Council Sri Lanka, and the Institute of Electrical and Electronics Engineers.

Prof. Sureswaran Ramadass is Professor Emeritus at the Malaysian University of Science and Technology. He is also Chief Scientist at Crystalviewhd Sdn Bhd (formerly known as NLTVC Sdn Bhd). Crystalviewhd is a Next-Generation Internet Communications research and development company. He is also Managing Director of VHGlobal Sdn Bhd. VHGlobal is an advanced patient-centric global telehealth platform. Before this, he was Founding Director and Professor at the National Advanced IPv6 Centre of Excellence (NAV6), Universiti Sains Malaysia. He obtained his BsEE/CE (Magna Cum Laude) and master's degree in Electrical and Computer Engineering from the University of Miami in 1987 and 1990. He graduated as a top student in the College of Engineering. He obtained his Ph.D. from Universiti Sains Malaysia in 2000 while serving as a full-time faculty in the School of Computer Sciences.

Prof. Dr. Premkumar Rajagopal received his B.B.A. from RMIT University in Melbourne in the year 1996, followed by an MBA from Universiti Utara Malaysia in 1998. In 2006, he graduated with his PhD in Management from Universiti Sains Malaysia 2006. The current President of Malaysia University of Science and Technology, Prof. Dr. Premkumar is a detail-oriented University President with 14 years of experience in the Education Industry. He has a proven ability to build relationships and maintain partnerships with academic partners internationally to increase overall productivity and grow profit channels. He is a results-oriented CEO with a demonstrated record of streamlining operations, increasing profits, and maximizing market penetration. He has been an experienced Logistics and Supply Chain Manager with over 12 years of experience in the electronic industry (INTEL TECHNOLOGY). His professional experience has also earned him the recognition from International Supply Chain Education Alliance (ISCEA), as he was appointed the President of the ISCEA Malaysia in 2020.

Eng. H.M.K.K.M.B. Herath currently holds the position of Lecturer at the Faculty of Engineering, situated within the Sri Lanka Technological Campus (SLTC). His expertise lies in various course modules, including robotics engineering, autonomous systems, and embedded system development. In 2019, Herath achieved a significant academic milestone by completing his Bachelor of Technology Honors in Mechatronics Engineering from The Open University of Sri Lanka. Driven by his passion for continuous growth and knowledge, Herath pursued further studies, and in 2023, he attained his Master of Science degree from the University of Moratuwa in Sri Lanka. His professional affiliations include memberships at esteemed organizations such as the Institution of Engineers Sri Lanka, the Engineering Council Sri Lanka, and the Institute of Electrical and Electronics Engineers.

He has also taken on the role of an editorial advisor for several book projects and actively participated in course development at OUSL. Herath is Lead Coordinator of the Computational Intelligence and Robotics Research Group at SLTC. His research interests span across diverse fields, encompassing biomedical engineering, brain–computer interfacing, human–computer interaction, and artificial intelligence.

1 Introduction to Gaze-Based Communication

Gaze-based communication is a type of communication that uses eye movements as a means of conveying messages. It is often used by individuals with limited or no speech, such as motor neuron disease, cerebral palsy, or other conditions affecting verbal communication. Gaze-based communication systems typically use specialized hardware, such as eye trackers, to detect and interpret the user's eye movements [1]. The user can then select items on a computer screen, for example, by fixating on them or by using other eye movements such as blinks or saccades. Gaze-based communication can be used in various settings, including home, school, and the workplace [2, 3]. It can allow individuals with communication disabilities to interact with others, express their needs and preferences, and participate in social activities. There are several types of gaze-based communication systems, ranging from simple systems that use only eye movements to more complex systems that incorporate speech synthesis, predictive text, and other features to help users communicate more efficiently and effectively [4–6].

Gaze-based communication can assist individuals with activities of daily living (ADLs) in various ways [7–10]. ADLs are the basic daily tasks that individuals perform to care for themselves, such as bathing, dressing, grooming, and eating [11–14]. Here are some examples of how gaze-based communication can be used to assist with ADLs:

1. Choosing clothing: A gaze-based communication system can allow an individual to select clothing items from a digital wardrobe on a computer screen using eye movements. This can help the individual to maintain independence and make choices about their appearance.
2. Eating and drinking: A gaze-based communication system is used to select food and drink items from a digital menu on a computer screen. The system can indicate when the individual is finished eating or drinking.
3. Personal hygiene: A gaze-based communication system can assist with brushing teeth or washing hands. The system can display images or videos that guide the individual through the steps of the task, and the individual can indicate when they have completed each step.
4. Household tasks: A gaze-based communication system can control appliances such as lights, fans, and televisions. The system can also control devices such as wheelchairs or scooters, allowing individuals to move around their homes independently.

DOI: 10.1201/9781003373940-1

Overall, gaze-based communication can be a powerful tool to help individuals with communication disabilities maintain independence and participate in ADLs. It allows them to express their needs and preferences, make choices, and interact with their environment meaningfully.

Gaze-based communication can also assist caregivers in performing their tasks more efficiently and effectively. Caregiving tasks include assisting with ADLs, monitoring vital signs, administering medications, and providing emotional support [15–17]. Here are some examples of how gaze-based communication can be used to assist with caregiving tasks:

1. Monitoring vital signs: A gaze-based communication system can display vital signs such as heart rate, blood pressure, and oxygen saturation. This allows caregivers to monitor the individual's health status and respond quickly to changes.
2. Administering medications: A gaze-based communication system can display medication schedules and reminders. Caregivers can also use the system to document when medications have been given and track any side effects.
3. Providing emotional support: A gaze-based communication system can display images, videos, or messages that provide emotional support to the individual. For example, a caregiver can use the system to display a message of encouragement or a favorite song to help the individual feel more positive.
4. Providing instruction: A gaze-based communication system can display instructional videos or images that guide the caregiver through wound care or physical therapy exercises. This can help ensure that the tasks are performed correctly and consistently.

Gaze-based communication can be a valuable tool for caregivers in providing high-quality care to individuals with communication disabilities [18, 19]. It allows them to monitor health status, administer medications, provide emotional support, and provide instruction efficiently and effectively.

Eye-gaze-based communication is essential because it allows individuals with communication disabilities to express themselves, participate in social interactions, and maintain independence in daily activities. Without this type of communication, individuals with communication disabilities may be unable to engage with their environment fully and may experience social isolation, frustration, and a decreased quality of life. Here are some specific reasons why eye-gaze-based communication is essential:

1. Expression: Eye-gaze-based communication allows individuals with communication disabilities to express their thoughts, feelings, and needs. This is essential for maintaining social connections and relationships, as well as for advocating for oneself and making decisions about one's own life.
2. Independence: Eye-gaze-based communication allows individuals with communication disabilities to maintain independence in daily activities. It will enable them to make choices, control their environment, and perform tasks without constant assistance.

3. Access: Eye-gaze-based communication provides access to education, employment, and other opportunities that may be unavailable to individuals with communication disabilities without this type of communication.
4. Improved quality of life: Eye-gaze-based communication can improve the overall quality of life for individuals with communication disabilities by reducing frustration, increasing social interactions, and promoting greater participation in daily activities.

Eye-gaze-based communication is crucial for individuals with communication disabilities to express themselves, maintain independence, and participate fully in society. It can significantly affect their quality of life and well-being [20–22].

Eye tracking is essential for several reasons, including research, usability testing, and the development of gaze-based communication technology [23]. Here are some specific reasons why eye tracking is necessary:

Research: Eye tracking can provide insights into how humans perceive and interact with their environment. Researchers can study visual attention, decision-making, and cognitive processes by analyzing eye movements. This can lead to a better understanding of human behavior and inform the development of new technologies and products.

Usability testing: Eye tracking can be used to evaluate the usability of websites, software applications, and other digital interfaces. By analyzing where users look and how long they spend on different interface elements, designers can identify usability issues and make improvements to enhance the user experience.

Marketing and advertising: Eye tracking can be used to measure the effectiveness of marketing and advertising materials. By analyzing where people look and how long they spend looking at different elements of an advertisement, marketers can optimize the design to maximize engagement and impact.

Gaze-based communication: Eye tracking is essential for developing gaze-based communication technology. By tracking eye movements, individuals with communication disabilities can use their gaze to control a computer or other device, allowing them to communicate and interact with their environment in new ways.

Eye tracking is a valuable tool for understanding human behavior, improving usability, and developing new technologies. It has a wide range of applications in research, industry, and healthcare and is likely to become even more critical as technology advances [24].

Human eye movements refer to the involuntary and voluntary movements of the eyes. There are several types of eye movements [24], each of which serves a different function. Here are some examples of human eye movements:

1. Saccades: These rapid eye movements occur when the eyes shift their focus from one object to another. Saccades are necessary for scanning and exploring the environment.
2. Smooth pursuit: This type of eye movement occurs when the eyes follow a moving object. Smooth pursuit is essential for tracking moving objects and maintaining visual fixation.

3. Vergence: This is the movement of the eyes in opposite directions to maintain binocular vision (the ability to see with both eyes). Vergence is essential for depth perception.
4. Nystagmus: This is an involuntary movement of the eyes, characterized by repetitive back-and-forth or circular motions. Nystagmus can be a symptom of neurological conditions or other underlying health issues.
5. Fixation: This is maintaining a steady gaze on a stationary object. Fixation is essential for visual acuity and reading, and other visual tasks.

The study of human eye movements, also known as oculomotor research, has important implications for various fields, including neuroscience, psychology, and engineering [25, 26]. Researchers can gain insights into cognition, perception, and human behavior by understanding how the eyes move and interact with the environment.

1.1   THE EYES

The human eye is a complex organ responsible for detecting light and transmitting visual information to the brain [27]. It is composed of several interconnected structures, including the following:

1. Cornea: The transparent, outermost eye layer covers the iris and pupil. It helps to focus light as it enters the eye.
2. Iris: This is the colored part of the eye that controls the size of the pupil, which regulates the amount of light that enters the eye.
3. Pupil: This is the circular open in the center of the iris that allows light to enter the eye.
4. Lens: This is a clear, flexible structure behind the iris and pupil. It helps to focus light onto the retina.
5. Retina: This is the innermost layer of the eye, containing photoreceptor cells that convert light into electrical signals transmitted to the brain through the optic nerve.
6. Optic nerve: This bundle of nerve fibers carries visual information from the retina to the brain.
7. Vitreous humor: This gel-like substance fills the space between the lens and the retina.
8. Sclera: This is the white outer layer of the eye that provides structural support and protects the delicate inner structures.
9. Conjunctiva: This thin, transparent membrane covers the front of the eye and lines the inside of the eyelids.
10. Eyelids and eyelashes: This helps to protect the eye from dust and other foreign objects and helps to spread tears across the surface of the eye to keep it moist.

The eyeball has six muscles arranged in three pairs, each pair having an antagonistic relationship with the other [28–32]. These muscles work together to move the

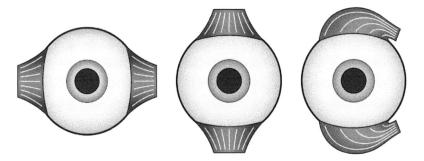

FIGURE 1.1   Three pairs of muscles can compensate for all movements of the head.

eyeball in different directions and maintain proper alignment. The six muscles are as follows:

1. The medial rectus muscle moves the eyeball inward toward the nose. It works in opposition to the lateral rectus muscle.
2. The lateral rectus muscle moves the eyeball outward, away from the nose. It works in opposition to the medial rectus muscle.
3. The superior rectus muscle moves the eyeball upward toward the forehead. It works in opposition to the inferior rectus muscle.
4. The inferior rectus muscle moves the eyeball downward toward the chin. It works in opposition to the superior rectus muscle.
5. Superior oblique muscle moves the eyeball downward and outward, away from the nose. It works in opposition to the inferior oblique muscle.
6. The inferior oblique muscle moves the eyeball upward and outward toward the ear. It works in opposition to the superior oblique muscle.

These six muscles are controlled by three cranial nerves: the oculomotor nerve, the trochlear nerve, and the abducens nerve. The proper coordination of these muscles is essential for appropriate eye movement and binocular vision, as shown in three pairs of antagonistic muscles, as shown in Figure 1.1.

Figure 1.2 depicts the simplified schematics of the eye. The working process of the eye can be broken down into several steps. First, the light enters the eye through the cornea, which is the transparent, outermost layer of the eye. The cornea helps to focus the light as it enters the eye [33]. Second, the iris, the colored part of the eye, controls the size of the pupil, which is the circular opening in the center of the iris. The pupil regulates the light that enters the eye [34]. Third, the light passes through the lens, a clear, flexible structure behind the iris and pupil. The lens further focuses the light onto the retina. Next, the retina is the innermost layer of the eye and contains photoreceptor cells called rods and cones. These cells convert the light into electrical signals sent to the brain through the optic nerve. Finally, the brain then interprets these electrical signals as visual images. It is important to note that the vision process is not solely dependent on the eye. The brain plays a crucial role

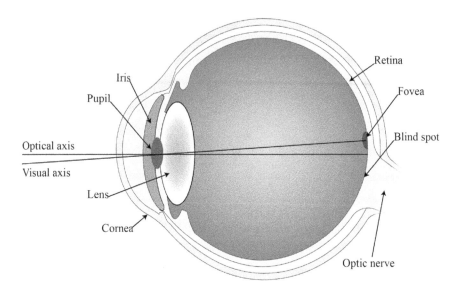

FIGURE 1.2   Schematics of the eye.

in interpreting the electrical signals sent from the eye and constructing the visual images we perceive [35]. Additionally, other structures in the eye, such as the muscles that control eye movement and the tear glands that produce tears, also contribute to the overall function of the eye.

Compensation eye movement is a term used to describe the eye movements that occur to maintain visual stability when the head or body is in motion. These eye movements are essential for preventing the visual scene from becoming blurred or distorted during head or body movements. There are two main types of compensation eye movements:

1. The vestibule-ocular reflex (VOR) is a reflexive eye movement that responds to head movements. It works by stabilizing the eyes on a visual target during head movements. When the head turns to the left, the eyes move in the opposite direction to keep the visual target focused.
2. Optokinetic reflex (OKR): The OKR is a reflexive eye movement that responds to large-scale visual motion. It works by moving the eyes toward the motion to maintain visual stability. For example, if you are looking out the window of a moving train, the OKR will move your eyes toward the passing scenery to prevent blurring.

These two reflexive eye movements work together to ensure that the visual scene remains stable during head and body movements. The VOR maintains visual stability during quick head movements, while the OKR compensates for slower or larger-scale visual motion. Compensation eye movements are a crucial component of our visual system and essential for maintaining visual stability during movement.

Without them, the visual scene would appear blurry and distorted during minor head or body movements.

When the eye moves, it rotates around its center rather than changing its position in space. This rotation is called a saccade, a quick, jerky eye movement that allows us to scan our environment and shift our focus from one object to another. The length of a saccade is defined by the angle of the pupil's normal at the beginning and end of the movement. The pupil's normal is an imaginary line that runs perpendicular to the cornea's surface, which is the transparent front part of the eye. By measuring the angle of the pupil's normal at the beginning and end of the saccade, we can determine the length and direction of the eye movement. The length of a saccade can vary depending on the task and the individual [36]. For example, saccades are typically shorter and more frequent when reading, while saccades may be longer and less frequent when scanning a room. Understanding the mechanics of saccadic eye movements is essential for studying visual perception and eye movement disorders and developing technologies such as eye-tracking systems.

1.2 EYE TRACKERS

Eye trackers are devices that monitor and record eye movements [37]. They use sensors that detect the eye's position and track its movements in real time [38]. Eye-gaze trackers are a type of eye tracker used to monitor and record the direction of a person's gaze [39]. They use sensors that detect the eye's position and track its movements in real time, allowing researchers and developers to determine where a person is looking on a computer screen or other display [40]. There are several types of eye-gaze trackers, including the following:

1. Pupil-based eye trackers: These eye trackers use the position and movement of the pupil to determine where a person is looking.
2. Corneal reflection eye trackers: These eye trackers use the reflection of light off the cornea to determine where a person is looking.
3. Electrooculography (EOG) eye trackers: These eye trackers use electrodes placed around the eye to detect changes in the electrical field generated by eye movements.

Eye-gaze trackers are used in a variety of applications, including the following:

- Human–computer interaction (HCI): Eye-gaze trackers are used to develop technologies that allow people to control computers and other devices using only their gaze.
- Neuroscience: Neuroscience eye-gaze trackers study visual perception, attention, and cognitive processes.
- Marketing and advertising: Eye-gaze trackers are used in marketing and advertising to study behavior and preferences.
- Sports training: Eye-gaze trackers analyze and improve athletes' visual attention and decision-making skills.

Generally, eye-gaze trackers are powerful tools for studying and understanding human behavior and cognition and for developing new technologies and applications that can improve our ADL [41]. Also, there are several types of eye trackers [42–47], including:

1. Video-based eye trackers: These eye trackers use a camera to capture images of the eye and track its movements based on the position of the pupil and the reflection of infrared light.
2. Infrared-based eye trackers: These eye trackers use infrared light to illuminate the eye and track its movements based on the pupil's position and the infrared light's reflection.
3. Magnetic-based eye trackers: These eye trackers use sensors to detect changes in the magnetic field around the eye and track its movements based on these changes.

Video-based eye trackers are a type of eye tracker that uses a camera to capture images of the eye and track its movements based on the position of the pupil and the reflection of infrared light. They are among the most common eye trackers widely used in research, medicine, and HCI, as shown in Figure 1.3. Video-based eye trackers work by illuminating the eye with infrared light and capturing images of the eye using a camera [48]. The position of the pupil is then tracked based on the reflection of the infrared light, allowing researchers and developers to determine the direction and speed of eye movements in real time. Video-based eye trackers are versatile tools in various applications, from basic research to commercial product development. They provide valuable insights into the complex mechanisms of eye movements and visual perception and new opportunities for improving HCI and other fields.

Mobile eye trackers are designed to be used in natural [49] and real-world environments [50], as shown in Figure 1.4. They are portable and lightweight and can be

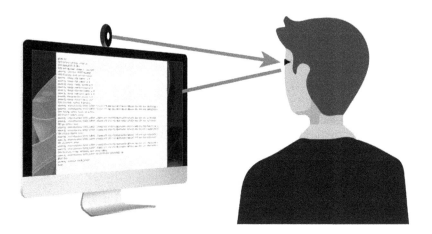

FIGURE 1.3 Stationary eye trackers, one stand-alone system and one integrated into a display.

FIGURE 1.4 Eye-tracking glasses.

worn like glasses, allowing researchers and developers to monitor and record eye movements in various settings. Mobile eye trackers use a combination of video-based, infrared-based, or magnetic-based tracking technologies to determine the position and movement of the eye. They typically have a small camera mounted on the eyeglasses frame, which captures images of the eye and tracks its movements in real time. Overall, mobile eye trackers provide a powerful tool for studying and understanding human behavior and cognition in natural environments and for developing new technologies and applications to improve our daily lives. They can revolutionize various fields, from sports training to market research to clinical assessment.

Video-based eye trackers can also be used for iris detection, which is the process of identifying and recognizing an individual based on the unique pattern of their iris [51, 52]. This is often used as a security measure, as the pattern of the iris is unique to each individual and can be challenging to replicate. Video-based eye trackers for iris detection work by capturing images or video of the eye and analyzing the unique pattern of the iris. The iris is the colored part of the eye that surrounds the pupil, and it contains a unique pattern of ridges, furrows, and freckles that can be used to identify an individual. To capture images of the iris, video-based eye trackers use a specialized camera to capture high-resolution eye images. The camera is typically equipped with infrared illumination, which allows it to capture clear images of the iris even in low-light conditions [53]. The images are then processed using specialized software that analyzes the unique pattern of the iris and compares it with a database of known iris patterns. Overall, video-based eye trackers for iris detection provide a highly accurate and secure method of identifying and verifying individuals. They are becoming increasingly popular in various applications, as they offer a high level of security and can be integrated with existing access control and security systems.

Video-based eye trackers can also be used for pupil detection, which is the process of tracking the movement and dilation of the pupil over time. Pupil detection is often used in research settings to study visual perception, cognitive processing, and other aspects of human behavior—video-based eye trackers for pupil detection work using a camera to capture high-resolution eye images. The camera is typically equipped with infrared illumination, which allows it to capture clear images of the pupil even in low-light conditions. The images are then processed using specialized software that detects the location and size of the pupil in each image. By tracking the movement and dilation of the pupil over time, video-based eye trackers for pupil detection can provide valuable insights into a range of cognitive and perceptual processes [54]. For example, they can be used to study attention, arousal, and emotional responses to visual stimuli. They can also be used to track the reading process, as changes in pupil size and movement are associated with changes in cognitive load and processing difficulty. Overall, video-based eye trackers for pupil detection provide a powerful tool for studying and understanding human behavior and cognition. They can revolutionize various fields, from gaming and virtual reality (VR) to healthcare and education.

The vector from the glint to the center of the pupil is a crucial factor in calculating the gaze direction in many eye-tracking systems, as shown in Figure 1.5. This vector is used to determine the position of the eye in space, which can then be used to calculate the direction of gaze relative to a particular point or object of interest. The glint is a small, bright reflection that appears on the eye's surface due to the reflection of an external light source. By tracking the movement of the glint over time, eye-tracking systems can determine the position and orientation of the eye in space [55]. The center of the pupil is also tracked, and the vector between the glint

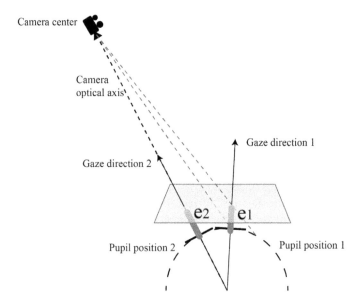

FIGURE 1.5 The vector from the glint to the pupil's center is the basis for calculating the gaze direction.

and the center of the pupil is used to calculate the direction of the gaze [56]. In some eye-tracking systems, additional information, such as the position of the head and the distance between the eyes, is also used to calculate the direction of the gaze [57, 58]. This information is typically captured using sensors such as accelerometers and gyroscopes, which can detect the orientation and movement of the head. Once the direction of gaze has been calculated, it can be used for various applications, including HCI, VR, and medical diagnosis. Eye-tracking systems are becoming increasingly sophisticated and accurate, and they have the potential to revolutionize a variety of fields in the coming years.

The corneal reflection method of eye tracking typically requires head fixation to keep the eye stable. However, alternative approaches allow for free movement of the head and eyes, making them more suitable for HCI applications [59–61]. One such approach is known as the video-based eye-tracking method. Video-based eye-tracking systems use cameras to capture high-resolution images of the eye, which are then processed to track the pupil's movement and other eye features. By analyzing the changes in the position and size of these features over time, video-based eye-tracking systems can accurately determine the direction of gaze without the need for head fixation. Another approach that allows for free movement is using multiple cameras to capture eye images from different angles. This approach, known as the multi-camera eye-tracking method, allows for the accurate tracking of eye movements even when the head is in motion. Combining the images from multiple cameras can provide a three-dimensional (3D) reconstruction of the eye and accurately determine the direction of gaze. In recent years, there has been significant progress in developing eye-tracking systems that can be used in HCI applications without needing head fixation. These systems are becoming increasingly sophisticated and accurate, and they have the potential to revolutionize the way we interact with computers and other digital devices [62].

1.3   EYE-GAZE TRACKING FOR HCI

Eye-gaze tracking has become an increasingly popular method for HCI in recent years. By tracking the direction of gaze, computers and other digital devices can interpret a user's intentions and respond accordingly, creating a more natural and intuitive interface. One of the primary applications of eye-gaze tracking in HCI is assistive technology for people with disabilities [59]. For example, individuals with physical disabilities that limit their ability to use traditional input devices such as a mouse or keyboard can use eye-gaze tracking to control a computer or other digital device. Eye-gaze tracking can also be used in virtual and augmented reality (AR) applications, allowing users to interact with digital environments using their eyes. Eye-gaze tracking can also improve the user experience in various other applications. For example, eye-gaze tracking can be used in web browsing to determine which parts of a web page a user looks at, allowing for more effective targeting and user interface design [63]. In gaming, eye-gaze tracking can be used to control game characters or to create a more immersive gaming experience [64]. Overall, eye-gaze tracking has the potential to revolutionize the way we interact with computers and other digital devices. As eye-tracking technology improves, we can expect widespread adoption in various applications, leading to more natural and intuitive interfaces that better meet users' needs.

Gaze prediction is an essential aspect of eye-gaze tracking for HCI. It uses algorithms and machine learning techniques to predict where users will likely look next based on their previous eye movements and other contextual factors. By predicting the user's gaze, computers and other digital devices can anticipate the user's intentions and respond more quickly and effectively. There are several approaches to gaze prediction in eye-gaze tracking for HCI [60]. One common approach is to use statistical models based on eye movement data from previous users. These models can be trained to predict where users are likely to look next based on factors such as the layout of the user interface, the position of the user's head, and the user's previous eye movements. Another approach is to use machine learning techniques to learn patterns in the user's eye movements and predict their gaze based on these patterns [65]. This approach typically involves training a neural network or other machine learning algorithm on a large dataset of eye movement data and then using the trained model to predict the user's gaze in real time. Recent advances in deep learning have led to significant improvements in gaze prediction accuracy. For example, researchers have developed deep learning models that can predict gaze with an accuracy of over 90%, even in challenging conditions such as low light or when the user is wearing glasses. Overall, gaze prediction is an essential aspect of eye-gaze tracking for HCI, and it has the potential to significantly improve the user experience in a wide range of applications. As eye-tracking technology continues to improve, we can expect to see more advanced and accurate gaze prediction algorithms that further enhance the capabilities of eye-gaze tracking for HCI.

Eye-gaze tracking for HCI has the potential to significantly improve the quality of life for people with disabilities or other challenges that make traditional input devices difficult to use. Some of the daily living activities that can be made easier with eye-gaze tracking include the following [66–68]:

1. Communication: Eye-gaze tracking can control speech-generating devices, allowing people with conditions such as cerebral palsy or Amyotrophic Lateral Sclerosis (ALS) to communicate more easily with others.
2. Writing and typing: People with difficulty using their hands can use eye-gaze tracking to write emails, documents, and other text-based content.
3. Web browsing: Eye-gaze tracking can navigate the Internet and browse websites more efficiently, allowing people with disabilities or other challenges to access information and stay connected.
4. Gaming: Eye-gaze tracking can be used to control game characters, allowing people with disabilities or other challenges to enjoy video games and participate in online gaming communities.
5. Environmental control: Eye-gaze tracking can control devices such as lights, televisions, and other home appliances, allowing people with disabilities to live more independently.

Also, eye-gaze tracking has the potential to significantly improve the quality of life for people with disabilities or other challenges. As eye-tracking technology continues to improve, we can expect to see more advanced and accessible applications that further enhance the capabilities of eye-gaze tracking for daily living activities.

1.4 APPROACH TO IMPLICIT INTENTION UNDERSTANDING WITH EYE-GAZE COMMUNICATION

Implicit intention understanding with eye-gaze communication refers to the ability of computers or other devices to interpret a person's gaze and use it to infer their intentions [69]. This approach is based on the idea that people often look at the things they are interested in or want to interact with, and by analyzing their gaze patterns, computers can infer their intentions. One application of implicit intention understanding with eye-gaze communication is in the field of human–robot interaction (HRI) [70–72]. In HRI, robots and other autonomous systems must understand human intentions to interact with people effectively. By analyzing a person's gaze, a robot can infer their interest and adjust their behavior accordingly.

Another application of implicit intention understanding with eye-gaze communication is in assistive technology. For example, a computer system with eye-gaze tracking technology can interpret a person's gaze to control devices such as wheelchairs, prosthetic limbs, or home automation systems.

There are several challenges associated with an implicit intention understanding with eye-gaze communication. One challenge is that people often look at things for various reasons, and it can be difficult for computers to infer their intentions accurately. Another challenge is that multiple factors can influence gaze patterns, such as cultural norms, personal preferences, and visual distractions, making it challenging to interpret a person's gaze accurately.

Despite these challenges, significant progress has been made in developing algorithms and machine learning techniques for implicit intention understanding with eye-gaze communication. As eye-tracking technology continues to improve, we can expect to see more advanced and accurate systems capable of interpreting a person's gaze and using it to infer their intentions in various applications.

Developing algorithms and machine learning techniques for implicit intention understanding with eye-gaze communication involves several steps, including data collection, feature extraction, classification, and validation. Several machine learning algorithms can be used for implicit intention understanding with eye-gaze communication, including decision trees, support vector machines (SVMs), neural networks, and so on. The choice of algorithm depends on the specific task or application and the characteristics of the eye-tracking data being used. Overall, developing algorithms and machine learning techniques for implicit intention understanding with eye-gaze communication is an active area of research, with many promising approaches being developed and tested in various applications. As eye-tracking technology continues to improve, we can expect to see more advanced and accurate systems capable of inferring a person's intentions based on their gaze behavior.

Wearable technology can play a significant role in caring for older people and helping them with their ADLs. Wearable devices, such as smartwatches, fitness trackers, and other health monitoring devices, can provide important information about an older person's health status, activity levels, and daily routines. This information can be used to develop personalized care plans and to monitor the person's health and well-being over time. For example, wearable devices can track an older person's physical activity, sleep patterns, and heart rate, providing valuable information about their overall health status. This information can be used to develop exercise plans, monitor medication adherence, and identify potential health issues before they become serious.

Wearable devices can also provide reminders and prompts for essential tasks, such as taking medication, attending medical appointments, or completing daily routines. These reminders can be delivered through smartwatch notifications or other wearable devices, helping older people stay on track and maintain their independence.

In addition to these practical applications, wearable technology can provide significant social and emotional benefits for older people. For example, wearable devices can facilitate social connections, such as video calls with family members or friends, or provide access to entertainment and educational content. Overall, wearable technology has the potential to play a significant role in caring for older people and supporting their ADLs, improving their quality of life, and helping them maintain their independence for longer. As technology advances, we expect to see even more innovative and effective wearable devices designed specifically for older people and their unique needs.

Implicit purpose communication with older adults doing ADLs in a homecare setting with a caregiver can involve various technologies and communication strategies. The goal of implicit purpose communication is to provide support and assistance to older adults while minimizing the feeling of intrusion and dependence on the caregiver. One technology that can be used for implicit purpose communication is a smartwatch or other wearable device that tracks an older person's activity levels, medication schedule, and additional important health information. This information can be shared with the caregiver, who can provide support and reminders without constantly checking in or disrupting the older person's routine.

Another communication strategy that can be used is nonverbal cues, such as eye gaze or facial expressions, to indicate when the older person needs assistance or experiencing discomfort or pain. Caregivers can be trained to recognize these cues and respond appropriately, providing the necessary support without the older person having to ask for help explicitly. In addition to these technologies and communication strategies, it is also essential to establish a trusting and respectful relationship between the caregiver and the older person. This can involve regular communication and check-ins, involving the older person in decision-making and allowing them to maintain a sense of independence and control over their daily routine. Overall, implicit purpose communication with older adults in a homecare setting with a caregiver involves using various technologies and communication strategies to provide support and assistance while minimizing intrusion and maintaining the older person's independence and autonomy.

Implicit intention recognition refers to the ability of technology or systems to infer a user's intentions without the user explicitly stating them. In the context of HCI, implicit intention recognition can facilitate natural and seamless interaction between humans and machines, improving the overall user experience. One way to achieve implicit intention recognition is through sensors, such as cameras, microphones, or other biometric sensors, which can capture user behavior and physiological responses. Machine learning algorithms can then analyze these data and infer the user's intentions based on patterns and correlations. For example, in eye-gaze communication, implicit intention recognition can be used to understand what the user is looking at and their intended action. By analyzing patterns in eye movement and gaze behavior, machine learning algorithms can predict the user's intentions, allowing for more natural and intuitive interaction with the system. Implicit intention recognition can also be used in other HCI contexts, such as speech recognition, gesture recognition, or brain–computer interfaces (BCIs). Sensors and machine learning algorithms can infer the user's intentions based on their speech, movements, or brain activity. Overall, implicit intention recognition has the potential to significantly improve the usability and effectiveness of HCI systems by allowing for more natural and seamless interaction between humans and machines.

Eye-gaze movements can be analyzed to infer the user's intention in ADLs. By tracking the user's eye movements, it is possible to understand where the user is looking, how long they are looking at something, and whether they are actively engaging with the environment or passively observing. In the context of ADL, eye-gaze tracking can infer the user's intention when performing tasks such as cooking, cleaning, or using technology. For example, tracking the user's gaze as they prepare a meal makes it possible to understand their ingredients, how much they are using, and their intended outcome. This information can assist or guide, such as recipe suggestions or reminding the user to check the oven temperature. Eye-gaze tracking can also understand the user's attention and engagement level during ADL. For example, by tracking the user's gaze while they watch a video or read a book, it is possible to understand whether they are actively engaged with the content or if their attention is starting to wane. This information can then be used to adjust the content or provide recommendations to keep the user engaged and interested. Eye-gaze tracking is a powerful tool for inferring the user's intention in ADL. By analyzing the user's gaze behavior, it is possible to gain insights into their goals, attention, and engagement, which can be used to provide personalized assistance and support.

The visual attention system is a network of cognitive processes and brain regions that allow us to selectively attend to relevant information in our environment. It lets us focus on specific aspects of our surroundings while filtering out irrelevant or distracting information. The visual attention system can be broadly divided into two types: Bottom-up and top-down attention. The saliency of sensory stimuli, such as color, contrast, or motion, drives bottom-up attention. When a sensory stimulation is particularly salient, it automatically attracts our attention, even if we are unaware. Top-down attention, on the other hand, is guided by our goals, expectations, and prior knowledge. It allows us to selectively attend to information relevant to our current task or goal, even if it is not particularly salient. For example, suppose we are looking for a specific object in a cluttered scene. In that case, we can use top-down attention to filter out irrelevant information and focus on the relevant aspects of the scene. The visual attention system involves a complex interplay of neural networks and brain regions, including the parietal cortex, frontal cortex, and superior colliculus. These regions work together to process and prioritize sensory information, allocate attentional resources, and guide our behavior in response to visual stimuli.

The visual attention system is critical in our ability to interact with and navigate our environment. It allows us to selectively attend to relevant information, filter out distractions, and respond quickly and efficiently to changing situations.

1.5   MOTIVATION

The motivation behind using eye-gaze tracking in HCI is to provide a more natural and intuitive way for users to interact with digital devices. Traditional input devices such as mice, keyboards, and touchscreens can be cumbersome and unintuitive for specific tasks, especially for people with physical disabilities or impairments. Eye-gaze tracking provides an alternative input method that allows users to control devices simply by looking at different parts of the screen or interface. This technology can benefit individuals with motor impairments or conditions such as motor neuron disease or cerebral palsy who may have difficulty using traditional input methods. In addition to improving accessibility, eye-gaze tracking can enhance the user experience in other ways. For example, it can enable a more precise and efficient selection of targets on a screen, especially for small or complex interfaces. It can also enable more natural and context-sensitive interactions, such as using gaze direction to trigger specific actions or adjust settings based on the user's attentional state. Overall, the motivation behind using eye-gaze tracking in HCI is to provide a more natural, intuitive, and accessible way for users to interact with digital devices.

1.6   BACKGROUND TO THE STUDY

The use of eye-gaze tracking in HCI has been an active area of research for several decades, with numerous studies investigating its potential applications and benefits. One of the earliest applications of eye-gaze tracking in HCI was in human factors engineering. It was used to study visual attention and task performance in complex environments such as aviation and military operations. Researchers used eye tracking to measure the time it takes to complete tasks, the frequency of visual fixations, and the visual search patterns of users as they interacted with various interfaces. In recent years, eye-gaze tracking has gained popularity for improving accessibility in digital environments, especially for people with motor impairments or disabilities. Studies have shown that eye-gaze tracking can be used as an alternative input method for controlling devices, selecting targets on a screen, and navigating complex interfaces. Eye-gaze tracking has also been used in cognitive psychology and neuroscience research to investigate visual attention and perception. Researchers have used eye tracking to study visual search, attentional bias, and the effects of distractors on task performance. In addition to its research applications, eye-gaze tracking has been integrated into various commercial products and services, such as assistive technologies for people with disabilities, video games, and advertising analytics. Overall, the background research on eye-gaze tracking in HCI has demonstrated its potential as a versatile and powerful tool for improving user experience and accessibility in digital environments.

The eye-gaze-intended inference technique is a powerful tool that can enhance human awareness and enable communication for persons with disabilities using an HCI interface. This technique is beneficial for individuals who have difficulty with traditional forms of communication, such as speech or hand gestures. The eye-gaze-intended inference technique involves eye-tracking technology to determine where a person looks on a screen or interface. By analyzing the patterns of eye movements and gaze direction, the system can infer the user's intended actions or communication. For example, if the user looks at a particular button or icon on the screen, the system can interpret that as a command to perform a certain action. This technique has many benefits for persons with disabilities. It allows them to communicate more effectively with human aids, as they can use their eyes to convey their intentions and needs. It also enhances their independence, as they can use the system to control various devices and interfaces without relying on others for assistance. Overall, the eye-gaze-intended inference technique is an innovative and powerful tool that can potentially transform the lives of persons with disabilities. With the help of this technique, they can communicate more effectively and participate more fully in society.

The eye-gaze technique can offer many benefits for persons with disabilities. Eye-gaze technology uses sensors to track the movement of a person's eyes and determine where they are looking. This technology can benefit individuals with difficulty with traditional forms of communication, such as speech or hand gestures, due to physical or neurological impairments. Here are some of the benefits that the eye-gaze technique can offer for persons with disabilities:

1. Improved communication: For individuals who cannot speak or use their hands to communicate, the eye-gaze technique can provide a way to convey their thoughts and intentions. By looking at specific objects or symbols on a screen, the person can communicate with others and express their needs and desires.

2. Increased independence: The eye-gaze technique can give individuals with disabilities more independence by allowing them to control devices and interfaces without needing assistance from others. They can use their eyes to navigate menus, select options, and perform other tasks that would otherwise require assistance.

3. Enhanced mobility: Eye-gaze technology can control wheelchairs and other mobility devices, giving individuals with mobility impairments more control over their movements and greater freedom to explore their environment.

4. Improved education and learning: The eye-gaze technique can provide educational materials and interactive learning experiences for individuals with disabilities. By tracking their eye movements, the system can determine their level of engagement and adjust the content to meet their needs.

5. Better quality of life: By providing new ways to communicate, interact with the world, and participate in society, the eye-gaze technique can improve the overall quality of life for persons with disabilities. It can help them feel more included, empowered, and engaged.

REFERENCES

1. Majaranta, P., & Bulling, A. (2014). Eye tracking and eye-based human–computer interaction. Advances in Physiological Computing, 39–65.
2. Singh, H., & Singh, J. (2012). Human eye tracking and related issues: A review. International Journal of Scientific and Research Publications, 2(9), 1–9.
3. Karlsson, P., Allsop, A., Dee-Price, B. J., & Wallen, M. (2018). Eye-gaze control technology for children, adolescents and adults with cerebral palsy with significant physical disability: Findings from a systematic review. Developmental Neurorehabilitation, 21(8), 497–505.
4. Giannopoulos, I., Kiefer, P., & Raubal, M. (2015, August). GazeNav: Gaze-based pedestrian navigation. In Proceedings of the 17th International Conference on Human-Computer Interaction with Mobile Devices and Services (pp. 337–346). New York: Association for Computing Machinery.
5. Galante, A., & Menezes, P. (2012). A gaze-based interaction system for people with cerebral palsy. Procedia Technology, 5, 895–902.
6. Wanjari, A. G., & Khode, S. S. (2014). The eye gaze communication system. International Journal of Research Studies in Science, Engineering and Technology [IJRSSET], 1(1), 4–9.
7. Madhusanka, B. G. D. A., & Ramadass, S. (2021). Implicit intention communication for activities of daily living of elder/disabled people to improve well-being. IoT in Healthcare and Ambient Assisted Living, 325–342.
8. Madhusanka, B. G. D. A., Ramadass, S., Rajagopal, P., & Herath, H. M. K. K. M. B. (2022). Attention-aware recognition of activities of daily living based on eye gaze tracking. In Internet of Things for Human-Centered Design: Application to Elderly Healthcare (pp. 155–179). Singapore: Springer Nature.
9. Sunny, M. S. H., Zarif, M. I. I., Rulik, I., Sanjuan, J., Rahman, M. H., Ahamed, S. I.,. . . Brahmi, B. (2021). Eye-gaze control of a wheelchair mounted 6DOF assistive robot for activities of daily living. Journal of NeuroEngineering and Rehabilitation, 18(1), 1–12.
10. Li, S., & Zhang, X. (2017). Implicit intention communication in human–robot interaction through visual behavior studies. IEEE Transactions on Human-Machine Systems, 47(4), 437–448.
11. Mlinac, M. E., & Feng, M. C. (2016). Assessment of activities of daily living, self-care, and independence. Archives of Clinical Neuropsychology, 31(6), 506–516.
12. Lawton, M. P., & Brody, E. M. (1969). Assessment of older people: Self-maintaining and instrumental activities of daily living. The Gerontologist, 9(3_Part_1), 179–186.
13. Edemekong, P. F., Bomgaars, D. L., Sukumaran, S., & Levy, S. B. (2020). Activities of daily living (ADLs). Treasure Island: StatPearls Publishing.
14. Hetz, S. P., Latimer, A. E., & Martin Ginis, K. A. (2009). Activities of daily living performed by individuals with SCI: Relationships with physical fitness and leisure time physical activity. Spinal Cord, 47(7), 550–554.
15. Saari, M., Xiao, S., Rowe, A., Patterson, E., Killackey, T., Raffaghello, J., & Tourangeau, A. E. (2018). The role of unregulated care providers in home care: A scoping review. Journal of Nursing Management, 26(7), 782–794.
16. Chi, N. C., & Demiris, G. (2017). The roles of telehealth tools in supporting family caregivers: Current evidence, opportunities, and limitations. Journal of Gerontological Nursing, 43(2), 3–5.
17. Reinhard, S. C., Given, B., Petlick, N. H., & Bemis, A. (2008). Supporting family caregivers in providing care. Patient safety and quality: An evidence-based handbook for nurses.
18. Mahmud, S., Lin, X., & Kim, J. H. (2020, January). Interface for human machine interaction for assistant devices: A review. In 2020 10th Annual Computing and Communication Workshop and Conference (CCWC) (pp. 0768–0773). Las Vegas, NV: IEEE.

19. Linse, K., Aust, E., Joos, M., & Hermann, A. (2018). Communication matters—pitfalls and promise of hightech communication devices in palliative care of severely physically disabled patients with amyotrophic lateral sclerosis. Frontiers in Neurology, 9, 603.

20. Borgestig, M., Al Khatib, I., Masayko, S., & Hemmingsson, H. (2021). The impact of eye-gaze controlled computer on communication and functional independence in children and young people with complex needs–a multicenter intervention study. Developmental Neurorehabilitation, 24(8), 511–524.

21. Majaranta, P. (Ed.). (2011). Gaze Interaction and Applications of Eye Tracking: Advances in Assistive Technologies: Advances in Assistive Technologies. Hershey, PA: IGI Global.

22. Holmqvist, E., Thunberg, G., & Peny Dahlstrand, M. (2018). Gaze-controlled communication technology for children with severe multiple disabilities: Parents and professionals' perception of gains, obstacles, and prerequisites. Assistive Technology, 30(4), 201–208.

23. Jacob, R. J., & Karn, K. S. (2003). Eye tracking in human-computer interaction and usability research: Ready to deliver the promises. In The mind's eye (pp. 573–605). North-Holland.

24. Schütz, A. C., Braun, D. I., & Gegenfurtner, K. R. (2011). Eye movements and perception: A selective review. Journal of Vision, 11(5), 9–9.

25. Radach, R., Hyona, J., & Deubel, H. (Eds.). (2003). The Mind's Eye: Cognitive and Applied Aspects of Eye Movement Research. North Holland: Elsevier.

26. Monty, R. A., & Senders, J. W. (Eds.). (2017). Eye movements and psychological processes (Vol. 22). Routledge.

27. Marr, D. (2010). Vision: A computational investigation into the human representation and processing of visual information. MIT press.

28. Carpi, F., & De Rossi, D. (2007). Bioinspired actuation of the eyeballs of an android robotic face: Concept and preliminary investigations. Bioinspiration & Biomimetics, 2(2), S50.

29. Walls, G. L. (1962). The evolutionary history of eye movements. Vision Research, 2(1–4), 69–80.

30. Miller, J. M., & Robinson, D. A. (1984). A model of the mechanics of binocular alignment. Computers and Biomedical Research, 17(5), 436–470.

31. Chin, S. (2018). Visual vertigo: Vertigo of oculomotor origin. Medical Hypotheses, 116, 84–95.

32. Shaad, D. J. (1938). Binocular vision and orthoptic procedure. Archives of Ophthalmology, 20(3), 477–501.

33. Sliney, D. H. (1983). Eye protective techniques for bright light. Ophthalmology, 90(8), 937–944.

34. Tomy, R. M. (2019). Pupil: Assessment and diagnosis. Kerala Journal of Ophthalmology, 31(2), 167–171.

35. Calder, A. J., Lawrence, A. D., Keane, J., Scott, S. K., Owen, A. M., Christoffels, I., & Young, A. W. (2002). Reading the mind from eye gaze. Neuropsychologia, 40(8), 1129–1138.

36. Hayhoe, M. M., Bensinger, D. G., & Ballard, D. H. (1998). Task constraints in visual working memory. Vision Research, 38(1), 125–137.

37. Ware, C., & Mikaelian, H. H. (1986, May). An evaluation of an eye tracker as a device for computer input2. In Proceedings of the SIGCHI/GI Conference on Human Factors in Computing Systems and Graphics Interface (pp. 183–188). New York: Association for Computing Machinery.

38. Wang, D., Mulvey, F. B., Pelz, J. B., & Holmqvist, K. (2017). A study of artificial eyes for the measurement of precision in eye-trackers. Behavior Research Methods, 49, 947–959.

39. Venugopal, D., Amudha, J., & Jyotsna, C. (2016, May). Developing an application using eye tracker. In 2016 IEEE International Conference on Recent Trends in Electronics, Information & Communication Technology (RTEICT) (pp. 1518–1522). Bangalore: IEEE.
40. Kassner, M., Patera, W., & Bulling, A. (2014, September). Pupil: An open source platform for pervasive eye tracking and mobile gaze-based interaction. In Proceedings of the 2014 ACM International Joint Conference on Pervasive and Ubiquitous Computing: Adjunct Publication (pp. 1151–1160). New York: Association for Computing Machinery.
41. Duchowski, A. T. (2002). A breadth-first survey of eye-tracking applications. Behavior Research Methods Instruments and Computers, 34(4), 455–470.
42. Holmqvist, K., & Blignaut, P. (2020). Small eye movements cannot be reliably measured by video-based P-CR eye-trackers. Behavior Research Methods, 52, 2098–2121.
43. Wyatt, H. J. (2010). The human pupil and the use of video-based eyetrackers. Vision Research, 50(19), 1982–1988.
44. Blignaut, P. (2014). Mapping the pupil-glint vector to gaze coordinates in a simple video-based eye tracker. Journal of Eye Movement Research, 7(1).
45. Coetzer, R. C., & Hancke, G. P. (2014). Development of a robust active infrared-based eye tracker. IET Computer Vision, 8(6), 523–534.
46. Price, D., Kaputa, D., Sierra, D. A., & Enderle, J. (2009, April). Infrared-based eye-tracker system for saccades. In 2009 IEEE 35th Annual Northeast Bioengineering Conference (pp. 1–2). Cambridge, MA: IEEE.
47. Kim, D., Richards, S. W., & Caudell, T. P. (1997, March). An optical tracker for augmented reality and wearable computers. In Proceedings of IEEE 1997 Annual International Symposium on Virtual Reality (pp. 146–150). Albuquerque, NM: IEEE.
48. Mantiuk, R., Kowalik, M., Nowosielski, A., & Bazyluk, B. (2012). Do-it-yourself eye tracker: Low-cost pupil-based eye tracker for computer graphics applications. In Advances in Multimedia Modeling: 18th International Conference, MMM 2012, Klagenfurt, Austria, January 4–6, 2012. Proceedings 18 (pp. 115–125). Berlin, Heidelberg: Springer.
49. Mokatren, M., Kuflik, T., & Shimshoni, I. (2018). Exploring the potential of a mobile eye tracker as an intuitive indoor pointing device: A case study in cultural heritage. Future Generation Computer Systems, 81, 528–541.
50. Asan, O., & Yang, Y. (2015). Using eye trackers for usability evaluation of health information technology: A systematic literature review. JMIR Human Factors, 2(1), e4062.
51. Holmqvist, K., Örbom, S. L., & Zemblys, R. (2022). Small head movements increase and colour noise in data from five video-based P–CR eye trackers. Behavior Research Methods, 54(2), 845–863.
52. Youssef, R. A. B., Mohamed, A. S. E. D., & Ahmed, M. K. (2007, March). Reliable high speed iris detection for video based eye tracking systems. In The International MultiConference of Engineers and Computer Scientists (IMECS) (pp. 1877–1882). Hong Kong: IAENG.
53. Wildes, R. P. (1997). Iris recognition: An emerging biometric technology. Proceedings of the IEEE, 85(9), 1348–1363.
54. Tatler, B. W., Kirtley, C., Macdonald, R. G., Mitchell, K. M. A., & Savage, S. W. (2014). The active eye: Perspectives on eye movement research. Current trends in eye tracking research, 3–16.
55. Blignaut, P. (2013, October). A new mapping function to improve the accuracy of a video-based eye tracker. In Proceedings of the South African Institute for Computer Scientists and Information Technologists Conference (pp. 56–59). New York: Association for Computing Machinery.
56. Hennessey, C., Noureddin, B., & Lawrence, P. (2006, March). A single camera eye-gaze tracking system with free head motion. In Proceedings of the 2006 Symposium on Eye Tracking Research & Applications (pp. 87–94). New York: Association for Computing Machinery.

57. Valenti, R., Sebe, N., & Gevers, T. (2011). Combining head pose and eye location information for gaze estimation. IEEE Transactions on Image Processing, 21(2), 802–815.

58. Todorović, D. (2006). Geometrical basis of perception of gaze direction. Vision Research, 46(21), 3549–3562.

59. Sharma, A., & Abrol, P. (2013). Eye gaze techniques for human computer interaction: A research survey. International Journal of Computer Applications, 71(9).

60. Chandra, S., Sharma, G., Malhotra, S., Jha, D., & Mittal, A. P. (2015, December). Eye tracking based human computer interaction: Applications and their uses. In 2015 International Conference on Man and Machine Interfacing (MAMI) (pp. 1–5). Bhubaneswar: IEEE.

61. Morimoto, C. H., Koons, D., Amit, A., Flickner, M., & Zhai, S. (1999, October). Keeping an eye for HCI. In XII Brazilian Symposium on Computer Graphics and Image Processing (Cat. No. PR00481) (pp. 171–176). Campinas: IEEE.

62. Li, D., Babcock, J., & Parkhurst, D. J. (2006, March). openEyes: A low-cost head-mounted eye-tracking solution. In Proceedings of the 2006 Symposium on Eye Tracking Research & Applications (pp. 95–100). New York: Association for Computing Machinery.

63. Móro, R., Daráz, J., & Bieliková, M. (2014, September). Visualization of gaze tracking data for UX testing on the web. In HT (Doctoral Consortium/Late-breaking Results/Workshops).

64. Munoz, J., Yannakakis, G. N., Mulvey, F., Hansen, D. W., Gutierrez, G., & Sanchis, A. (2011, August). Towards gaze-controlled platform games. In 2011 IEEE Conference on Computational Intelligence and Games (CIG'11) (pp. 47–54). Seoul: IEEE.

65. Klaib, A. F., Alsrehin, N. O., Melhem, W. Y., Bashtawi, H. O., & Magableh, A. A. (2021). Eye tracking algorithms, techniques, tools, and applications with an emphasis on machine learning and Internet of Things technologies. Expert Systems with Applications, 166, 114037.

66. Eid, M. A., Giakoumidis, N., & El Saddik, A. (2016). A novel eye-gaze-controlled wheelchair system for navigating unknown environments: Case study with a person with ALS. IEEE Access, 4, 558–573.

67. Ishiguro, Y., Mujibiya, A., Miyaki, T., & Rekimoto, J. (2010, April). Aided eyes: Eye activity sensing for daily life. In Proceedings of the 1st Augmented Human International Conference (pp. 1–7). New York: Association for Computing Machinery.

68. Fathi, A., Li, Y., & Rehg, J. M. (2012). Learning to recognize daily actions using gaze. ECCV (1), 7572, 314–327.

69. Zander, T. O., Gaertner, M., Kothe, C., & Vilimek, R. (2010). Combining eye gaze input with a brain–computer interface for touchless human–computer interaction. International Journal of Human–Computer Interaction, 27(1), 38–51.

70. Admoni, H., & Scassellati, B. (2017). Social eye gaze in human-robot interaction: A review. Journal of Human-Robot Interaction, 6(1), 25–63.

71. Saran, A., Majumdar, S., Short, E. S., Thomaz, A., & Niekum, S. (2018, October). Human gaze following for human-robot interaction. In 2018 IEEE/RSJ International Conference on Intelligent Robots and Systems (IROS) (pp. 8615–8621). Madrid: IEEE.

72. Shishkin, S. L., Zhao, D. G., Velichkovsky, B. M., & Isachenko, A. V. (2017). Gaze-and-brain-controlled interfaces for human-computer and human-robot interaction. Psychology in Russia, 10(3), 120.

2 Assistive Technologies to Implicit Intention Communication Through Visual Behavior for Daily Living Activities

Implicit intention communication through visual behavior refers to using nonverbal cues, such as body language, facial expressions, and gestures, to convey intentions or messages to others. Daily living activities include reaching for a utensil at the dinner table to indicate a desire to eat or pointing toward an object to indicate a need or preference [1]. Implicit intention communication through visual behavior is an essential aspect of human communication, as it allows individuals to communicate with others without the need for explicit verbal communication [2]. This can be particularly useful when verbal communication [3] is difficult or impossible, such as in noisy environments or with individuals who speak a different language. Examples of visual behaviors [4] that can be used to communicate intentions in daily living activities include the following:

1. Pointing: Pointing to an object can indicate a desire or preference for that object.
2. Facial expressions: Smiling, frowning, or making other facial expressions can communicate emotions and intentions.
3. Eye contact: Making eye contact can indicate interest, attention, or a desire for communication.
4. Gestures such as waving, nodding, or shaking the head can convey messages needed for verbal communication.
5. Body language: Posture, positioning, and body movement can convey messages about intentions, emotions, and attitudes.

Overall, implicit intention communication through visual behavior is a powerful tool for individuals to communicate their needs, desires, and intentions in daily activities. By paying attention to nonverbal cues, individuals can better understand and communicate with each other, even when verbal communication is not possible or practical.

DOI: 10.1201/9781003373940-2

2.1 BACKGROUND OF IMPLICIT INTENTION COMMUNICATION THROUGH VISUAL BEHAVIOR

The concept of implicit intention communication through visual behavior has been studied in various fields, including psychology, sociology, and linguistics [5]. It is a fundamental aspect of human communication in all cultures and societies. Studies have shown that nonverbal communication makes up a significant portion of all human communication, with some estimates suggesting that up to 93% of communication is nonverbal [6–8]. Nonverbal communication can convey various messages, including emotional states, attitudes, intentions, and social status [9, 10]. Researchers have identified nonverbal cues that can communicate preferences through visual behavior, including facial expressions, eye contact, body language, and gestures [11–13]. These cues can convey various intentions, from expressing interest or attraction to indicating a need or desire [14]. Implicit intention communication through visual behavior is essential when verbal communication may be difficult or impossible, such as in noisy environments or with individuals who do not speak the same language. It is also necessary for individuals with communication difficulties, such as those with autism [15] spectrum disorders, who may rely heavily on nonverbal cues to communicate their intentions and needs.

Overall, the study of implicit intention communication through visual behavior highlights the importance of nonverbal communication in human interaction and emphasizes the need for individuals to be aware of and skilled in reading and using nonverbal cues in daily living activities.

2.1.1 NONVERBAL COMMUNICATION

Nonverbal communication refers to using nonverbal cues, such as body language, facial expressions, tone of voice, and gestures, to convey messages to others [16]. It is a fundamental aspect of human communication and plays a significant role in how we interact and understand each other.

Nonverbal cues can convey a wide range of information, including emotions, attitudes, intentions, and social status. For example, a smile can indicate happiness or friendliness, while a frown can indicate sadness or disapproval. The tone of voice can convey emotions, such as anger or sarcasm, while gestures can share messages, such as pointing to an object to indicate a desire for it [17, 18]. Nonverbal communication can also complement verbal communication, reinforcing or contradicting verbal statements. For example, if someone says they are happy, but their facial expression is sad, the nonverbal cues may suggest that their verbal statement is not genuine [19].

Nonverbal communication is essential when verbal communication may be difficult or impossible [20], such as in noisy environments or with individuals who do not speak the same language. It is also necessary for individuals with communication difficulties, such as those with autism spectrum disorders [21, 22], who may rely heavily on nonverbal cues to communicate their intentions and needs. Nonverbal communication is a complex and multifaceted aspect of human interaction that plays a crucial role in understanding and connecting [23]. Understanding and reading, and using nonverbal cues, are important to effective communication. This research has identified several different types of nonverbal communication.

2.1.1.1 Facial Expression

Facial expressions are a form of nonverbal communication that can convey various emotions and social cues. For example, a smile can signal happiness or friendliness, while a frown can indicate sadness or disapproval [24–27]. Other facial expressions, such as raised eyebrows or a furrowed forehead, can show surprise or concern [28, 29]. Facial expressions [30, 31] are essential to human communication and can provide valuable information about a person's emotional state, intentions, and attitudes.

2.1.1.2 Gestures

Gesture recognition uses computer algorithms and technology to interpret and understand human gestures and movements [32, 33]. This can involve analyzing data from cameras or other sensors to detect and recognize specific gestures or body movements, such as hand signals, facial expressions, or body posture [34, 35].

Gesture recognition technology has many applications [36], including gaming, healthcare, robotics, and security systems. For example, gesture recognition can be used to control video games or VR systems [37] using hand movements or body posture or to monitor and analyze patient activities in healthcare settings to help with rehabilitation or injury prevention [38]. In security systems, gesture recognition can identify and track individuals based on their body movements or facial expressions. Overall, gesture recognition is an exciting area of research and development with many potential applications in various fields.

2.1.1.3 Paralinguistic

Paralinguistics [39] refers to the nonverbal aspects of spoken communication, such as tone of voice, pitch, volume, and pace [40]. These paralinguistic cues can convey meaning and emotion not given through words. For example, a speaker's tone of voice and intonation can indicate sarcasm or excitement, while their pace and volume can indicate urgency or emphasis [41]. Paralinguistic cues are essential to communication and can significantly influence how a message is perceived and understood. They can also convey social cues and establish a rapport with others. For example, a friendly tone of voice and a warm greeting can develop a positive relationship with someone. In contrast, a stern tone of voice can convey authority or disapproval. Understanding and effectively using paralinguistic cues can significantly enhance communication and help build stronger relationships.

2.1.1.4 Body Language and Posture

Body language and posture are nonverbal cues that convey information about a person's thoughts, feelings, and intentions. Body language refers to a person's various physical movements and gestures, such as facial expressions, hand gestures, and body posture. Posture refers to how a person holds their body, including their position, alignment, and tension [42]. Body language and posture can convey various emotions and social cues [43]. For example, slouching and avoiding eye contact may indicate discomfort or insecurity, while standing tall with an open posture may give confidence and assertiveness. Other body language cues, such as crossed arms or tapping feet, can indicate boredom, impatience, or defensiveness.

Understanding and effectively using body language and posture can be valuable communication tools and help build rapport with others [43]. By paying attention to these nonverbal cues, we can gain insight into a person's emotional state and adjust our communication style accordingly. Additionally, by being aware of our body language and posture, we can communicate our thoughts and feelings more effectively and create a positive impression on others.

2.1.1.5 Proxemics

Proxemics studies how people use and perceive space in social situations [44]. It involves the analysis of interpersonal distances, as well as the use of physical space and territory to communicate social and cultural messages [45]. In many cultures, different distances are maintained between people based on the nature of the social relationship and the interaction context. For example, in some cultures, close physical proximity indicates intimacy or friendship; in others, a greater distance is maintained to show respect or deference.

Proxemics can also be influenced by other factors, such as the size and layout of physical spaces, the use of objects and furniture, and the degree of personal freedom considered appropriate in a given context. The study of proxemics has important implications for communication and social interaction [46], as it can help us to understand how people use and respond to space in different contexts. By being aware of the role of proxemics in communication, we can better navigate social situations and communicate effectively with people from different cultural backgrounds.

2.1.1.6 Eye Gaze

Eye gaze refers to the direction and duration of a person's eye movements, including where they are looking and for how long. Eye gaze can convey a wide range of social cues and emotions, an essential aspect of nonverbal communication [47]. For example, direct eye contact can signal confidence, trustworthiness, and interest in the other person, while avoiding eye contact may indicate shyness, disinterest, or deception. Additionally, eye gaze can regulate conversation, indicate turn-taking, and express emotions such as surprise, confusion, or anger.

Research has shown that eye gaze can also powerfully affect social interactions and behavior. For example, maintaining eye contact can increase trust and rapport between individuals, while breaking eye contact or looking away can signal discomfort or disapproval [48]. Eye gaze is a complex and vital aspect of nonverbal communication and can significantly influence how social interactions are perceived and understood. By paying attention to eye gaze and other nonverbal cues, we can gain valuable insights into the thoughts, feelings, and intentions of others and communicate more effectively in a wide range of contexts.

2.1.1.7 Haptics

Haptics refers to the study of touch and its role in communication and perception. It involves the analysis of tactile sensations and their effects on human behavior and emotions. Haptics can convey a wide range of social and emotional messages, an important aspect of nonverbal communication [49]. For example, a hug or a pat on the back can signal support or affection, while a handshake can convey respect or professionalism. Using haptic feedback in technology, such as touch screens or gaming controllers, can enhance user experience and improve performance [50].

Research has shown that touch can powerfully affect human behavior and emotions. For example, a friendly touch can increase trust and rapport, while an aggressive touch can elicit fear or anxiety. The study of haptics has important implications for communication, psychology, and technology. By understanding the role of touch in communication and perception, we can develop more effective strategies for building relationships, designing technology, and promoting positive social interactions.

2.1.1.8 Appearance

Appearance refers to how a person looks and presents themselves, including clothing, grooming, and physical features [51]. It is an essential aspect of nonverbal communication, as it can convey social and cultural messages and influence how others perceive and interact with us. People often use appearance to express their identity and share their social status, values, and personality [52]. For example, clothing can signal a person's occupation, social class, or cultural affiliation, while hairstyle and makeup can convey personal style and self-expression.

Research has shown that appearance can have a powerful effect on how others perceive and treat people. For example, people perceived as attractive or well-groomed may be seen as more competent, trustworthy, and socially skilled than those who are not. Appearance is essential to nonverbal communication and can significantly influence social interactions and relationships. We can improve our communication skills and develop more positive relationships with those around us by paying attention to our appearance and how others perceive it.

2.1.2 BACKGROUND OF IMPLICIT INTENTION COMMUNICATION

Implicit intention communication refers to the process by which people communicate their intentions indirectly, often through nonverbal cues such as body language, tone of voice, or facial expressions [53]. This form of communication is often used when people are reluctant to express their intentions directly, because of social norms, cultural taboos, or personal reasons. The study of implicit intention communication has a long history in psychology and communication research [54, 55]. Early research in this area focused on the role of nonverbal cues in interpersonal attraction and social influence. Later research expanded on this work to explore how implicit intention communication is used in various social contexts, including negotiation, conflict resolution, and persuasion.

In recent years, the study of implicit intention communication has gained renewed interest with the emergence of new technologies and communication platforms. For example, researchers have explored how people use emojis and other nonverbal cues in digital communication to convey their intentions and emotions [56]. Overall, the study of implicit intention communication is an important area of research in communication and psychology. By understanding how people communicate their intentions implicitly, we can develop better strategies for effective communication and build more positive social relationships.

Implicit interaction refers to using computer systems and technology designed to operate without requiring active engagement from users. This type of interaction is often used to support people with disabilities or impairments, such as those with motor disabilities or visual impairments, who may have difficulty using traditional user interfaces.

In the context of HCI [57, 58], implicit interaction can take many forms, such as gaze-based interaction, speech recognition, or touchless interfaces. These interfaces are designed to respond to the user's actions and behavior naturally and intuitively, without requiring direct input. For example, gaze-based interaction systems use eye-tracking technology to detect the user's gaze and allow them to control the computer interface with their eyes-speech recognition systems to control the computer through spoken commands without requiring physical input. Touchless interfaces use motion sensors and other technologies to detect the user's movements and gestures, allowing them to control the computer without touching the screen or keyboard. Overall, implicit interaction is an important area of research in HCI, as it can provide a more accessible and inclusive user experience for people with disabilities or impairments. By developing more advanced and sophisticated implicit interaction techniques, we can improve the usability and accessibility of computer systems and technology for all users.

The gaze-based interaction can require little physical effort from users, which makes it an attractive option for people with motion impairments or disabilities. However, it is essential to note that age, illness, or injury can also affect the ability to control gaze. In some cases, people with disabilities or impairments may require assistance or additional support to use gaze-based interaction systems effectively. This may include specialized equipment or training to help users develop the skills and techniques to control their gaze and interact with the system. Additionally, it is essential to consider the usability and accessibility of gaze-based interaction systems for older adults and people with disabilities. Designers and developers need to ensure that these systems are designed with the needs and abilities of these users in mind and that they are accessible and easy to use for all users, regardless of their age or physical abilities.

Comprehending intent is critical to developing artificial cognitive agents like robots [59] that can interact with humans and offer different services. To be effective, these agents must understand the intentions and needs of humans and respond appropriately to their requests. One way to achieve this is through natural language processing (NLP) [60], which involves using machine learning and other techniques to analyze and understand human language. NLP can help robots understand the meaning and context of human speech, as well as the intentions and emotions behind it.

Another approach is to use computer vision and other sensing technologies to interpret human gestures, facial expressions, and body language. These technologies can help robots infer the intentions and needs of humans based on their physical cues and behaviors. In addition, to understanding intent, artificial cognitive agents must also be able to respond appropriately and effectively to human requests. This requires advanced planning and decision-making capabilities and adapting and learning from new situations. Overall, developing artificial cognitive agents that can comprehend and respond to human intent is an important area of research in robotics and artificial intelligence. As these technologies continue to advance, they have the potential to revolutionize how we interact with machines and make a wide range of services more accessible and effective for humans.

Yu et al. [61] conducted an experiment where participants were asked to interact with a social robot to persuade them to change their dietary habits. The study examined how the language and behavior of the robot affected participants' willingness to adopt healthier eating habits. The study showed that the language robot's language and behavior significantly impacted participants' willingness to adopt healthier eating habits. Participants who interacted with a robot with more persuasive language and displayed positive behaviors were likelier to change their diet.

The authors concluded that social robots could become effective persuasive agents in HRIs. They suggest that social robots could be used in various settings, such as healthcare and education, to help people adopt healthier habits and behaviors. Overall, the study highlights the potential of social robots as persuasive agents and underscores the importance of designing robots that can effectively communicate with and influence humans. The method for recognizing human purpose is shown in Figure 2.1.

Identifying human intentions can be challenging for robots, especially when multiple actions are required to achieve a goal. However, using machine learning and other artificial intelligence techniques, robots can learn to recognize behavior patterns and identify their intentions. For example, a robot could observe a person

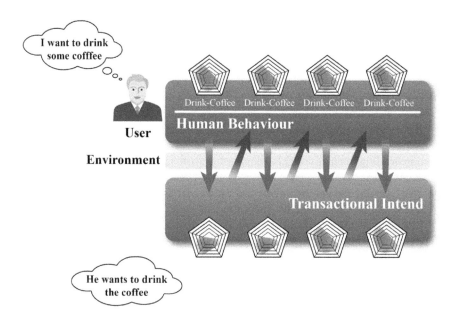

FIGURE 2.1   Example of human implicit intention understanding.

Source: adopted from Yu et al.[61].

taking various measures to get a coffee cup, such as walking to the kitchen, opening a cabinet, and reaching for a coffee mug. By analyzing this sequence of actions and connecting the object information (e.g., the person is going for a coffee mug), the robot could infer that the person intends to get a cup of coffee.

To achieve this, the robot must be equipped with sensors and cameras to perceive its environment and sophisticated algorithms to analyze and interpret the data it collects. Additionally, the robot must be trained on significant human actions and intentions datasets to accurately recognize and respond to different situations. While identifying human intentions can be complex, advances in artificial intelligence and robotics are making it increasingly possible for robots to understand and interact with humans more naturally and intuitively.

Gaze-based interaction paradigms refer to HCI where the user's gaze is used as the primary input for controlling assistive technologies such as wheelchairs, prosthetic limbs, and other devices. This approach can benefit people with physical disabilities or impairments that make using traditional input devices such as keyboards or joysticks difficult. To develop a gaze-based interaction paradigm, researchers typically use eye-tracking technology to detect the direction and duration of a person's gaze. By analyzing these data, they can create algorithms and user interfaces that allow the person to control the assistive technology using their eyes.

One example of a gaze-based interaction paradigm for assistive technology is the GazeCoin system [62] developed by researchers at the University of Essex. This system uses eye-tracking technology and machine-learning algorithms to allow people with motor impairments to control a wheelchair using their gaze. Another example is the EyeHarp system [63], developed by researchers at the Universitat Pompeu Fabra in Spain. This system uses eye-tracking technology to allow people with motor impairments to play a musical instrument using their gaze. Overall, gaze-based interaction paradigms have the potential to significantly improve the quality of life for people with physical disabilities or impairments. By allowing them to control assistive technologies using their gaze, these systems can provide greater independence, autonomy, mobility, and new opportunities for self-expression and creativity.

Electroencephalography (EEG) [64–66] is a technique used to measure the brain's electrical activity. It involves placing electrodes on the scalp and recording the electrical signals generated by the brain. One advantage of EEG is that it is non-invasive and has a high resolution, meaning that it can capture changes in brain activity in milliseconds. This makes it useful for studying brain activity linked to ideas, emotions, and behavior. One method of analyzing EEG data is to use event-related potentials (ERPs), electrical signals that occur in response to specific events or stimuli. By analyzing these ERPs, researchers can identify brain activity patterns associated with different cognitive processes, such as attention, memory, and language. For example, researchers might use EEG and ERP analysis to study how the brain processes language. They might present participants with a series of words or sentences and record their brain activity using EEG. By analyzing the ERPs associated with different aspects of language processing (e.g., semantic processing and syntactic processing), they can gain insights into how the brain represents and processes language. EEG and ERP analysis are powerful tools for studying brain activity and can provide valuable insights into various cognitive functions and behaviors.

2.1.3 VISUAL BEHAVIOR STUDIES OF IMPLICIT INTENTION

Visual behavior studies of implicit intention involve analyzing patterns of eye gaze and other visual behaviors to infer the intentions of an individual, even when those intentions are not explicitly stated. For example, researchers might use eye-tracking technology to study how people look at and interact with objects in their environment. By analyzing eye-gaze patterns and other visual behaviors, they can infer the individual's intentions, preferences, and goals.

One example of visual behavior studies of implicit intention is the study of visual attention in driving. Researchers might use eye-tracking technology to study how drivers visually scan their environment while driving. By analyzing patterns of eye gaze and other visual behaviors, they can gain insights into how drivers anticipate and respond to potential hazards on the road.

Another example is the study of visual attention in social interactions [67]. Researchers might use eye-tracking technology to study how people look at and respond to social cues such as facial expressions and body language. By analyzing patterns of eye gaze and other visual behaviors, they can gain insights into how people infer the intentions and emotions of others in social interactions. Overall, visual behavior studies of implicit intent can provide valuable insights into how people interact with their environment and each other. By analyzing eye-gaze patterns and other visual behaviors, researchers can better understand how people infer intentions and make decisions based on implicit cues.

Gaze-based HRI is still a relatively uncommon method of interaction, particularly at the level of inferring the intention of the human user [68]. HRI fundamentally differs from HCI in involving interactions between autonomous and cognitive robotic systems and humans in dynamic real-world settings. This presents new challenges for developing HRI-based systems, including accounting for human behavior's complex and dynamic nature and ensuring that robotic systems can accurately infer human intentions.

One of the challenges of developing gaze-based HRI systems is that they must be able to accurately interpret patterns of eye gaze and other visual behavior to infer the intentions of the human user. This requires the use of computer vision and machine learning techniques to analyze and interpret visual data in real time. Another challenge is ensuring that HRI systems can adapt to the dynamic nature of human behavior and respond appropriately to changes in the environment or the user's intentions. This requires the development of sophisticated algorithms and control systems capable of processing and responding to large amounts of sensory data in real time.

Despite these challenges, there is growing interest in developing gaze-based HRI systems, particularly in healthcare, education, and entertainment. As technology advances, we will likely see more sophisticated and effective gaze-based HRI systems that can accurately infer the intentions of human users in a wide range of settings.

Gaze-operated systems have been developed for various applications, including wheelchair control, mobile devices, quadcopters, and laparoscopes. In the case of a gaze-operated wheelchair, the user's eye movements are tracked and translated into control signals that control the direction and speed of the wheelchair [69]. This allows individuals with limited mobility to operate the wheelchair using only their eyes without manual controls.

Similarly, in the case of remotely controlled mobile devices, quadcopters, and laparoscopes, gaze-operated systems can be used to control the movement and direction of the device. This can be particularly useful in situations where manual control is difficult or impossible, such as in hazardous environments or during surgical procedures. Overall, the use of gaze-operated systems has the potential to significantly improve accessibility and mobility for individuals with disabilities and enhance the efficiency and safety of a wide range of applications in fields such as healthcare, transportation, and aerospace. As technology advances, we will likely see more sophisticated and effective gaze-operated systems developed for an even more comprehensive range of applications.

Understanding the context of task performance and the role of attention, including visual attention, is critical in HCI. When designing interfaces and interactions between humans and computers, it is important to consider the specific context in which the task will be performed. This includes factors such as the user's physical environment, experience with technology, cognitive abilities, and goals and motivations for completing the task. By considering these factors, designers can create interfaces tailored to the user's needs and capabilities, resulting in a more efficient and effective interaction. Visual attention is particularly significant as it is critical in determining how users interact with digital interfaces [70]. By understanding the mechanisms of visual attention and how they can be influenced by factors such as task demands, cognitive load, and interface design, designers can create interfaces that are more visually salient and easier to use. Overall, the study of context and attention is critical in HCI, as it enables designers to create interfaces tailored to the user's needs, resulting in more efficient and effective interactions. Factors that give inspiration and motivation for this include the following:

1. In some situations, users may have their hands occupied with other tasks or limited or no use of their limbs due to disabilities. This can make using traditional input devices, such as keyboards, mice, or touchscreens, difficult or impossible. In such situations, alternative input methods may be necessary for users to interact with digital interfaces. One example of an alternative input method is gaze-based interaction, which uses eye movements to control the interface. This can be particularly useful for users with limited or no use of their limbs, as it allows them to interact with the interface using only their eyes. Other alternative input methods include voice recognition, which will enable users to control the interface using spoken commands, and haptic feedback, which provides tactile feedback to the user to enhance their interaction. Overall, the development of alternative input methods is critical in enabling users with disabilities to access digital interfaces and to participate fully in the digital world. As technology advances, we will likely see even more innovative and effective alternative input methods developed to meet the needs of users with diverse abilities and needs.

2. Eye movements are generally faster and more precise than movements of other body parts, such as the hands or the head. This makes eye-based

interaction a potentially efficient and effective way to control digital interfaces. When using a cursor to interact with a digital interface, the user must
visually locate and fixate on the target point and then use a pointing device
to move the cursor to that point and activate it. This process can be time-
consuming and requires a high degree of precision. In contrast, eye-based
interaction allows the user to fixate directly on the target point, eliminating
the need for a cursor or other pointing device. This can be particularly useful
for users with disabilities or other conditions that make it difficult or impossible to use traditional input methods. However, eye-based interaction also
presents challenges, such as the need for accurate eye-tracking technology
and ensuring that the interface responds appropriately to the user's gaze.
Eye-based interaction can be a powerful tool for interacting with digital
interfaces. Still, it is essential to consider the needs and abilities of the user
carefully and to design interfaces optimized for eye-based interaction.

3. Traditional input methods such as keyboards and pointing devices can cause
   fatigue and even physical injury with prolonged use, particularly for users
   with disabilities or other conditions that affect their mobility. Eye-based
   interaction, on the other hand, can provide a low-fatigue and low-risk alternative. By using eye gaze to control digital interfaces, users can avoid the
   physical strain associated with traditional input methods and maintain a
   comfortable and sustainable level of interaction. However, it is essential to
   note that eye-based interaction has unique challenges, such as the need for
   accurate and reliable eye-tracking technology, the potential for eye strain
   or fatigue with prolonged use, and the need for appropriate interface design
   and user training. Eye-based interaction can be a valuable addition to the
   range of input modalities available in HCI. Still, it is important to consider
   the needs and abilities of the user carefully and to design interfaces optimized for eye-based interaction.

Eye-tracking technology is becoming more widely available and is utilized for various
purposes, including directing the action of physically controlled agents like robots.
Eye-tracking technology is a precise and dependable method of monitoring a user's
gaze point on a computer screen or any other visual stimuli. Like other familiar input
sources such as a mouse, keyboard, or joystick, eye-gaze direction may be employed
as an input modality in robot control systems. In settings where utilizing hands or
speech may not be possible or safe, eye tracking may provide a natural and straightforward approach for people to engage with robots. There are several possible uses for
eye-tracking robot control, including industry, healthcare, and assistive technologies.
Eye tracking, for instance, may be used to operate a robotic arm to carry out delicate
surgery, help people with impairments with daily duties, or even enable remote employees to handle robots in dangerous settings. It is crucial to remember that eye-tracking
technology still has considerable drawbacks, especially regarding accuracy and resil-
ience under various circumstances. When using eye-tracking technology in delicate
applications, it is crucial to consider user privacy and data security concerns.

Human beings can fixate their gaze on a specific object or location, allowing the
brain to process and comprehend the visual information that is being presented.

These periods of fixating the eyes on a particular visual component are called fixations. During fixation, the eyes are relatively still, allowing the visual system to gather more detailed information about the object being viewed. This process is crucial for visual perception and recognition, as it will enable the brain to analyze and interpret the details of the object. In eye-tracking studies, fixations are often used to measure attention, as they indicate which objects or regions of interest are being attended to by the viewer. By tracking participants' fixation patterns, researchers can gain insights into how humans perceive and process visual information and how this information is used in decision-making and other cognitive tasks. Fixation patterns can also create more compelling user interfaces and displays, as they can reveal which areas of a visual stimulus are most salient or relevant to the viewer. This information can be used to optimize the design of displays and interfaces, making them more efficient and user-friendly.

The gaze can reveal a person's visual attention and provide insights into their cognitive processes and intentions [71]. By tracking a person's gaze, researchers can determine which visual stimuli or objects a person is attending to and for how long. This information can be used to infer the person's goals, intentions, and motivations. For example, if a person is fixating on a particular object, it may suggest that they are interested in or planning to interact with it. In addition, gaze can also provide clues about a person's emotional state and level of engagement [72]. For example, if a person avoids eye contact, it may indicate that they feel anxious or uncomfortable. The gaze is a powerful indicator of a person's cognitive and emotional processes. It can provide valuable information in various fields, including psychology, neuroscience, marketing, and HCI.

2.2   OVERVIEW OF EYE-GAZE TRACKING

Eye-gaze tracking is a technique that involves using specialized hardware and software to monitor and record the movements of a person's eyes. Eye-gaze tracking technology can be used to measure a variety of eye movements, including fixations, saccades, and smooth pursuits. Eye-gaze-tracking systems typically use cameras or sensors to track the position of the eyes relative to the head, allowing the system to determine where the person is looking on a screen or in the real world. These systems can also measure the duration and frequency of fixations, the speed and direction of saccades, and the smoothness of pursuits. Eye-gaze tracking has various applications in various fields, including psychology, neuroscience, marketing, HCI, and robotics [73]. For example, eye-gaze tracking can be used to study visual attention and perception, assess cognitive and emotional processes, and develop more compelling user interfaces and displays. In recent years, eye-gaze tracking technology has become more accessible, with new products and systems being developed for consumer and industrial use. Eye-gaze tracking is now used in various applications, including assistive technology, gaming, and VR. However, it is essential to note that eye-gaze tracking technology still has some limitations, particularly regarding accuracy and reliability under varying conditions. It is also important to consider ethical and privacy concerns when using eye-gaze tracking technology, particularly in sensitive applications. The video eye gaze is tracked with the picture domain and the gazing area, as shown in Figure 2.2.

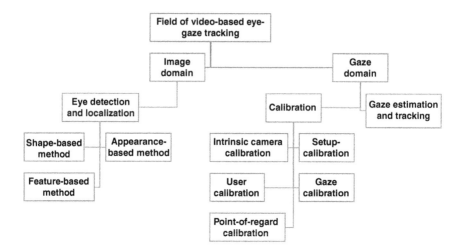

FIGURE 2.2   The field of video-based eye-gaze tracking.

2.2.1 IMAGE DOMAIN

Video-based eye-gaze tracking typically involves detecting and localizing the position of the eyes in each frame of the video. This process can be divided into two main steps: Eye detection and eye location. Eye detection refers to identifying the presence of eyes in an image or video frame. This can be done using various techniques, including template matching, Haar cascades, and machine learning algorithms [74]. Eye location, on the other hand, involves determining the precise position of the eyes within the image or video frame. This can be done using various techniques, including geometric models, pupil tracking, and corneal reflection tracking. The classification of eye detection and location techniques is often carried out concurrently, as the two processes are closely related and dependent on each other [75]. For example, eye location accuracy depends on eye detection accuracy, and vice versa. Various factors can affect the performance of eye detection and location techniques, including lighting conditions, head pose, and occlusions. Therefore, researchers are continually developing new strategies and algorithms to improve the accuracy and robustness of video-based eye-gaze-tracking systems. The techniques of detecting eyes and locating them are listed in Figure 2.2 in particular.

2.2.1.1 Shape-Based Method

Shape-based eye detection is a technique used in computer vision and image processing to detect the presence and location of eyes in images or videos. This technique analyzes the shape and appearance of the eyes and their surrounding areas [76]. In shape-based eye detection, the eyes are typically modeled as elliptical shapes, with the pupil located near the ellipse's center. The algorithm uses template matching, edge detection, and feature extraction techniques to search for image regions matching this shape and location. Shape-based eye detection can be used in various applications, including eye-gaze tracking, facial recognition, and biometric identification [77]. One advantage of this technique is that it can be used in real time, making it suitable for applications such as video-based eye-tracking and driver-monitoring systems. However, there are some limitations to shape-based eye detection. For example, the accuracy of the technique can be affected by variations in lighting, head pose, and occlusions, such as glasses or hair. Additionally, some people may have eye shapes or facial features unsuitable for this technique. Overall, shape-based eye detection helps detect and localize eyes in images and videos. Still, it should be used with other methods to improve accuracy and robustness.

2.2.1.2 Appearance-Based Method

Appearance-based eye detection is a technique used in computer vision and image processing to detect the presence and location of eyes in images or videos based on their appearance rather than their shape. This technique uses machine learning algorithms to learn the appearance of eyes from training images and then applies this knowledge to detect eyes in new images [78]. In appearance-based eye detection, the algorithm typically uses a classifier trained on a dataset of eye images, with positive examples (i.e., images of eyes) and negative examples (i.e., images without eyes). The classifier is trained to distinguish between these two classes based on features extracted from the images, such as texture, color, and gradient information. Once the classifier is introduced, it can detect eyes in new images or videos by scanning the image or video frame for regions that match the appearance of the eyes. This technique can be used in real-time applications such as eye-gaze tracking, facial recognition, and biometric identification. One advantage of appearance-based eye detection is that it can be more robust to variations in lighting, head pose, and occlusions, such as glasses or hair, than shape-based techniques. However, it requires much training data and can be computationally expensive. Overall, appearance-based eye detection helps detect and localize eyes in images and videos, particularly in applications that require real-time performance and robustness to varying conditions.

2.2.1.3 Feature-Based Method

Feature-based eye detection is a technique used in computer vision and image processing to detect the presence and location of eyes in images or videos based on specific features unique to the eyes, such as the iris, eyelids, and eyelashes. This technique relies on identifying these features and using them to locate the position of the eyes. In feature-based eye detection, the algorithm typically uses techniques such as edge detection, contour analysis, and template matching to find the features of the eyes [79]. For example, the iris can be detected using circular Hough transforms or pattern recognition techniques, while the eyelids and eyelashes can be detected using edge detection and contour analysis. Once the features of the eyes are identified, the position and orientation of the eyes can be determined using geometric models or machine learning algorithms. This technique can be used in real-time applications such as eye-gaze tracking, driver-monitoring systems, and biometric identification. One advantage of feature-based eye detection is that it can be more accurate and robust to variations in lighting, head pose, and occlusions such as glasses or hair than other techniques. However, it can also be computationally expensive and requires much training data. Overall, feature-based eye detection helps detect and localize

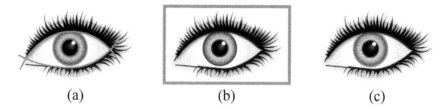

(a)   (b)   (c)

FIGURE 2.3 Methods of detecting eyes and location. (a) Open eye shape and contours by fitting a geometric eye region model; (b) eye photometric look using machine learning and template matching technology; (c) unique local characteristics, for example, limbus borders, for a particular eye area.

eyes in images and videos, particularly in applications that require high accuracy and robustness to varying conditions. Various detection techniques and locations of the eyes are presented in Figures 2.2 and 2.3.

2.2.2 GAZE DOMAIN

The gaze field is a critical component of a video gaze-tracking system and refers to the region of space that is visible to the user's eyes and can be tracked by the system. The gaze field consists of two primary functions: Calibration and gaze tracking. Calibration maps the user's eye movements to a specific region of space. This is typically done by asking the user to look at a series of points on a screen while the system records the position of their gaze [80]. These data then create a calibration function that maps eye movements to positions in the gazing field. Once the calibration function has been established, the system can then track the user's gaze as they look at different objects in the gazing field. This is typically done using one or more cameras that capture images of the user's eyes and track their movements in real time. Gaze tracking can be used for various applications, including eye-gaze-controlled interfaces, HCI, and usability testing. By monitoring the user's gaze, the system can determine where the user is looking on a screen or in the environment, which can be used to control the movement of a cursor, select objects on a screen, or provide feedback to the user. Overall, the gazing field is a critical element of a video gaze-tracking system, providing the foundation for accurate and reliable gaze tracking in various applications. Calibration and gaze tracking are critical functions of the gazing field, enabling the system to map eye movements to positions in space and follow the user's gaze in real time.

2.2.2.1 Calibration

Gaze calibration establishes a mapping function between the user's eye movements and the corresponding positions in the visual space. Gaze calibration ensures accurate and reliable gaze tracking in a video gaze-tracking system. During gaze calibration, the user is typically asked to look at a series of targets displayed on a screen or in the environment [81, 82]. At the same time, the system records the position of their gaze. The targets may be presented at different locations, distances, and angles to cover the entire gaze field and capture a range of eye movements. The data collected during gaze calibration are then used to create a calibration function that maps eye movements to positions in the visual space.

This calibration function is typically stored in the system and used to track the user's gaze during subsequent use. There are various techniques for gaze calibration, including point-based calibration, area-based calibration, and hybrid calibration [83]. Point-based calibration involves asking the user to look at specific points on a screen or in the environment. In contrast, area-based calibration asks the user to look at a broader screen area or environment. Hybrid calibration combines elements of both point-based and area-based calibration. The accuracy and reliability of gaze tracking in a video gaze-tracking system depend on the quality of the calibration [84, 85]. Therefore, it is important to ensure that the calibration is performed carefully and accurately and that the system is recalibrated periodically to maintain accuracy over time.

Point-of-regard (PoR) [86] calibration is a type of gaze calibration that aims explicitly to map the user's eye movements to the position on the screen or in the environment where they are looking. PoR calibration is critical for accurate and reliable gaze tracking in a video gaze-tracking system, especially for applications that require precise targeting or selection of visual elements on the screen or in the environment. PoR calibration typically involves presenting the user with a series of calibration targets on the screen or in the environment and asking them to fixate on each target. The targets may be offered at different locations, sizes, and distances to cover the entire screen or environment and capture a range of eye movements.

The system records the position of the user's gaze relative to each calibration target. It uses these data to establish a mapping function between eye movements and the corresponding position on the screen or in the environment. This calibration function then tracks the user's gaze during subsequent system use. It is important to perform PoR calibration carefully and accurately to ensure the reliability and accuracy of the gaze-tracking system. This may involve using high-quality calibration targets, providing proper lighting conditions, and minimizing distractions that could affect the user's eye movements. Overall, PoR calibration is a critical component of gaze tracking in a video gaze-tracking system, enabling accurate and reliable targeting and selection of visual elements on the screen or in the environment. Table 2.1 describes the different types of mapping to calibration.

2.2.2.2 Gaze Estimation and Tracking

Gaze estimation and tracking refer to identifying where a person is looking by analyzing their eye movements and direction. This technology is used in various applications, such as driver-monitoring systems, gaming, and assistive technologies [87]. Gaze estimation involves using cameras to capture images or videos of the user's face and eyes and then analyzing the eye position, movement, and shape to determine the gaze direction. This can be done using machine learning algorithms trained on large eye image datasets.

TABLE 2.1

PoR Calibration of Geometric Mapping and Implicit Mapping

Geometric mapping	Video gaze-tracking systems calibrate PoR via geometric mapping. Geometric mapping uses geometry to match the user's gaze to the screen or surroundings. Geometric mapping PoR calibration usually requires the user to stare at several calibration targets at known screen points or surroundings. The device records the user's gaze relative to each calibration target. These data map eye movements to screen or environmental positions. The mapping function calculates the user's gaze on the screen or surroundings by triangulating the user's eye location relative to two or more calibration targets. This needs exact knowledge of the calibration targets' location and orientation close to each other and the user's sight. Spatial analysis careful PoR calibration is dependable. Nevertheless, it may be susceptible to variables, including the user's gaze angle, distance from the calibration targets, and target accuracy. Geometric mapping PoR calibration helps video gaze-tracking systems accurately target and select visual components on the screen or surroundings. It needs extensive calibration and validation to maintain accuracy and dependability in varied use conditions. Figure 2.4(a) describes a PoR calibration of geometrical mapping.
Implicit mapping	Video gaze-tracking systems also employ implicit mapping for PoR calibration. Implicit mapping trains a machine learning system to associate eye movements with screen or environmental positions. The user usually looks at a succession of calibration targets at known points on the screen or surroundings to conduct implicit mapping PoR calibration. The device then captures the user's gaze relative to each calibration target and trains a machine-learning algorithm to associate eye movements with screen or environmental positions. The machine learning method may employ neural networks, decision trees, or SVMs to learn the mapping function between eye motions and screen or environmental positions. The system may include lighting conditions, user posture, and head movement to increase mapping accuracy.
	Implicit mapping PoR calibration is versatile as the machine learning system can learn and adapt to user eye movements and ambient conditions. It may need more training data and computer resources than geometric mapping PoR calibration and be more susceptible to data quality and training biases. Implicit mapping PoR calibration is a potential method for video gaze-tracking systems that allow adjustable targeting and selection of visual items on the screen or in the surroundings. It needs extensive training and validation to achieve accuracy and dependability in varied use circumstances. Figure 2.4(b) describes a PoR calibration of implicit mapping.

Gaze tracking, on the other hand, involves continuously monitoring the user's gaze direction over time. This can be done using specialized eye-tracking hardware, such as infrared sensors or EOG electrodes. Gaze estimation and tracking have many potential applications, including improving HCI, enhancing virtual and AR

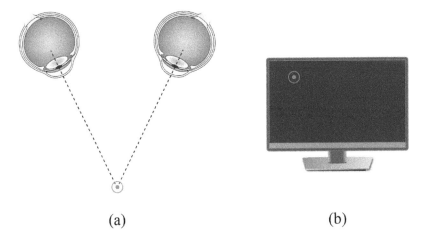

(a)   (b)

FIGURE. 2.4   PoR calibration of (a) geometric mapping and (b) implicit mapping.

experiences, and assisting people with disabilities. However, privacy concerns are associated with these technologies, as they can be used to monitor and track individuals without their consent.

2.2.3   HCI-BASED GAZE INTERACTION

HCI-based gaze interaction refers to gaze estimation and tracking technologies enabling users to interact with computers and other digital devices through eye movements. This technology can provide an alternative to traditional input methods, such as a mouse or keyboard, and can be particularly useful for people with motor disabilities. HCI-based gaze interaction systems typically involve a camera or eye-tracking device that captures images of the user's eyes and determines their gaze direction. This information can then control various aspects of the computer interface, such as moving the mouse cursor, clicking on buttons, scrolling through documents, or typing text.

One common use of HCI-based gaze interaction is in assistive technologies for people with disabilities. For example, individuals with motor impairments that make it difficult to use a traditional mouse or keyboard may be able to use gaze interaction to control their computer or communicate with others. HCI-based gaze interaction also has potential applications in gaming, virtual and AR, and automotive technology, where it can enhance user experience and improve safety. However, there are also challenges associated with HCI-based gaze interaction, such as the need for accurate and reliable gaze estimation and the need to develop intuitive and effective user interfaces that can be controlled through eye movements.

Video-based eye-gazing techniques can be categorized into two main types: two-dimensional (2D) and three-dimensional (3D). 2D eye tracking involves using a single camera to capture a 2D image of the user's face and eyes and then analyzing the image to estimate gaze direction. This approach is generally less expensive and more practical than 3D tracking, but it can be less accurate, particularly when the user's head or body is moving. 3D eye tracking, on the other hand, uses multiple cameras or depth sensors to capture a 3D model of the user's face and eyes, which can be used to estimate gaze direction more accurately. This approach is generally more expensive and requires more specialized hardware than 2D tracking, but it can provide higher accuracy and better performance in dynamic environments.

2D and 3D eye-tracking techniques have advantages and limitations, and the choice of which approach to use will depend on the application's specific requirements [88]. For example, 2D tracking may be suitable for applications without critical accuracies, such as gaze-based advertising. In contrast, 3D tracking may be more appropriate for applications that require high accuracy and precision, such as eye surgery or pilot training.

Gaze estimation of the 2D mapping technique involves using a camera to capture images or video of the user's face and eyes, then mapping the eyes' position onto a 2D plane. This approach is based on the assumption that the user's gaze direction can be accurately estimated by analyzing the position and movement of the eyes relative to the 2D image. To perform 2D gaze estimation, the camera is typically placed in front of the user, and the image of the user's face and eyes is analyzed using computer vision algorithms. These algorithms may involve detecting the position and shape of the pupils, measuring the distance between the pupils, or exploring the movement of the eyes over time.

Once the position of the eyes has been determined in the 2D image, this information can be used to estimate the user's gaze direction. This may involve mapping the position of the eyes onto a virtual screen or grid or using the position of the eyes to control a cursor or other interface element. While 2D gaze estimation is generally less accurate than 3D tracking, it can still provide a useful and practical method for enabling gaze-based interaction with computers and other digital devices. However, it is essential to note that 2D gaze estimation may be affected by factors such as head movement, lighting conditions, and the user's glasses or contact lenses, which can all impact the accuracy of the estimated gaze direction.

Gaze estimation of the 3D mapping technique involves using multiple cameras or depth sensors to capture a 3D model of the user's face and eyes, which can be used to estimate gaze direction accurately. This approach assumes that the user's gaze direction can be accurately estimated by analyzing the 3D position and movement of the eyes relative to the user's head and body. To perform 3D gaze estimation, multiple cameras or depth sensors are typically used to capture a 3D model of the user's face and eyes. This information can then be used to calculate the position and movement of the eyes in 3D space relative to the user's head and body.

Once the position and movement of the eyes have been determined in 3D space, this information can be used to estimate the user's gaze direction with high accuracy. This may involve mapping the position of the eyes onto a virtual screen or grid or using the position of the eyes to control a cursor or other interface element. One advantage of 3D gaze estimation over 2D tracking is that it can provide higher accuracy and better performance in dynamic environments where the user's head or body may be moving. However, 3D gaze estimation generally requires more specialized hardware and software than 2D tracking and may be more expensive and complex.

The choice of gaze estimation technique will depend on the application's requirements, including accuracy, reliability, cost, and ease of use.

2.3   RECOGNIZING ACTIVITIES OF DAILY LIVING TO IMPROVE WELL-BEING

ADLs are basic self-care tasks that individuals must perform to care for themselves, including bathing, dressing, grooming, toileting, eating, and transferring. ADL functioning is a critical indicator of an individual's ability to live independently and perform basic self-care tasks. As people age, they may experience physical and cognitive decline that can affect their ability to perform ADLs independently [89]. This decline may be gradual, but it can ultimately lead to the need for long-term care or assistance from caregivers. Measuring an individual's level of ADL performance is an essential component of assessing their health status and care needs. It can help healthcare professionals develop appropriate care plans, identify areas of weakness, and provide interventions to maintain or improve their ADL functioning [90]. Regular assessments of ADL performance can help individuals and their families plan for future care needs and make informed decisions about long-term care options.

In government-subsidized assisted living facilities, caregivers may be required by law to gather ADL data for patients 24/7, especially for those with cognitive impairments such as Alzheimer's disease. Regular ADL assessments can help caregivers monitor changes in a patient's physical and cognitive abilities, identify any decline in ADL performance, and provide appropriate care and interventions. For patients with Alzheimer's disease [91] or other forms of dementia, ADL assessments can be critical. These individuals may have difficulty completing basic self-care tasks and may require assistance to prevent accidents and injuries. In addition to providing direct care to patients, caregivers in assisted living facilities may also use ADL data to communicate with healthcare professionals and coordinate care with other patient care team members, such as physicians, nurses, and occupational therapists. Overall, gathering ADL data is critical to providing high-quality care to patients in assisted living facilities, particularly those with cognitive impairments or other health conditions impacting their ability to perform basic self-care tasks independently.

Computer vision methods, including gaze-based systems, can recognize video images in conventional cameras or Kinect sensors [92]. These systems can be used in various applications, such as tracking eye movements for research purposes or detecting driver drowsiness in automobiles [93]. However, using these systems raises concerns about personal data protection and privacy. Data collection on an individual's eye movements could be considered sensitive personal data, and using such data could infringe on an individual's privacy rights. As a result, gaze-based systems may lose user confidence, mainly if individuals are uncomfortable with their eye movements being tracked and recorded. To address these concerns, organizations using gaze-based methods may need to implement robust data protection policies and procedures to ensure that individual privacy rights are respected.

Such policies might include obtaining explicit consent from individuals before collecting and processing sensitive data, implementing appropriate security measures to protect data, and providing individuals with access to their data and the ability to request its deletion. Overall, the use of computer vision methods in gaze-based systems can be beneficial in various applications. However, organizations must balance the potential benefits against the risks to personal data protection and privacy and take appropriate measures to protect individuals' privacy rights.

2.3.1 THE ADL RECOGNITION SYSTEM

An ADL recognition system is a computer-based system that uses sensors, cameras, and machine learning algorithms to detect and recognize an individual's ADL performance. These systems are designed to monitor and evaluate an individual's ability to perform basic self-care tasks, such as dressing, grooming, bathing, and eating. ADL recognition systems [94] typically consist of several components, including sensors and cameras placed in the individual's living space to monitor their movements and actions. The system then uses machine learning algorithms to analyze the data collected from the sensors and cameras, recognize patterns, and identify specific ADLs being performed.

These systems can be used in various settings, including assisted living facilities and home care environments, to provide real-time feedback on an individual's ADL performance. The data collected by the system can also be used to track changes in an individual's ability to perform ADLs over time, which can help caregivers and healthcare professionals identify early signs of decline and develop appropriate care plans. ADL recognition systems can improve the quality of care provided to individuals who require assistance with basic self-care tasks. However, ensuring that these systems are designed and implemented with appropriate privacy and security measures is important to protect individual data and privacy rights.

Technology advancements have led to the development of smart ambient systems designed to improve users' daily lives. These systems typically use embedded technology, such as sensors and actuators, to detect and respond to users' needs [95]. Innovative ambient systems are often used in home care environments, where they can help individuals with disabilities or other health conditions to perform ADLs and live independently. For example, a smart ambient system might include sensors that detect when an individual is having difficulty getting out of bed or moving around their home. The system could then activate an actuator, such as a lift chair, to assist the individual with getting up and moving around.

Smart ambient systems can also monitor an individual's health status and alert caregivers or healthcare professionals if there are concerns [96]. For example, a system might include sensors that monitor an individual's heart rate, blood pressure, or medication usage and alert healthcare professionals to significant changes or issues. Smart ambient systems can significantly improve the quality of life for individuals who require assistance with ADLs or other daily activities. However, ensuring these systems are designed and implemented with appropriate privacy and security measures is important to protect individual data and privacy rights.

The automatic detection of physical activity using sensors is a popular research topic in mobile and ubiquitous computing [97]. This technology is used in many applications, including life-assisted health monitoring systems, fall detection, and older support systems. Sensor-based activity identification is essential for these applications because it allows continuous monitoring of an individual's physical activity levels and detecting of significant changes or issues. For example, a fall detection system might use sensors to detect when an individual has fallen and alert caregivers or emergency services. Mobile and ubiquitous computing technologies, such as smartphones and wearable devices, have enabled the development of sensor-based activity identification systems that are portable and easy to use [98]. These systems typically use a combination of sensors, such as accelerometers, gyroscopes, and magnetometers, to detect and classify physical activities. Using sensor-based activity identification systems can improve the quality of life for individuals who require assistance with physical activities. However, ensuring these systems are designed and implemented with appropriate privacy and security measures is important to protect individual data and privacy rights. It is also important to consider the potential ethical implications of using these systems, such as issues related to autonomy and consent.

Using LoRaWAN battery-free wireless sensors [99] in structural health monitoring can positively impact both safety and sustainability in the construction industry. By continuously monitoring the health of structures, engineers and construction professionals can detect any potential issues or damage early on, allowing them to take proactive measures to prevent further damage or failure. This can help improve the safety and longevity of structures, as shown in Figure 2.5, reducing the risk of accidents or costly repairs. In addition, battery-free wireless sensors can help reduce

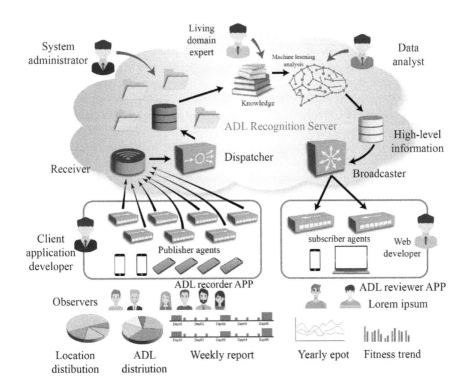

FIGURE 2.5   Architecture of the ADLs recognition system.

Source: Adopted from [101].

costs and environmental impact in several ways. First, they eliminate the need for frequent battery replacements, reducing maintenance costs and the amount of electronic waste produced. Second, their low-power communication capabilities minimize energy consumption, making them more sustainable and environmentally friendly. Overall, using LoRaWAN battery-free wireless sensors in structural health monitoring can benefit the construction industry, including improved safety, reduced costs, and a more sustainable approach to monitoring structures over time.

Understanding the patterns of movement, places, and sleep patterns of older people can provide valuable insights into their overall health and well-being and identify potential health risks or issues. Machine learning algorithms can analyze large datasets and identify patterns and trends that may not be immediately apparent to humans [100]. Using these algorithms to analyze data from elderly populations, researchers can identify patterns of activity and behavior associated with certain health conditions or risks. For example, machine learning algorithms could be used to identify patterns in sleep patterns that may be indicative of sleep disorders or other health issues. Similarly, they could be used to identify patterns of movement that may be associated with an increased risk of falls or other injuries. Overall, using intelligent features and algorithms for machine learning in analyzing data from the elderly can improve our understanding of their health and well-being while enabling us to identify and address potential health risks or issues early on.

Using probabilistic methods in analyzing sensor data from participants engaged in ADLs is a promising approach to understanding behavior patterns and identifying potential health risks or issues. In the case of "preparing and consuming a hot drink," using variations of coffee or tea, the probabilistic method can help identify patterns in the sensor data that are associated with normal or abnormal behavior. For example, the process may be used to determine the time it takes to prepare a hot drink, the sequence of actions involved, and the frequency and duration of pauses during the process.

Researchers can identify anomalies or deviations from normal behavior that may indicate potential health risks or issues by analyzing these behavior patterns. For example, suppose a participant takes an unusually long time to prepare a hot drink or needs help completing the task. This may be a sign of cognitive decline or physical impairment. Using probabilistic methods in analyzing sensor data from ADL participants can provide valuable insights into behavior patterns and identify potential health risks or issues early on. This can enable healthcare professionals and caregivers to proactively address these issues and improve the quality of life for elderly individuals.

Using a monitoring system containing various non-intrusive sensors in supplementary care homes can be a valuable tool to enhance care for elderly individuals. These sensors can collect data on multiple aspects of daily living, such as activity levels, sleep patterns, and medication adherence. By collecting these data, caregivers and healthcare professionals can gain insights into the overall health and well-being of elderly individuals and identify any potential health risks or issues early on. For example, sensors that detect falls or changes in activity levels can help identify individuals who may be at risk for falls or other injuries.

Additionally, sensors that monitor medication adherence can help ensure that elderly individuals take their medications as prescribed, improving health outcomes and reducing the risk of complications. Overall, using non-intrusive sensors in supplementary care homes can improve the quality of care for elderly individuals by providing caregivers and healthcare professionals with valuable insights into their health and well-being. This can enable them to take proactive measures to address potential health risks or issues and ensure that elderly individuals receive the best possible care.

The ProSAFE [102] project's recommendation for a non-intrusive surveillance solution for older people is a significant development in the field of eldercare. Non-intrusive surveillance solutions can help ensure older people's safety and well-being while respecting their privacy and independence. Such solutions may include using sensors, cameras, or other monitoring devices to detect potential risks or issues and alert caregivers or healthcare professionals to take appropriate action. For example, sensors that detect falls or changes in activity levels can help identify individuals who may be at risk for falls or other injuries. Using non-intrusive surveillance solutions can also provide peace of mind for family members or caregivers who may be concerned about the safety and well-being of their loved ones. These solutions can help ensure that older people are safe and well-cared for by providing real-time monitoring and alerts, even when caregivers or healthcare professionals are absent. Overall, the recommendation of non-intrusive surveillance solutions for older people by the ProSAFE project is a positive development in the field of eldercare, as it can help ensure the safety and well-being of older individuals while respecting their privacy and independence.

Activity recognition using sensor systems typically involves two main activities: Monitoring and wearability of the sensor. Monitoring consists in collecting data from sensors integrated into the environment, such as attaching sensors to items in ADLs or static locations in the house (e.g., walls, wardrobes, and doors) to monitor user-smart interactions. This type of monitoring can provide valuable insights into behavior patterns and identify potential health risks or issues early on. The wearability of the sensor involves attaching sensors to the user's body, such as wristbands, necklaces, or other wearable devices. This type of sensor is typically used to monitor physical activity levels, sleep patterns, heart rate, and other vital signs. Wearable sensors can provide real-time feedback on the user's health status and help identify potential health risks or issues early on.

Robust sensors integrated into the environment can provide a wealth of data on user behavior and interactions with their environment, which can be analyzed using machine learning algorithms to identify patterns and anomalies. Wearable sensors can also provide valuable data on physical activity levels and other health metrics, which can be used to identify potential health risks or issues. Overall, using robust and wearable sensors in activity recognition can improve the quality of care for elderly individuals by providing valuable insights into their health and well-being. These insights can enable healthcare professionals and caregivers to take proactive measures to address potential health risks or issues early on and ensure that elderly individuals are receiving the best possible care.

Research in activity recognition has explored various approaches to detect ADLs and identify abnormal behavior using machine learning and formal modeling techniques. One such approach is the Markov decision model, which can be used to model the probabilistic nature of ADLs and identify abnormal behavior based on deviations from expected behavior patterns. These models can provide valuable insights into the underlying structure of ADLs and enable caregivers and healthcare professionals to detect potential health risks or issues early on.

Another approach is categorizing into abnormal compartment models, which involves dividing ADLs into different categories based on their complexity and level of risk. This approach can help identify high-risk activities that require closer monitoring and provide insights into the potential consequences of abnormal behavior. Formal modeling of the system studied can also provide valuable insights into its operation and interaction. This approach involves creating a mathematical model of the system and using it to simulate different scenarios and test the effectiveness of other interventions. This can help identify potential weaknesses in the system and enable healthcare professionals and caregivers to improve the quality of care provided. Overall, using machine learning and formal modeling techniques in activity recognition can provide valuable insights into the underlying structure of ADLs, identify potential health risks or issues early on, and improve the quality of care for elderly individuals.

The proportion of elderly individuals in society is increasing in many countries worldwide, including most of Europe's nations. According to the World Health Organization (WHO), falls and fall-related injuries are major health concerns among elderly individuals, with the risk increasing as individuals age. Specifically, the WHO reports that the risk of falls and fall-related injuries increases from 28% to 42% as individuals age from above 70 years. Falls can result in serious injuries such as fractures, head injuries, and other health complications that can significantly impact the quality of life of elderly individuals. Therefore, there is a pressing need to develop effective solutions to prevent falls and fall-related injuries among elderly individuals. This includes using innovative technologies such as sensor systems and machine learning algorithms to monitor the activity of elderly individuals and identify potential health risks or issues early on. By leveraging these technologies, healthcare professionals and caregivers can take proactive measures to prevent falls and improve the quality of care provided to elderly individuals.

Fall detection systems are designed to detect when a person has fallen and may require assistance. These systems can be classified into two main categories: Contextual and wearable strategies. Contextual fall detection systems use environmental sensors, such as cameras, microphones, and pressure sensors, to see falls. These sensors are typically placed in a room or area where the person is likely to fall, such as a bathroom or bedroom. The sensors can detect the sound or motion of a fall and send an alert to a caregiver or monitoring system.

On the other hand, wearable fall detection systems use sensors attached to the person's body, such as a wristband or pendant. These sensors can detect changes in motion or orientation indicative of a fall. The wearable device alerts a caregiver or monitoring system when a fall is detected. Both types of fall detection systems have their advantages and disadvantages. Contextual methods may be more effective at detecting falls in specific environments, but they may not be as precise as wearable systems. On the other hand, wearable systems may be more accurate at detecting falls, but they may require the person to wear a device at all times, which may be inconvenient or uncomfortable.

Smartphones are becoming increasingly popular as a tool for fall detection because they come equipped with built-in accelerometers, which can detect changes in motion and orientation. Users can turn their devices into wearable fall detection systems using a smartphone app without additional hardware. The accelerometer can see when the phone is dropped or when the user experiences a sudden change in motion, which can indicate a fall. Smartphones have several advantages over traditional wearable fall detection systems. They are easy to carry around, and many people always have smartphones. Additionally, smartphone fall detection systems are often less expensive than traditional wearable devices. However, there are also some limitations to using a smartphone as a fall detection system. For example, the accelerometer may not be as sensitive or accurate as a dedicated wearable device. In addition, the phone may need to be within a certain distance of the user for the fall detection to work correctly, which could be a problem if the user needs to remember or leave the phone behind. Overall, while smartphones may be a promising tool for fall detection, there may be better substitutes for dedicated wearable devices in all situations.

Several simulators enable ADL analysis using ADL sequences as input for temporal simulation of movement or sensor readings. These simulators can help assess ADL analysis software's performance and develop and test new algorithms for fall detection and other applications. Some simulators work by generating synthetic ADL sequences based on statistical models of typical human movements and behaviors. These sequences can then simulate sensor readings and other data that real-world ADLs might generate. Other simulators use recorded data from real-world ADLs to create simulations that can be used for testing and analysis.

One advantage of using simulators for ADL analysis is that they provide a controlled testing and evaluation environment. Researchers can test their algorithms under various conditions and with different input data, allowing them to identify strengths and weaknesses and improve their performance. Another advantage is that simulators can help reduce the cost and time involved in collecting and processing real-world ADL data. Instead of relying on expensive sensors and other equipment to collect data from real people, researchers can use simulations to generate data for testing and analysis. Overall, simulators are a valuable tool for ADL analysis and fall detection research, and their use is likely to continue to grow as these fields evolve.

Assistive robots have the potential to help restore ADLs for elderly and disabled individuals, allowing them to maintain or regain independence. However, one of the main challenges in developing effective assistive robots is the need for a good and intuitive HRI system. HRI refers to the methods and interfaces to enable communication and collaboration between humans and robots. For assistive robots to be effective, they must be able to understand and respond to human needs and preferences in a way that is easy to use and understand. This requires developing intuitive and adaptable interfaces to individual users' needs.

Several approaches have been proposed for developing effective HRI systems for assistive robots. One method is to use NLP and speech recognition technology to allow users to communicate with the robot using voice commands. Another approach is to use touchscreens or other interactive displays to enable users to interact with the robot using gestures or other input methods. In addition to developing intuitive HRI systems, it is also important to consider ethical and social issues related to assistive robots. For example, they ensure that the robot respects the user's privacy and autonomy and does not cause harm or distress. Developing effective and intuitive HRI systems is critical for successfully deploying assistive robots for ADL support. Ongoing research in this area will likely lead to continued progress in the field.

Gaze-based communication is an approach to HRI that uses eye-tracking technology to enable users to communicate with the robot using their eyes. This approach has several potential benefits for assistive robotics and ADL support. One of the main benefits of gaze-based communication is that it is a low-effort method that does not require significant physical or cognitive exertion on the user's part. This makes it particularly useful for elderly or disabled individuals with limited mobility or physical limitations. Another benefit is that gaze-based communication retains the user's visual capacity, allowing them to maintain visual awareness of their environment while still interacting with the robot. This can be particularly important for ADL support, as it will enable the user to monitor their surroundings while still receiving assistance from the robot. Overall, gaze-based communication in HRI is expected to simplify the interaction between users and assistive robots, increasing the acceptance of these technologies and promoting users' independence in ADLs. As eye-tracking technology advances, we expect further development and refinement of gaze-based communication approaches for assistive robotics and other applications.

While gaze-based communication shows promise for HRI in assistive robotics and ADL support, integrating this technology into usable, practical, and intuitive HCI remains challenging. One of the main issues with gaze-based communication is that it can take time to implement in a way that is accurate and easy to use. Eye-tracking technology can be sensitive to lighting conditions, head movements, and other factors, making it challenging to interpret users' gaze directions and intentions reliably. Another challenge is developing intuitive and intuitive interfaces for users to learn and use effectively. While gaze-based communication may be a low-effort method, it still requires users to learn and use new skills and techniques for interacting with the robot.

Ongoing research aims to develop more effective and user-friendly HCI for gaze-based communication in assistive robotics and ADL support. One approach is to use machine learning algorithms to improve the accuracy of gaze tracking and enable more natural and intuitive communication between users and robots. While integrating gaze-based communication into usable and intuitive HCI remains unresolved, ongoing research and development will likely lead to continued progress and innovation in assistive robotics and ADL support.

One of the potential benefits of gaze-based communication in assistive robotics and ADL support is the ability to implicitly comprehend the user's intentions by monitoring their visual attention. This can allow the robot to anticipate the user's needs and provide assistance more effectively. Another benefit of gaze-based communication is that it does not interfere with the user's healthy visual conduct or prevent them from monitoring their surroundings. Instead, it provides an additional means of communication that can be used for more complex or nuanced interactions with the robot.

The ultimate goal of gaze-based communication and other HCI approaches in assistive robotics is to simplify the interaction between users and robots, making it more intuitive, efficient, and effective. By improving the adoption of assistive technology and promoting users' independence in daily life, these technologies can potentially improve the quality of life for elderly and disabled individuals. As research continues, we expect ongoing progress and innovation in developing more effective and user-friendly HCI for assistive robotics and ADL support.

2.4 CONTRIBUTION TO THE RESEARCH

This explains the three problems that the study contributes to in designing and developing an artificial neural network (ANN)-based system for gaze-based communication:

1. Data collection and annotation: Collecting and annotating a large eye-tracking dataset is critical in developing an accurate and effective ANN-based system for gaze-based communication. However, this process can be time-consuming and expensive, and the data quality and annotations can significantly impact the system's performance. The study proposes a methodology for collecting and annotating eye-tracking data that is efficient and effective while maintaining a high level of accuracy.
2. Feature selection and extraction: To accurately interpret the user's gaze direction and intentions, an ANN-based system for gaze-based communication must use relevant and informative features. However, selecting and extracting these features can be challenging, as the eye-tracking data may contain noise, variability, and redundancy. The study proposes a set of feature selection and extraction techniques that can improve the accuracy and efficiency of the system.
3. Neural network architecture and training: The architecture and training of the ANN are critical factors in determining the accuracy and performance of the system. However, designing an optimal neural network architecture and training procedure can take time, as it involves a trade-off between model complexity and generalization ability. The study proposes a neural network architecture and training methodology that can effectively handle the complexity and variability of the eye-tracking data while maintaining high accuracy and generalization ability.

Generally, the study addresses these three critical problems in designing and developing an ANN-based system for gaze-based communication, which can improve the accuracy and effectiveness of assistive robotics and ADL support technologies. Also, the following results of this research are identified:

1. Development of a novel ANN for estimating gaze points
2. Development of an implicit intention algorithm for gaze-based communication
3. Improve elder care by using gaze-based communication

2.4.1 DEVELOPMENT OF A NOVEL ANN FOR ESTIMATING GAZE POINTS

Developing an ANN for estimating gaze points involves several key steps, including data collection, feature extraction, network architecture design, and training. Once the ANN has been trained, it can be used as the real-time gaze point of new eye-tracking data. This can be useful in various applications, including assistive robotics and ADL support, where accurate and efficient gaze-based communication can improve the user's independence and quality of life.

2.4.2 DEVELOPMENT OF AN IMPLICIT INTENTION ALGORITHM FOR GAZE-BASED COMMUNICATION

Developing an implicit intention algorithm for gaze-based communication involves several key steps, including data collection, feature extraction, and algorithm design. Once the implicit intention algorithm has been developed and validated, it can interpret the user's intentions in real time based on their eye movements. This can be useful in various applications, including assistive robotics and ADL support, where accurate and efficient interpretation of the user's intentions can improve the user's independence and quality of life.

2.4.3 IMPROVE ELDER CARING BY USING GAZE-BASED COMMUNICATION

Gaze-based communication can significantly improve elder care by increasing seniors' independence and quality of life. Here are some ways in which gaze-based communication can be beneficial:

1. Improved communication: Many seniors may have difficulty communicating verbally due to dementia, stroke, or Parkinson's disease. Gaze-based communication provides an alternative means of communication that is intuitive and requires minimal effort. This can help seniors express their needs, preferences, and emotions more effectively, improving their quality of life.

2. Enhanced safety: Seniors are at an increased risk of falls and other accidents. Gaze-based fall detection systems can help prevent falls by alerting caregivers to activate safety features such as handrails or bed alarms. In addition, gaze-based monitoring of seniors' ADLs can help detect changes in behavior that may indicate a health issue or a need for assistance.

3. Increased independence: Seniors often value their freedom and may be reluctant to accept assistance from caregivers. Gaze-based technology can help seniors maintain their independence by enabling them to perform ADLs more quickly and efficiently. For example, the gaze-based interface controls appliances, adjusts lighting or temperature, or navigates the internet.

4. Reduced caregiver burden: Caregiving can be physically and emotionally demanding, particularly for family members with other responsibilities such as work and family. Gaze-based communication can help reduce caregiver burden by enabling seniors to communicate their needs more effectively and reducing the need for constant monitoring.

Generally, using gaze-based communication can help improve the elder care experience by enhancing communication, safety, and independence and reducing caregiver burden.

REFERENCES

1. Bieńkiewicz, M. M., Brandi, M. L., Goldenberg, G., Hughes, C. M., & Hermsdörfer, J. (2014). The tool in the brain: Apraxia in ADL. Behavioral and neurological correlates of apraxia in daily living. Frontiers in Psychology, 5, 353.
2. Breazeal, C., Kidd, C. D., Thomaz, A. L., Hoffman, G., & Berlin, M. (2005, August). Effects of nonverbal communication on efficiency and robustness in human-robot teamwork. In 2005 IEEE/RSJ International Conference on Intelligent Robots and Systems (pp. 708–713). Edmonton, AB: IEEE.
3. Jakobson, R. (1972). Verbal communication. Scientific American, 227(3), 72–81.
4. Madhusanka, B. G. D. A., & Ramadass, S. (2021). Implicit intention communication for activities of daily living of elder/disabled people to improve well-being. IoT in Healthcare and Ambient Assisted Living, 325–342.
5. Hymes, D. (1964). Introduction: Toward ethnographies of communication 1. American Anthropologist, 66(6_PART2), 1–34.
6. Jung, H. S., & Yoon, H. H. (2011). The effects of nonverbal communication of employees in the family restaurant upon customers' emotional responses and customer satisfaction. International Journal of Hospitality Management, 30(3), 542–550.
7. Wagner, H. L. (1993). On measuring performance in category judgment studies of nonverbal behavior. Journal of Nonverbal Behavior, 17, 3–28.
8. Leathers, D. G., & Eaves, M. (2015). Successful Nonverbal Communication: Principles and Applications. New York: Routledge.
9. Argyle, M. (2013). Bodily communication. Routledge.
10. Sundaram, D. S., & Webster, C. (2000). The role of nonverbal communication in service encounters. Journal of Services Marketing, 14(5), 378–391.
11. Hans, A., & Hans, E. (2015). Kinesics, haptics and proxemics: Aspects of non-verbal communication. IOSR Journal of Humanities and Social Science (IOSR-JHSS), 20(2), 47–52.
12. Foley, G. N., & Gentile, J. P. (2010). Nonverbal communication in psychotherapy. Psychiatry (Edgmont), 7(6), 38.
13. Okon, J. J. (2011). Role of non-verbal communication in education. Mediterranean Journal of Social Sciences, 2(5), 35–40.
14. Li, S., & Zhang, X. (2017). Implicit intention communication in human–robot interaction through visual behavior studies. IEEE Transactions on Human-Machine Systems, 47(4), 437–448.
15. Georgescu, A. L., Kuzmanovic, B., Roth, D., Bente, G., & Vogeley, K. (2014). The use of virtual characters to assess and train non-verbal communication in high-functioning autism. Frontiers in Human Neuroscience, 8, 807.

16. Phutela, D. (2015). The importance of non-verbal communication. IUP Journal of Soft Skills, 9(4), 43.
17. Pantic, M., Pentland, A., Nijholt, A., & Huang, T. (2006, November). Human computing and machine understanding of human behavior: A survey. In Proceedings of the 8th International Conference on Multimodal Interfaces (pp. 239–248). New York: Association for Computing Machinery.
18. Trevarthen, C. (1984). Emotions in infancy: Regulators of contact and relationships with persons. Approaches to Emotion, 129–157.
19. Gladstein, G. A. (1974). Nonverbal communication and counseling/psychotherapy: A review. The Counseling Psychologist, 4(3), 34–57.
20. Xu, Y., Staples, S., & Shen, J. J. (2012). Nonverbal communication behaviors of internationally educated nurses and patient care. Research and Theory for Nursing Practice, 26(4), 290–308.
21. Lauritsen, M. B. (2013). Autism spectrum disorders. European Child & Adolescent Psychiatry, 22, 37–42.
22. World Health Organization. (2019). Autism spectrum disorders (No. WHO-EM/MNH/215/E). World Health Organization. Regional Office for the Eastern Mediterranean.
23. Amphaeris, J., Blumstein, D. T., Shannon, G., Tenbrink, T., & Kershenbaum, A. (2023). A multifaceted framework to establish the presence of meaning in non-human communication. Biological Reviews, 98, 1887–1909.
24. Bull, P. (2001). Nonverbal communication: The state of the art. The Psychologist, 14(12), 644–647.
25. Riggio, R. E. (1992). Social interaction skills and nonverbal behavior. Applications of Nonverbal Behavioral Theories and Research, 3–30.
26. Shafique, Z., Wang, H., & Tian, Y. (2023). Nonverbal communication cue recognition: A pathway to more accessible communication. In Proceedings of the IEEE/CVF Conference on Computer Vision and Pattern Recognition (pp. 5665–5673). Vancouver, BC: IEEE.
27. Friedman, H. S. (1979). Nonverbal communication between patients and medical practitioners. Journal of Social Issues, 35(1), 82–99.
28. Ekman, P. (1973). Cross-cultural studies of facial expression. Darwin and Facial Expression: A Century of Research in Review, 169222(1).
29. Hiatt, S. W., Campos, J. J., & Emde, R. N. (1979). Facial patterning and infant emotional expression: Happiness, surprise, and fear. Child Development, 1020–1035.
30. Morishima, S. (1996). Modeling of facial expression and emotion for human communication system. Displays, 17(1), 15–25.
31. Herath, H. M. K. K. M. B., Karunasena, G. M. K. B., & Mittal, M. (2022). Monitoring the impact of stress on facial skin using affective computing. In Predictive Analytics of Psychological Disorders in Healthcare: Data Analytics on Psychological Disorders (pp. 55–85). Singapore: Springer Nature.
32. Meshram, A. P., & Rojatkar, D. D. (2017). Gesture recognition technology. Journal of Emerging Technologies and Innovative Research (JETIR), 4(1), 135–138.
33. Geer, D. (2004). Will gesture recognition technology point the way?. Computer, 37(10), 20–23.
34. Kret, M. E., Roelofs, K., Stekelenburg, J. J., & De Gelder, B. (2013). Emotional signals from faces, bodies and scenes influence observers' face expressions, fixations and pupil-size. Frontiers in Human Neuroscience, 7, 810.
35. Sanjeewa, E. D. G., Herath, K. K. L., Madhusanka, B. G. D. A., Priyankara, H. D. N. S., & Herath, H. M. K. K. M. B. (2021). Understanding the hand gesture command to visual attention model for mobile robot navigation: service robots in domestic environment. In Cognitive Computing for Human-Robot Interaction (pp. 287–310). Academic Press.

36. Madhusanka, B. G. D. A., Ramadass, S., Rajagopal, P., & Herath, H. M. K. K. M. B. (2022). Attention-aware recognition of activities of daily living based on eye gaze tracking. In Internet of Things for Human-Centered Design: Application to Elderly Healthcare (pp. 155–179). Singapore: Springer Nature.

37. Segen, J., & Kumar, S. (1998, August). Fast and accurate 3D gesture recognition interface. In Proceedings Fourteenth International Conference on Pattern Recognition (Cat. No. 98EX170) (Vol. 1, pp. 86–91). Los Alamitos, CA: IEEE.

38. Rautaray, S. S., & Agrawal, A. (2012). Real time multiple hand gesture recognition system for human computer interaction. International Journal of Intelligent Systems and Applications, 4(5), 56–64.

39. Abercrombie, D. (1968). Paralanguage. British Journal of Disorders of Communication, 3(1), 55–59.

40. Elena, S. (2021). Paralinguistic means and their role in the organization and understanding of a literary text. ACADEMICIA: An International Multidisciplinary Research Journal, 11(12), 89–92.

41. Stamp, J. T. (2011). Body posture defined by environment (Doctoral dissertation, Montana State University-Bozeman, College of Arts & Architecture).

42. Embgen, S., Luber, M., Becker-Asano, C., Ragni, M., Evers, V., & Arras, K. O. (2012, September). Robot-specific social cues in emotional body language. In 2012 IEEE RO-MAN: The 21st IEEE International Symposium on Robot and Human Interactive Communication (pp. 1019–1025). Paris: IEEE.

43. Lewis, H. (2012). Body Language: A Guide for Professionals. New Delhi: SAGE Publications India.

44. Agnus, O. M. (2012). Proxemics: The study of space. IRWLE, 8(1), 1–7.

45. Cristani, M., Paggetti, G., Vinciarelli, A., Bazzani, L., Menegaz, G., & Murino, V. (2011, October). Towards computational proxemics: Inferring social relations from interpersonal distances. In 2011 IEEE Third International Conference on Privacy, Security, Risk and Trust and 2011 IEEE Third International Conference on Social Computing (pp. 290–297). Boston, MA: IEEE.

46. McCall, C. (2017). Mapping social interactions: The science of proxemics. Social Behavior from Rodents to Humans: Neural Foundations and Clinical Implications, 295–308.

47. Ruhland, K., Peters, C. E., Andrist, S., Badler, J. B., Badler, N. I., Gleicher, M.,. . . McDonnell, R. (2015, September). A review of eye gaze in virtual agents, social robotics and HCI: Behaviour generation, user interaction and perception. In Computer Graphics Forum (Vol. 34, No. 6, pp. 299–326). Oxford, UK: Blackwell Publishing Ltd.

48. Hutchinson, T. E., White, K. P., Martin, W. N., Reichert, K. C., & Frey, L. A. (1989). Human-computer interaction using eye-gaze input. IEEE Transactions on Systems, Man, and Cybernetics, 19(6), 1527–1534.

49. El Saddik, A., Orozco, M., Eid, M., & Cha, J. (2011). Haptics Technologies: Bringing Touch to Multimedia. Berlin, Heidelberg: Springer Science & Business Media.

50. Yohanan, S., & MacLean, K. E. (2008, April). The haptic creature project: Social human-robot interaction through affective touch. In Proceedings of the AISB 2008 Symposium on the Reign of Catz & Dogs: The Second AISB Symposium on the Role of Virtual Creatures in a Computerised Society (Vol. 1, pp. 7–11). Aberdeen: University of Aberdeen.

51. Berry, B. (2016). The Power of Looks: Social Stratification of Physical Appearance. New York: Routledge.

52. Uba, L. (2003). Asian Americans: Personality Patterns, Identity, and Mental Health. New York: Guilford Press.

53. Moladande, M. W. C. N., & Madhusanka, B. G. D. A. (2019, March). Implicit intention and activity recognition of a human using neural networks for a service robot eye. In 2019 International Research Conference on Smart Computing and Systems Engineering (SCSE) (pp. 38–43). Colombo, Sri Lanka: IEEE.

54. Madhusanka, B. G. D. A., Ramadass, S., Rajagopal, P., & Herath, H. M. K. K. M. B. (2022). Biofeedback method for human-computer interaction to improve elder caring: Eye-gaze tracking. In Predictive Modeling in Biomedical Data Mining and Analysis (pp. 137–156). Academic Press.

55. Madhusanka, B. G. D. A., Ramadass, S., Premkumar, R., & Herath, H. M. K. K. M. B. (2022). Concentrated gaze base interaction for decision making using human-machine interface. Multimedia Computing Systems and Virtual Reality, 257–279.

56. Erle, T. M., Schmid, K., Goslar, S. H., & Martin, J. D. (2022). Emojis as social information in digital communication. Emotion, 22(7), 1529.

57. Vaughan, T. M., Heetderks, W. J., Trejo, L. J., Rymer, W. Z., Weinrich, M., Moore, M. M.,. . . Wolpaw, J. R. (2003). Brain-computer interface technology: A review of the Second International Meeting. IEEE Transactions on Neural Systems and Rehabilitation Engineering: A Publication of the IEEE Engineering in Medicine and Biology Society, 11(2), 94–109.

58. Herath, H. M. K. K. M. B., de Mel, W. R., & Mittal, M. (2023). Brain-computer interfacing for flexion and extension of bio-inspired robot fingers. International Journal of Cognitive Computing in Engineering, 4, 89–99.

59. Wykowska, A., Chaminade, T., & Cheng, G. (2016). Embodied artificial agents for understanding human social cognition. Philosophical Transactions of the Royal Society B: Biological Sciences, 371(1693), 20150375.

60. Kang, Y., Cai, Z., Tan, C. W., Huang, Q., & Liu, H. (2020). Natural language processing (NLP) in management research: A literature review. Journal of Management Analytics, 7(2), 139–172.

61. Yu, Z., Kim, S., Mallipeddi, R., & Lee, M. (2015, July). Human intention understanding based on object affordance and action classification. In 2015 International Joint Conference on Neural Networks (IJCNN) (pp. 1–6). Killarney: IEEE.

62. Bozkir, E., Eivazi, S., Akgün, M., & Kasneci, E. (2020, December). Eye tracking data collection protocol for VR for remotely located subjects using blockchain and smart contracts. In 2020 IEEE International Conference on Artificial Intelligence and Virtual Reality (AIVR) (pp. 397–401). Utrecht: IEEE.

63. Vamvakousis, Z., & Ramirez, R. (2012, May). Temporal control in the EyeHarp gaze-controlled musical interface. In NIME. MI: University of Michigan.

64. Herath, H. M. K. K. M. B., & de Mel, W. R. (2021). Controlling an anatomical robot hand using the brain-computer interface based on motor imagery. Advances in Human-Computer Interaction, 2021, 1–15.

65. Allison, B. Z., Wolpaw, E. W., & Wolpaw, J. R. (2007). Brain–computer interface systems: Progress and prospects. Expert Review of Medical Devices, 4(4), 463–474.

66. Herath, H. M. K. K. M. B., Dhanushi, R. G. D., & Madhusanka, B. G. D. A. (2022). High-performance medicine in cognitive impairment: Brain–computer interfacing for prodromal Alzheimer's disease. In Predictive Modeling in Biomedical Data Mining and Analysis (pp. 105–121). Cambridge: Elsevier.

67. Atkinson, M. A., Simpson, A. A., & Cole, G. G. (2018). Visual attention and action: How cueing, direct mapping, and social interactions drive orienting. Psychonomic Bulletin & Review, 25, 1585–1605.

68. Paletta, L., Pszeida, M., Ganster, H., Fuhrmann, F., Weiss, W., Ladstätter, S., . . . Reiterer, B. (2019, September). Gaze-based human factors measurements for the evaluation of intuitive human-robot collaboration in real-time. In 2019 24th IEEE International Conference on Emerging Technologies and Factory Automation (ETFA) (pp. 1528–1531). Zaragoza: IEEE.

69. Letaief, M., Rezzoug, N., & Gorce, P. (2021). Comparison between joystick-and gaze-controlled electric wheelchair during narrow doorway crossing: Feasibility study and movement analysis. Assistive Technology, 33(1), 26–37.

70. Wang, Q., Yang, S., Liu, M., Cao, Z., & Ma, Q. (2014). An eye-tracking study of website complexity from cognitive load perspective. Decision Support Systems, 62, 1–10.

71. Borji, A., & Itti, L. (2012). State-of-the-art in visual attention modeling. IEEE Transactions on Pattern Analysis and Machine Intelligence, 35(1), 185–207.

72. Frischen, A., Bayliss, A. P., & Tipper, S. P. (2007). Gaze cueing of attention: Visual attention, social cognition, and individual differences. Psychological Bulletin, 133(4), 694.

73. Kim, K. N., & Ramakrishna, R. S. (1999, October). Vision-based eye-gaze tracking for human computer interface. In IEEE SMC'99 Conference Proceedings. 1999 IEEE International Conference on Systems, Man, and Cybernetics (Cat. No. 99CH37028) (Vol. 2, pp. 324–329). Tokyo: IEEE.

74. Hansen, D. W., & Ji, Q. (2009). In the eye of the beholder: A survey of models for eyes and gaze. IEEE Transactions on Pattern Analysis and Machine Intelligence, 32(3), 478–500.

75. Qvarfordt, P., & Zhai, S. (2005, April). Conversing with the user based on eye-gaze patterns. In Proceedings of the SIGCHI Conference on Human Factors in Computing Systems (pp. 221–230). New York: Association for Computing Machinery.

76. Soetedjo, A. (2012). Eye detection based-on color and shape features. International Journal of Advanced Computer Science and Applications, 3(5).

77. Khan, W., Hussain, A., Kuru, K., & Al-Askar, H. (2020). Pupil localisation and eye centre estimation using machine learning and computer vision. Sensors, 20(13), 3785.

78. Tan, K. H., Kriegman, D. J., & Ahuja, N. (2002, December). Appearance-based eye gaze estimation. In Sixth IEEE Workshop on Applications of Computer Vision, 2002 (WACV 2002). Proceedings. (pp. 191–195). Orlando, FL: IEEE.

79. Peng, K., Chen, L., Ruan, S., & Kukharev, G. (2005). A robust agorithm for eye detection on gray intensity face without spectacles. Journal of Computer Science & Technology, 5.

80. Jacob, R. J. (1993). Eye movement-based human-computer interaction techniques: Toward non-command interfaces. Advances in Human-computer Interaction, 4, 151–190.

81. Kondou, Y., & Ebisawa, Y. (2008, July). Easy eye-gaze calibration using a moving visual target in the head-free remote eye-gaze detection system. In 2008 IEEE Conference on Virtual Environments, Human-Computer Interfaces and Measurement Systems (pp. 145–150). Istanbul: IEEE.

82. Wang, K., Wang, S., & Ji, Q. (2016, March). Deep eye fixation map learning for calibration-free eye gaze tracking. In Proceedings of the Ninth Biennial ACM Symposium on Eye Tracking Research & Applications (pp. 47–55). New York: Association for Computing Machinery.

83. Wang, K., & Ji, Q. (2018). 3D gaze estimation without explicit personal calibration. Pattern Recognition, 79, 216–227.

84. Hennessey, C. A., & Lawrence, P. D. (2009). Improving the accuracy and reliability of remote system-calibration-free eye-gaze tracking. IEEE Transactions on Biomedical Engineering, 56(7), 1891–1900.

85. Morimoto, C. H., & Mimica, M. R. (2005). Eye gaze tracking techniques for interactive applications. Computer Vision and Image Understanding, 98(1), 4–24.

86. Pirri, F., Pizzoli, M., & Rudi, A. (2011, June). A general method for the point of regard estimation in 3D space. In CVPR 2011 (pp. 921–928). IEEE.

87. Villanueva, A., & Cabeza, R. (2008). A novel gaze estimation system with one calibration point. IEEE Transactions on Systems, Man, and Cybernetics, Part B (Cybernetics), 38(4), 1123–1138.

88. Larrazabal, A. J., Cena, C. G., & Martínez, C. E. (2019). Video-oculography eye tracking towards clinical applications: A review. Computers in Biology and Medicine, 108, 57–66.

89. Feng, Y., Chang, C. K., & Ming, H. (2017). Recognizing activities of daily living to improve well-being. IT Professional, 19(3), 31–37.

90. Katz, S. (1983). Assessing self-maintenance: Activities of daily living, mobility, and instrumental activities of daily living. Journal of the American Geriatrics Society, 31(12), 721–727.

91. Karantzoulis, S., & Galvin, J. E. (2011). Distinguishing Alzheimer's disease from other major forms of dementia. Expert Review of Neurotherapeutics, 11(11), 1579–1591.

92. Wibirama, S., Nugroho, H. A., & Hamamoto, K. (2017). Evaluating 3D gaze tracking in virtual space: A computer graphics approach. Entertainment Computing, 21, 11–17.

93. Sahayadhas, A., Sundaraj, K., & Murugappan, M. (2012). Detecting driver drowsiness based on sensors: A review. Sensors, 12(12), 16937–16953.

94. Bae, I. H. (2014). An ontology-based approach to ADL recognition in smart homes. Future Generation Computer Systems, 33, 32–41.

95. Chattopadhyay, A., Meyr, H., & Leupers, R. (2008). LISA: A uniform ADL for embedded processor modeling, implementation, and software toolsuite generation. In Processor description languages (pp. 95–132). Morgan Kaufmann.

96. Augusto, J. C., Nakashima, H., & Aghajan, H. (2010). Ambient intelligence and smart environments: A state of the art. Handbook of ambient intelligence and smart environments, 3–31.

97. Bastian, T., Maire, A., Dugas, J., Ataya, A., Villars, C., Gris, F.,. . . Simon, C. (2015). Automatic identification of physical activity types and sedentary behaviors from triaxial accelerometer: Laboratory-based calibrations are not enough. Journal of Applied Physiology, 118(6), 716–722.

98. Sakamura, K., & Koshizuka, N. (2005, November). Ubiquitous computing technologies for ubiquitous learning. In IEEE International Workshop on Wireless and Mobile Technologies in Education (WMTE'05) (pp. 11–20). Tokushima: IEEE.

99. Cai, Z., Chen, Q., Shi, T., Zhu, T., Chen, K., & Li, Y. (2022). Battery-free wireless sensor networks: A comprehensive survey. IEEE Internet of Things Journal, 10(6), 5543–5570.

100. Chahal, A., & Gulia, P. (2019). Machine learning and deep learning. International Journal of Innovative Technology and Exploring Engineering, 8(12), 4910–4914.

101. Nef, T., Urwyler, P., Büchler, M., Tarnanas, I., Stucki, R., Cazzoli, D.,. . . Mosimann, U. (2012). Evaluation of three state-of-the-art classifiers for recognition of activities of daily living from smart home ambient data. Sensors, 15(5), 11725–11740.

102. Rantz, M. J., Marek, K. D., Aud, M., Tyrer, H. W., Skubic, M., Demiris, G., & Hussam, A. (2005). A technology and nursing collaboration to help older adults age in place. Nursing Outlook, 53(1), 40–45.

3 An Integrated System for Improved Implicit Intention Communication for Older People on Daily Living Activities

An integrated system for improved implicit intention communication for older people on daily living activities would be a valuable tool to support independent living and enhance the quality of life for older adults [1]. Such a system would need to incorporate several key features to be effective, including the following:

1. User-friendly interface: The system should be easy to use and navigate, with simple commands and instructions that are clear and easy to understand.
2. Voice recognition: The system should recognize the user's voice and respond accordingly, enabling older adults to communicate their intentions without using complex or unfamiliar technology.
3. Context awareness: The system should be able to understand the context in which the user is operating, including their location, time of day, and any relevant environmental factors.
4. Personalization: The system should be tailored to the user's needs and preferences, considering their health status, cognitive abilities, and communication style.
5. Integration with other technologies: The system should be able to integrate with different assistive technologies [2], such as smart home devices, wearable sensors, and mobile apps, to provide a comprehensive solution for independent living.
6. Data privacy and security: The system should be designed with robust data privacy and security measures to protect users' personal information and ensure their safety.

In summary, an integrated system for improved implicit intention communication for older people on daily living activities would be a powerful tool to support independent living and improve the quality of life for older adults. By incorporating key

DOI: 10.1201/9781003373940-3

features such as a user-friendly interface, voice recognition, context awareness, personalization, integration with other technologies, and data privacy and security, such a system could revolutionize how older adults interact with technology and support their daily living activities [3].

Many older adults and people with disabilities may face communication barriers when using contemporary technology to support their daily activities. These barriers can arise from various factors, including limited mobility, cognitive impairment, visual or hearing impairment, and language barriers. To overcome these obstacles, it is essential to design assistive technologies that are accessible, intuitive, and easy to use for people with different communication needs. For example, technologies incorporating voice recognition, gesture recognition, or other alternative input methods can benefit people with limited mobility or dexterity. Similarly, technologies that use visual or audio cues can be helpful for people with hearing or visual impairments. Furthermore, it is essential to consider each user's individual needs and preferences when designing assistive technologies. This can involve personalizing and customizing the user interface to tailor it to the user's communication style, language, and cultural background. In summary, to overcome communication barriers in assistive technology for older adults and people with disabilities, designers need to prioritize accessibility, intuitive design, and personalization. By doing so, we can ensure that these technologies are effective tools for supporting independent living and enhancing the quality of life for all users.

HCI has the potential to anticipate and implicitly comprehend a user's intention, making it possible to deliver the necessary services automatically [4–6]. To achieve this goal, researchers have explored a range of human behaviors, such as gesture, voice/language, and EEG, to develop technologies that can accurately infer a user's intentions. As you mentioned, eye gaze is another natural indication that can reflect a person's intention when performing ADLs. Eye gaze can provide valuable information about where the user is looking, what they are paying attention to, and what they might be trying to do. For example, a user looking at a kitchen appliance could indicate they want to use it. A user looking at a door could indicate they want to go through it.

Eye-gaze tracking technology has advanced significantly in recent years, making it possible to track eye movements accurately and in real time [7]. This technology could be used to develop assistive technologies that can anticipate a user's intentions based on their eye-gaze patterns, making it possible to deliver the necessary services automatically. In summary, eye gaze is another natural indication that can reflect a person's intention when performing ADLs. By using eye-gaze tracking technology, it may be possible to develop assistive technologies that can anticipate a user's intentions based on their eye-gaze patterns, making it possible to deliver the necessary services automatically [8].

Visual attention and cognitive processes are closely related [9]. How we attend to visual stimuli can significantly impact our cognitive functions, such as memory, perception, and decision-making [10]. Visual attention refers to our ability to focus on specific visual stimuli in our environment while ignoring others. This process is critical for our ability to interact with our surroundings effectively. How we allocate our visual attention can influence our cognitive processes in several ways. For example, if we focus our attention on a particular object, it can enhance our ability to perceive details and remember them later.

Research [9, 11, 12] has shown that visual attention is closely related to cognitive processes such as working memory, selective attention, and executive functions. For example, individuals with attention deficit hyperactivity disorder often exhibit an impaired ability to sustain attention on a task, leading to deficits in working memory and executive functions. Therefore, understanding how visual attention and cognitive processes are related is critical for developing effective interventions and assistive technologies for individuals with cognitive impairments [13] or disabilities. By developing technologies that can support visual attention and enhance cognitive processes, we can improve the quality of life for individuals with cognitive impairments or disabilities and support their independent living.

The study in this chapter is mainly concerned with developing a new implicit intention communication paradigm that enables users to communicate their intentions naturally and efficiently in HCI through their eye gaze. The proposed framework aims to allow users to express their needs and desires more accurately and quickly, leading to more seamless interaction between the user and the technology. The study explores the relationship between eye-gaze patterns and user intentions in performing ADLs. The researchers aim to identify specific eye-gaze patterns associated with different user intentions, such as reaching for an object or moving to a specific location. By understanding these patterns, the researchers can develop algorithms that can infer user intentions based on their eye-gaze patterns automatically.

The proposed framework can potentially improve the accessibility and usability of HCI for individuals with cognitive or physical impairments. By enabling users to communicate their intentions naturally and efficiently through their eye gaze, it could help overcome some of the communication barriers currently in HCI. Additionally, the framework could have practical applications in various fields, such as robotics, healthcare, and education, where the ability to interpret user intentions accurately and quickly is essential.

Enabling users to communicate their intentions naturally and efficiently through their eye gaze can improve the accessibility and usability of HCI for individuals with cognitive or physical impairments. Individuals with disabilities may face challenges in using traditional methods of communication or interaction with technology, such as using a mouse or keyboard, due to physical limitations or cognitive impairments [14]. By using eye gaze to communicate, individuals with disabilities could have more natural and intuitive access to technology. For example, individuals with motor impairments that affect their ability to use traditional input devices may be able to control technology through their eye gaze. Similarly, individuals with cognitive impairments that affect their ability to communicate effectively through language may find it easier to express their intentions through eye gaze.

Moreover, this approach can potentially improve the quality of life for individuals with disabilities by enabling them to perform daily tasks more independently. For example, assistive technology that can infer a user's intentions based on their eye-gaze patterns could help individuals with mobility impairments to control their environment, such as turning on lights or adjusting the temperature, without relying on assistance from others. By enabling users to communicate their intentions naturally and efficiently through their eye gaze, this approach can make HCI more inclusive and accessible to individuals with cognitive or physical impairments, improving their ability to participate in daily life activities and enhancing their overall quality of life.

3.1   OLDER USERS AND ELDER CARING IN DAILY LIFE

Older users and elder caring in daily life are important issues that require attention and consideration. As people age, they may experience physical and cognitive changes affecting their ability to perform daily life activities independently [15, 16]. This can have a significant impact on their quality of life, as well as their ability to maintain their independence and dignity. Elder caring involves supporting older adults in performing ADLs and instrumental activities of daily living (IADLs) [17]. ADLs include basic self-care tasks such as bathing, dressing, and toileting, while IADLs involve more complex tasks such as managing finances, grocery shopping, and transportation. For older adults, receiving assistance with ADLs and IADLs is often essential for maintaining their independence and quality of life. Family members, friends, or professional caregivers may provide elder care support depending on the individual's needs and circumstances.

The IADLs are tasks that individuals perform to support their daily life and live independently in the community. These tasks are more complex than ADLs, which include basic self-care tasks such as eating, bathing, and dressing. IADLs require a higher level of cognitive functioning and often involve more complex decision-making skills. Some examples of IADLs include the following [18]:

1. Managing finances includes paying bills, balancing checkbooks, and managing investments.
2. Transportation involves driving or using public transportation to attend appointments, social events, or other activities.
3. Meal preparation and cooking: This involves planning and preparing nutritious meals and ensuring that an individual has ended up on hand.
4. Housekeeping: This includes tasks such as cleaning, laundry, and general household maintenance.
5. Shopping involves grocery shopping, running errands, and purchasing necessary items.
6. Medication management includes managing prescriptions, remembering to take medications on time, and ensuring that an individual has a sufficient supply of medications.

For older adults, the ability to perform IADLs is essential for maintaining their independence and quality of life. However, physical or cognitive changes associated with aging can make these tasks more challenging. In some cases, assistance from family members, friends, or professional caregivers may be necessary to help older adults perform IADLs. Additionally, technology can play a significant role in supporting older adults in performing IADLs independently. Assistive technology devices, such as home automation systems and remote monitoring devices, can help older adults manage their daily life tasks and live independently in their homes for as long as possible.

Technology can also play a significant role in elder care in daily life [19]. Assistive technology devices such as mobility aids, communication aids, and home automation systems can help older adults perform ADLs and IADLs independently, enhancing their quality of life and reducing their reliance on caregivers. Moreover, there is a growing trend toward developing technologies that enable older adults to age in place, allowing them to live independently in their homes for as long as possible. This involves using technology to monitor and support older adults' health, safety, and well-being through telehealth systems, remote monitoring devices, and smart home technologies. Addressing the needs of older users and elder caring in daily life requires a multifaceted approach considering the individual's physical, cognitive, social, and emotional needs. Technology can play a vital role in supporting older adults and their caregivers in maintaining their independence and quality of life.

Designing for elder care in daily life requires a multifaceted approach that considers the individual's physical, cognitive, social, and emotional needs. An elderly population is a diverse group with varying needs and abilities, and designers need to consider these factors when designing products or systems for elder care. For example, when designing products for elder care, designers need to consider the physical limitations of the elderly population, such as limited mobility, vision, and hearing impairments. Products should be designed with accessibility in mind, such as providing larger buttons, more explicit text, and audible feedback.

Cognitive abilities must also be considered in designing products for elder care [20]. Products should be designed to be intuitive, easy to use, and provide clear instructions. Designers can use familiar icons and symbols to make products more accessible to the elderly [21]. Social and emotional needs are also essential when designing elder care products [22]. Social isolation and loneliness are significant issues for the elderly, and designers can create products promoting social interaction and connection with family and friends [23, 24]. Products can also be designed to provide emotional support, such as reminding the elderly of essential dates and events or providing a sense of security. Overall, designing for elder care in daily life requires a human-centered approach that considers the individual's physical, cognitive, social, and emotional needs. By taking a multifaceted approach, designers can create products and systems that are usable, accessible, and meet the needs of the elderly population, leading to better outcomes for this vulnerable population.

3.2   HUMAN-CENTERED DESIGN AND USABILITY

Human-centered design (HCD) is an approach to design that puts the needs and experiences of people at the forefront of the design process [25, 26]. HCD is an iterative process that involves engaging with users throughout the design process to ensure that the end product is usable, accessible, and meets their needs. Usability is an essential component of HCD. Usability refers to the ease with which people can use a product or system to achieve their goals effectively and efficiently. Usability encompasses learning, efficiency, memorability, error prevention, and user satisfaction.

In HCD, usability is a critical consideration throughout the design process. Designers must ensure that the product or system is accessible and usable for all users, regardless of their physical or cognitive abilities. This requires careful consideration of the user's needs, preferences, and limitations. Usability testing is a standard method used in HCD to evaluate the usability of a product or system [27]. This involves observing users interacting with the product or system, identifying usability issues, and making design improvements based on user feedback. By incorporating usability into the design process, designers can create products and systems that are intuitive, accessible, and meet the needs of their users. This can result in increased user satisfaction, improved user engagement, and better user outcomes.

The HCD is an iterative process that involves engaging with users throughout the design process to ensure that the end product is usable, accessible, and meets their needs. The HCD process typically involves the following steps:

1. Understand the user and their needs: Designers need to understand the users and their needs by conducting research, such as surveys, interviews, and observation, to gain insights into how they use products and systems and their needs.
2. Define the problem: Based on the insights gained from user research, designers define the problem they want to solve and identify the goals and objectives of the product or system they want to design.
3. Ideate and prototype: Designers generate ideas and create prototypes that address the problem and meet the goals and objectives of the product or system.
4. Test and evaluate: Designers test the prototypes with users to evaluate their usability, identify usability issues, and make design improvements based on user feedback.
5. Implement and launch: Based on the testing and evaluation results, designers make final design decisions and implement the product or system launched into the market.
6. Iterate and improve: Once the product or system is launched, designers gather user feedback, analyze usage data, and make design improvements to improve the user experience.

By engaging with users throughout the design process, designers can ensure that the end product or system is usable, accessible, and meets the users' needs. This approach can lead to increased user engagement, increased customer satisfaction, and better user outcomes.

Usability testing is a critical method used in HCD to evaluate the usability of a product or system. It involves observing users interacting with the product or system, identifying usability issues, and making design improvements based on user feedback [28]. Usability testing typically involves the following steps:

1. Identify test participants: Test participants should be representative of the target user population for the product or system.
2. Develop test scenarios and tasks: Test scenarios and tasks should reflect real-world use and be relevant to the tested product or system.

3. Conduct the test: The user is observed as they perform the test scenarios and tasks. Data are collected through various methods, such as screen recordings, observations, and interviews.
4. Analyze the data: The data collected during the analysis identify usability issues, such as navigation difficulties, confusing interfaces, or error-prone interactions.
5. Make design improvements: Based on the usability issues identified during the test, design improvements are made to the product or system.
6. Repeat testing: The usability testing process is repeated to evaluate the effectiveness of the design improvements.

By conducting usability testing, designers can gain valuable insights into how users interact with their products or systems, identify usability issues, and make design improvements to enhance the user experience. This approach can lead to better user engagement, increased user satisfaction, and, ultimately, better user outcomes. Usability testing provides valuable insights into how users interact with a product or system. Designers can use this information to identify usability issues and make design improvements to enhance the user experience. By improving a product's or system's usability, designers can increase user engagement and satisfaction, leading to better user outcomes. Generally, usability testing is an essential component of HCD, and it plays a crucial role in ensuring that products and systems are usable, accessible, and meet the needs of their users. By incorporating usability testing into the design process, designers can create products and systems that are intuitive, efficient, and enjoyable to use, ultimately leading to better outcomes for users. Usability testing can help designers to do the following:

1. Identify usability issues: Usability testing helps identify usability issues that may not be apparent through other evaluation methods. These issues can include confusing navigation, unclear instructions, or frustrating interactions.
2. Understand behavior: By observing users interacting with a product or system, designers can better understand how users behave and what they need from it.
3. Evaluate design solutions: Usability testing can be used to evaluate the effectiveness of design solutions and identify areas where further improvements are needed.
4. Improve user satisfaction: By identifying usability issues and making design improvements, designers can improve the user experience and increase user satisfaction.

Cognitive abilities are critical in designing elder care products [29]. Cognitive skills refer to mental processes such as memory, attention, perception, and problem-solving. As people age, cognitive abilities decline, making learning and using new technology more challenging [30]. Designers must consider this when designing products for elder care, and they need to create products that are easy to use and do not require a significant cognitive load. One approach is to use familiar design patterns and interfaces that the elderly are already familiar with, such as using icons and symbols that are commonly recognized. Additionally, designers can use clear and straightforward language in product interfaces, providing clear instructions and minimizing the steps required to complete a task.

Another approach is to use feedback mechanisms such as sound or haptic feedback to provide immediate feedback to the user, which can help them understand whether they have completed a task correctly or not [31]. This can be particularly helpful for individuals with cognitive impairments. In summary, cognitive abilities are essential when designing elder care products. By creating products that are easy to use, require minimal cognitive load, and provide immediate feedback, designers can create products that meet the needs of the elderly population and improve their quality of life.

3.3 OBJECT IDENTIFICATION BASED ON ATTENTION

When a person's eyes are focused on a particular object, a cluster of gaze points on that object indicates visual attention [32]. Visual attention is the cognitive process of selectively concentrating on certain visual stimuli while ignoring others. It is an essential process for interpreting and understanding the world around us. Eye-tracking technology can measure visual attention by tracking the movement of a person's eyes and identifying the objects or areas where the person is looking. By analyzing gaze patterns, researchers can gain insights into a person's visual attention and determine what they focus on and for how long [33].

In elder care, eye-tracking technology can be used to design products and systems that are more intuitive and accessible for the elderly population. By understanding where users look and what they focus on, designers can create more natural interfaces requiring fewer cognitive resources. For example, suppose an elderly person struggles to find a particular button on a device. In that case, eye-tracking technology can identify where they are looking and what they are missing. Based on this information, designers can adjust the interface to make the button more prominent and easier to find. Visual attention is an important aspect of human cognition that can be measured using eye-tracking technology [34–36]. By understanding where users are looking and what they are focusing on, designers can create products and systems that are more intuitive and accessible for the elderly population.

After detecting each instance of visual attention using eye-tracking technology, a model of the ANN [37] can be used to group the gaze points of the object or area the person was looking at. This grouping helps to calculate an equal circle to represent the gaze cluster and better understand where the person's attention was focused. Once the gaze cluster is identified, object recognition techniques can be used to recognize the object or scene the person was looking at. This can be achieved by comparing the gaze cluster with the scene or object's image and identifying overlap areas. By analyzing the areas of overlap, the system can determine what the person was looking at and use this information to provide relevant assistance or feedback.

In the context of elder care, this technology can be used to create intelligent systems that can understand and respond to the visual attention of elderly users [38]. For example, suppose an elderly person struggles to find a particular item in their home. In that case, an intelligent system equipped with eye-tracking technology can identify what they are looking at and provide assistance or feedback to help them find the item. Overall, using ANN models and object recognition techniques can help improve the accuracy and usefulness of eye-tracking technology in understanding human visual attention. By combining these techniques with intelligent systems, designers can create products and systems that are more intuitive and accessible for the elderly population.

The classifier for deliberate gaze detection is based on an ANN, a machine-learning algorithm inspired by the structure and function of the human brain. The classification process involves using visual characteristics from natural visual behavior, not requiring users to perform abnormal visual behaviors such as prolonged gazing or purposeful blinking.

Figure 3.1 illustrates the process of classifying deliberate gaze using an ANN. The algorithm uses input data from eye-tracking technology, including gaze duration, fixation position, and saccade velocity, to determine whether the gaze is deliberated. The ANN model is trained using a dataset of intentional and non-deliberate gaze examples, allowing it to classify new instances of gaze behavior accurately. By using this approach, designers can create eye-tracking systems that are more natural and intuitive for users, improving the overall usability and accessibility of the system. This can be particularly beneficial in elder care, where users may have limited cognitive or physical abilities and struggle with more complex or demanding interfaces.

The features used in the classifier for deliberate gaze detection include the duration and focus of the gaze, which were chosen based on an analysis of literature and previous research. The classifier is trained using a dataset of deliberate and non-deliberate gaze examples, allowing it to learn the patterns and characteristics that distinguish intentional from unintentional gaze. During usage, the eye-tracking system records the gaze characteristics of the user and feeds them into the classifier. The classifier then analyzes these characteristics and produces an output indicating the degree of the intentionality of the gaze. This output can infer the user's visual attention and intent, allowing the system to respond appropriately and provide relevant assistance.

By incorporating this type of deliberate gaze detection into eye-tracking systems, designers can create more intuitive and responsive interfaces that better meet the

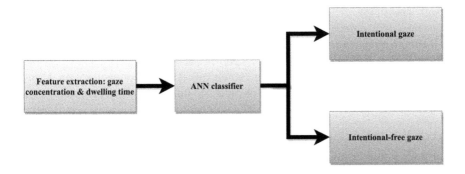

FIGURE 3.1   Detection of intentional gaze using an ANN classifier.

needs of elderly and disabled users. This can help improve their quality of life and promote greater independence in daily activities. In the eye-tracking system, visual attention is only attracted when the classifier recognizes a deliberate gaze. The classifier is trained to differentiate intentional gaze from unintentional gaze based on features such as gaze duration and focus. Once the system detects an intentional gaze, it can infer the user's visual attention and intent and respond appropriately to provide assistance or perform the requested task. This approach enables a more natural and intuitive mode of interaction for elderly and disabled users. It can help improve their quality of life by allowing greater independence in daily living activities.

3.4   HUMAN INTENTION INFERENCE

Human intention inference refers to the ability of a system to understand and predict a user's intentions based on their actions and behavior [39]. This can involve analyzing cues such as speech, facial expressions, body language, and eye gaze to infer the user's intent and respond appropriately [40]. Human intention inference is an important aspect of HCI, especially in applications where users may have limited mobility or communication abilities. By understanding a user's intentions, a system can provide more personalized and efficient assistance, improving usability and user satisfaction [41].

Nonverbal communication is any form that does not involve using words, such as facial expressions, body language, tone of voice, and gestures [42]. It can convey various emotions and attitudes and provide cues that help others understand a person's intentions and feelings. Research has shown that nonverbal cues can be even more powerful than verbal communication in some cases because they are often more difficult to fake or control consciously. For example, if someone tries to hide their emotions or intentions through words, their nonverbal cues may give them away.

Nonverbal communication can also provide important social cues that help people navigate social interactions and relationships. For example, someone's body language may indicate whether they are open and friendly or closed off and guarded. These cues can help others predict how someone will respond in different situations and guide their behavior accordingly. Nonverbal communication plays a vital role in interpersonal communication and can provide valuable information about a person's intentions, emotions, and attitudes, even when they are not explicitly communicated through words [43].

It sounds like an interesting study examining how nonverbal and indirect signals can facilitate more natural and effective interactions with older individuals. Implicit communication of purpose refers to how a person's actions, gestures, and expressions can convey their intentions and goals without explicit verbal communication. Using nonverbal and implicit signals can be particularly important when communicating with older individuals who may have difficulty hearing or processing verbal information or have cognitive or physical impairments that make it challenging to communicate in traditional ways. By using nonverbal cues and implicit communication of purpose, it may be possible to make interactions more intuitive and efficient while also reducing the risk of miscommunication or confusion.

For example, a caregiver or healthcare provider working with an older individual may use nonverbal cues such as gentle touches, facial expressions, and body language to convey empathy, understanding, and reassurance. They may also use indirect signals such as pointing, nodding, or gesturing to indicate a desired action or direction rather than relying solely on verbal instructions. Overall, this type of communication can be an effective way to facilitate more natural and effective interactions with older individuals and can help to improve the quality of care and support provided to this population.

The study uses an ANN model to identify human intention and assess the intended purpose of certain actions or behaviors. The study also uses a questionnaire based on contextual characteristics to help inform the intention recognition system. Once the intention recognition system is in place, carers or other professionals can use it to make choices or diagnoses based on the identified intentions. This description needs to clarify the specific scenarios in which the intention recognition system is being tested. Still, they are likely related to caregiving or support for older individuals [44].

The study explores how technology and machine learning can improve communication and decision-making in contexts where verbal communication may be difficult or limited. By using nonverbal cues and other contextual information, it may be possible to develop more accurate and effective systems for understanding and responding to the needs of older individuals or other populations with communication challenges.

This research uses nonverbal communication and computer vision technologies to recognize a human user's implied purpose. The study is specifically focused on supporting the movement of the eyes in older individuals, and the system is designed to determine the actions or requirements necessary to support this goal. The study uses an ANN model incorporating contextual information to recognize the user's intent to achieve this. The system uses nonverbal cues and other contextual factors to infer the user's purpose and needs and then responds accordingly to provide the best possible service. Overall, the study highlights the potential of technology and machine learning to support older individuals and others with communication or mobility challenges. By using nonverbal communication and contextual information to infer the user's intent, it may be possible to develop more effective and responsive systems for supporting the needs of this population. This could lead to improved quality of life and better access to care and support.

3.4.1 KNOWLEDGE OF HUMAN INTENTION

Human intention refers to the mental state or purpose that underlies a person's actions. It involves the conscious or subconscious desire to achieve a particular goal or outcome. Understanding human intention is essential in many fields, including psychology, neuroscience, artificial intelligence, and HCI. In psychology, researchers study human intent to understand the underlying motivations behind behavior. This helps develop theories of human behavior and mental processes [45].

In neuroscience, researchers study the neural basis of human intention to under-stand how the brain processes and generates intentions [46–48]. This has important implications for the development of neuroprosthetics and BCIs. In artificial intel-ligence and HCI, understanding human intention is crucial for developing intelli-gent systems that interact with humans more naturally and intuitively. This involves developing algorithms and models to recognize and interpret human intention from various sources, such as speech, gestures, and facial expressions.

ANN models are commonly used for classification tasks, such as spam filtering, document classification, and emotion prediction. This is because ANNs are well-suited for learning patterns in large datasets and can be trained to recognize complex relationships between input features and output labels. One of the key assumptions of an ANN model is that the input features are independent of each other, which allows the model to process each feature separately and combine them later in the prediction step. This property is known as "feature independence" and makes ANNs efficient and scalable for real-world applications, especially when real-time predictions are required.

ANN models can also be easily trained and optimized for different classification tasks by adjusting the model architecture, tuning the hyperparameters, and using different training algorithms. This makes them highly adaptable to various appli-cations, from image recognition to NLP. Overall, ANN models are a powerful tool for classification tasks, and their flexibility and scalability make them an attractive choice for many real-world applications.

In cases where the input features are correlated with each other and the output label, capturing the dependencies between the features can significantly improve the accuracy of classification models. This can be achieved using more advanced ANN architectures that allow non-linear relationships between the input features. One example of such an architecture is the ANN, which consists of multiple layers of interconnected neurons. ANNs can learn complex feature representations by com-bining lower-level features into higher-level features, capturing dependencies and interactions between the input features.

The architecture of an ANN can be visualized as a graph, where each node represents a neuron, and each edge represents a connection between neurons. The weights of the connections are adjusted during the training phase to optimize the model's performance. Figure 3.2 shows an example of an ANN architecture designed to capture dependencies between input features and improve prediction accuracy for classification tasks with correlated features. Using an ANN, the model can learn complex relationships between the input features and the output label, leading to more accurate predictions.

The experiment involves displaying different eye-gaze properties and measuring the features of intentional eye views. The experiment's duration is longer than five seconds, and the study uses an ANN classification algorithm to determine partici-pants' visual attention. The user's intention is displayed at the top of the screen. It remains there for more than five seconds, indicating that the user is paying attention to that particular aspect of the kitchen display.

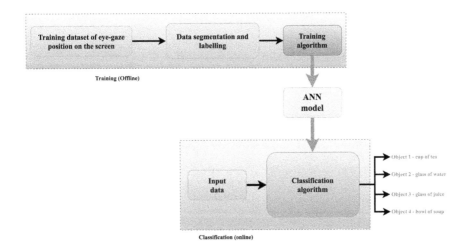

FIGURE 3.2 ANN algorithm block diagram.

ANN classification is a machine learning technique that trains a neural network to recognize patterns and relationships between input features and output labels. In this case, the input features are likely the eye-gaze properties, and the output label is the user's visual attention to different aspects of the kitchen display. Using an ANN classification algorithm, the study can identify which aspects of the kitchen display capture the participants' attention and how their attention changes over time. This information can be used to improve the design of kitchen displays and other interactive systems, making them more intuitive and user-friendly.

The experiment identified four specific items in a kitchen picture that participants were focusing their visual attention on. These items were a "cup of tea," "glass of water," "glass of juice," and "bowl of soup," and they were used to form the basis of the knowledge or intention that the experiment was trying to capture. All manipulator items were incorporated into a simulated picture to simulate a kitchen environment. However, due to the computer-intensive nature of the ANN classification training, it was carried out offline on a computer rather than in real time.

The training data and kitchen scenarios were used to accurately segment the items without limiting the system architecture. The generated models were then saved on the computer, and a classification algorithm was used to recognize the items in real time. The study focused on detecting visual attention and deliberate inferences, which are essential elements of the home environment. This information can be used to improve the design of interactive systems and make them more user-friendly.

Figure 3.3 shows a schematic of the ANN training and recognition phases used in the experiment. The training phase used the training data and kitchen scenarios to generate models to segment the items accurately. The recognition phase used the classification algorithm to recognize the items in real time based on the models developed during the training phase.

FIGURE 3.3   Artificial kitchen image with labeled objects.

3.5   INTENTIONAL COMMUNICATION THROUGH EYE GAZE

Intentional communication through eye gaze refers to using eye movements and gaze direction to convey information and communicate with others. This form of communication can be intentional, such as when a person deliberately looks at someone to signal their interest or attention, or unintentional, such as when a person's gaze is naturally drawn to something in their environment. Eye gaze can convey various information, such as emotions, intentions, and attitudes. For example, a prolonged gaze in a conversation can indicate interest or attentiveness, while a glance away may signal disinterest or discomfort.

Studies have shown that intentional communication through eye gaze can be particularly important for people with conditions that affect their ability to speak or communicate effectively, such as autism spectrum disorder. In these cases, eye gaze can be used as an alternative or augmentative communication method, allowing individuals to express their thoughts, feelings, and intentions without relying solely on spoken language. Researchers have also developed eye-gaze tracking technologies to enable communication with computers and other devices. For example, eye-gaze tracking can control a cursor on a computer screen, select items from a menu, or type out messages using an on-screen keyboard. Overall, intentional communication through eye gaze is a complex and multifaceted form of communication that plays a vital role in social interactions and can be used to enable communication for individuals who may have difficulty with spoken language.

It is important to check the accuracy of the results deduced from eye-gaze tracking, as factors can affect the reliability of the inference findings, such as distracting surroundings or poor gaze tracking. To ensure accuracy, the user should be involved in the process and asked to confirm or provide feedback on the inferences made from their eye-gaze patterns. This can be done by showing the outcome at the top of the screen and asking the user to indicate whether or not it aligns with their intention.

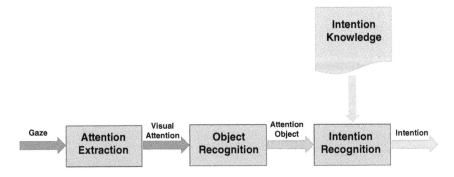

FIGURE 3.4 The gaze-based human intention inference.

In the experiment you described earlier, the user was asked to demonstrate their intention by utilizing the item for more than five seconds. This can also be a way to confirm the accuracy of the inferences made from eye-gaze tracking. While eye-gaze tracking can provide valuable information about a user's intentions and interests, it is important to remember that it is only sometimes 100% accurate. User feedback and confirmation can help ensure that the inferences made are reliable.

Figure 3.4 illustrates the gaze-based deduction of human intention, which involves four main components: Attention extraction, object recognition, intention recognition, and knowledge base. The first component, attention extraction, involves identifying and tracking the user's eye-gaze patterns and determining which objects or areas in the environment the user is attending to.

The second component, object recognition, involves using computer vision algorithms to identify and classify the objects or items the user is attending to. This may include recognizing specific objects, such as a cup or a book, or more general categories, such as food or household items. The third component, intention recognition, involves using the information from the first two components to infer the user's intention or goal. For example, if the user looks at a cup and then moves to the teacup, the system may imply that the user intends to make a cup of tea. The fourth component, the knowledge base, involves using a database or repository of information about the user's preferences, habits, and previous actions to refine the inferred intention further and make more accurate predictions about the user's goals and activities. Overall, the gaze-based deduction of human intention involves using computer vision and machine learning algorithms to analyze a user's eye-gaze patterns and infer their intentions and goals. This technology has potential applications in various fields, including HRI, AR, and assistive technology for people with disabilities.

3.6 FRAMEWORK FOR IMPLICIT INTENTION COMMUNICATION BASED ON GAZE

Figure 3.5 depicts the framework's overall structure for implicit intention communication based on gaze. The user views the scene from the kitchen, fed into the HCI system. The HCI system maintains a consistent view of the scene for the user throughout the intended procedure. The gaze tracking and attention extraction components

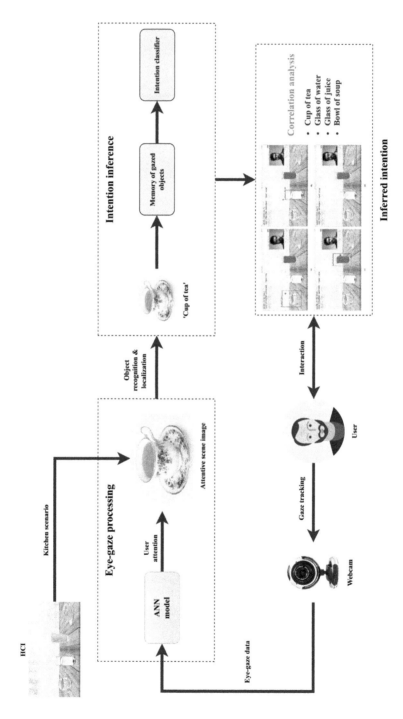

FIGURE 3.5   Gaze-based implicit intention communication framework.

analyze the user's eye-gaze patterns and extract information about which objects or areas in the environment the user is attending to. The object recognition component uses computer vision algorithms to recognize the objects or items the user is attending to. The intention recognition component infers the user's intention or goal based on the context and other available information. Finally, the feedback and confirmation component provides feedback to the user and asks for confirmation or clarification to ensure accuracy.

3.7   SETUP AND CONDUCT OF EXPERIMENTS

Figure 3.6 presents a feedback scenario to the user, replicating the situation in a home care system. The picture depicts a kitchen with visible items, and a camera tracks the user's eye-gaze patterns on the screen. The study focuses on identifying visual attention and intention in this scenario, which are essential components of the overall framework for implicit intention communication based on gaze. The goal is to use this information to infer the user's intentions and provide appropriate feedback or assistance in real time, as needed.

During the trial, participants sat in front of a monitor that displayed an image of a kitchen. They were asked to convey their intention by gazing at specific items using their eyes. In addition to tracking their gaze locations, ocular movements were also observed. The study used an ANN classification algorithm to identify the participants' visual attention and graphical objects were recognized from the camera's visual data. By analyzing these data, the researchers could infer the user's intentions and provide appropriate feedback or assistance based on the task.

Compared with the mouse model, one of the most common interaction models with excellent usability, the gaze modality utilizes natural visual behavior for care detection. While the mouse mode may not be accessible to most disabled people, it is still highly efficient in demonstrating the usefulness of the gaze modality due to its ubiquity and excellent usability. The remaining configuration of the mouse model

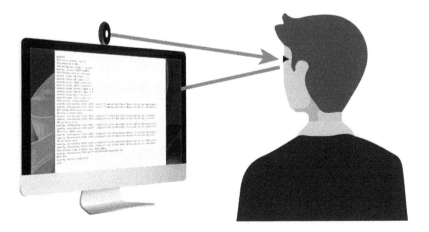

FIGURE 3.6   Experimental setup for gaze-based implicit intention communication.

used in the study was the same as the gaze model. This allowed for a direct comparison of the two interaction modalities and their effectiveness in detecting visual attention and inferring user intentions.

3.7.1 CNN-SVM Visual Attention Classification Training

Convolutional neural network (CNN)-SVM visual attention classification training involves combining CNNs and SVMs to classify visual attention [49, 50]. CNN is used to extract features from the input images, while SVM is used to classify the extracted features. The CNN is trained to learn features from the input images, which are then passed through a fully connected layer to generate a feature vector. This feature vector is then input to the SVM classifier, classifying the image into two classes: Attended or unattended.

During the training phase, the CNN is trained using a labeled image dataset, where each image is marked as either attended or unattended. The SVM is then trained using the feature vectors generated by the CNN and the corresponding class labels. The trained CNN-SVM model is then used to classify visual attention in new images. The input image is first passed through the trained CNN to generate a feature vector. The trained SVM classifies the image as attended or unattended when passed through. The CNN-SVM visual attention classification training approach detects visual attention and infers user intentions based on gaze data.

CNNs are designed to work with image data, and they reduce the number of parameters and connections required during training by exploiting the spatial correlation present in images. The convolutional layers in a CNN consist of filters that slide across the input image, extracting local features such as edges and corners. These features are combined and passed through fully connected layers to make predictions. By using convolutional layers, the number of trainable parameters in a CNN can be significantly reduced compared with a fully connected network, making it more computationally efficient to train. 300-W IMAVIS (image and vision computing) is a facial landmark detection dataset commonly used for face alignment tasks. However, it is not directly related to CNN-SVM visual attention classification training.

To provide more context, CNN-SVM is a standard method for object detection and classification tasks, including visual attention classification. CNN is used for feature extraction, and SVM is used for sorting. In CNN-SVM visual attention classification training, the CNN is typically pre-trained on large datasets such as ImageNet and then fine-tuned on the specific task of visual attention classification. The SVM is then trained on the extracted features to classify the visual attention. The specific architecture and parameters of the CNN-SVM model depend on the task and dataset.

The CNN consists of several convolutional layers followed by fully connected layers. The first convolutional block consists of two convolutional layers with 64 filters each, followed by a max pooling layer. The subsequent two blocks have convolutional layers with 128 and 256 filters, respectively, followed by a max pooling layer. The fourth block has three convolutional layers with 512 filters, followed by a max pooling layer. Finally, there are three fully connected layers with 4096, 4096, and 1000 neurons, respectively, followed by a softmax activation function to output the predicted class probabilities. The model is often fine-tuned on a specific dataset by replacing the last fully connected layer and training it on the new data. The final layer of the CNN model used in this investigation is a fully connected layer that feeds into the classification layer. The fully connected layer helps map the features extracted from the previous layers of the CNN to the specific classes in the classification layer. This is a common approach in CNN architectures used for classification tasks.

The suggested model for detecting visual attention consists of three main components: the pre-trained CNN, feature extraction, and SVM classifier. The pre-trained CNN is used to extract features from the input images. The feature extraction component takes the output from the pre-trained CNN and extracts the relevant features for the visual attention detection task. Finally, the SVM classifier classifies the extracted features as either attention or non-attention. The SVM classifier was chosen because it can handle high-dimensional data and deal with small datasets effectively. Figure 3.7 shows the architecture of the suggested model that combines the strengths of the pre-trained CNN and SVM classifier for accurate visual attention detection.

SVM is a powerful machine-learning approach for small datasets and high-dimensional feature spaces. SVM aims to find the best hyperplane that separates the different classes in the feature space. When the training data are not linearly separable in the original feature space, SVM uses a kernel trick to map the data to a higher-dimensional space where linear separation is possible. With sufficient training data, SVM can deliver accurate and robust classification results.

A multi-class SVM classifier is used to classify the gaze data into different classes based on the user's visual attention. The classifier is trained on the resultant vectors obtained from the pre-trained CNN model. The training is done with a training error of 0.02038 and a test error of 0.02045. The SVM classifier uses a linear function kernel to project the original linear and nonlinear dataset into a higher dimensional

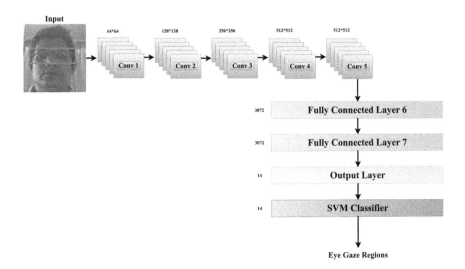

FIGURE 3.7   The architecture of the proposed visual attention detection model.

space, enabling it to separate the different classes more accurately. This approach allows for detecting visual attention with high accuracy and reliability.

3.8   EYE-GAZE ESTIMATION

Eye-gaze estimation refers to determining the direction in which a person is looking. It is a critical component of many computer vision applications, such as HCI, driver assistance systems, and VR. Eye-gaze estimation can be achieved through various techniques, including pupil tracking, corneal reflection, and head-mounted cameras [51–53]. Pupil tracking involves detecting and tracking the position of the pupil in real time. This technique is based on the fact that the position of the pupil changes as the gaze direction changes. By analyzing the movement of the pupil, the gaze direction can be estimated accurately. Pupil tracking can be done using infrared light and cameras near the eyes.

Corneal reflection is another technique for eye-gaze estimation. It involves illuminating the eye with a light source and detecting the reflection of the light from the cornea—the position of the reflection changes with changes in the gaze direction. By analyzing the movement of the reflection, the gaze direction can be estimated. Head-mounted cameras are also used for eye-gaze estimation. These cameras are attached to the head, capturing video of the user's face and eyes. The captured video is then analyzed to estimate the gaze direction. Head-mounted cameras are commonly used in VR applications, where the user's gaze direction controls the virtual environment. Overall, eye-gaze estimation is an essential component of many computer vision applications. By accurately estimating the direction of a person's gaze, computers can interact with users more naturally and efficiently.

CNN-SVM [54] models have been increasingly used for eye-gaze estimation because of their ability to handle large datasets and map images directly to gaze points without the need for hand-engineered features. These models are based on a combination of a CNN and an SVM classifier, with the CNN being used to extract relevant features from the input image and the SVM being used to map these features to gaze points. The CNN-SVM approach has shown promising results in accuracy and robustness in various eye-gaze estimation tasks.

Gaze estimation is an important field of research in HCI that aims to interpret users' visual attention and intentions by analyzing the direction of their gaze [55–57]. The applications of gaze estimation techniques are widespread, ranging from eye-tracking for assistive technologies to gaze-based interaction with computers and mobile devices to virtual and AR. By analyzing the eye regions in images or video streams captured by cameras, deep learning models such as CNN-SVM can accurately predict the position and movement of the user's gaze.

The eye localization process is a crucial step in gaze estimation, as it allows for the precise description of the eye position and subsequent estimation of the direction of gaze. This is typically achieved through a deformable eye model, which is applied to the image data to locate the eyes and estimate their position within the image. Once the eye position has been determined, other factors such as head pose, pupil size, and other eye-related features can be used to estimate the direction of gaze.

The facial landmark localization technique is a computer vision method that detects and localizes specific points on a face, such as the corners of the eyes, nose, and mouth [58, 59]. This technique is often used in gaze estimation to locate the position of the eyes in the image accurately. One approach to facial landmark localization is to use a random forest-embedded active shape model, which combines the flexibility of active shape models with the robustness of random forests. This method uses training images to learn facial landmarks' statistical shape and appearance and can accurately localize them in new images in real time.

3.8.1 EYE LANDMARK LOCALIZATION

Eye landmark localization identifies specific points or landmarks on the eye, such as the eye's corners, the pupil's center, and the iris's edge [60]. This process is important for gaze estimation, as it accurately determines where the user looks.

There are various methods for eye landmark localization, including machine learning, geometric, and hybrid approaches [61]. Machine learning approaches involve training a model on a large dataset of annotated eye images to predict the location of landmarks [62]. Geometric systems use mathematical models and feature extraction techniques to identify landmarks. Hybrid approaches combine both machine learning and geometric methods to achieve better accuracy.

While there have been significant advancements in eye detection and monitoring algorithms in recent years, many are designed to work in specific scenarios or with certain types of data. For example, some algorithms may be designed to work only with high-resolution images or videos, while others may be optimized for low-light conditions. Similarly, some algorithms may be better suited for detecting eyes in certain poses or orientations, while others may struggle with these scenarios.

Furthermore, there are many different types of eye detection and monitoring algorithms, each with strengths and weaknesses. Some algorithms may be better suited for real-time monitoring applications, while others may be more appropriate for post-processing and analysis. Overall, the effectiveness of any eye detection and monitoring algorithm will depend on the specific application and the types of data being analyzed. It is essential to carefully evaluate different algorithms and select the one that best meets the needs of the particular use case.

In the context of eye detection in face regions, an ANN model could be trained on a dataset of labeled images, where each image contains a face region and an annotation indicating the location of the eyes within that region. The ANN model could then learn to identify the patterns and features that indicate the presence of eyes in face regions. Once the ANN model has been trained, it can detect eyes automatically in new images or videos. This can be done by applying the model to each face region in the image or video and identifying the regions the model predicts contain eyes. Overall, using an ANN model for eye detection in face regions can be effective if it is carefully trained and tested on diverse data to ensure accuracy and reliability.

The teaching procedure is likely used to train a machine learning model (such as an ANN model) on a dataset of labeled images, where each image contains a face region and an annotation indicating the location of the eyes within that region. This procedure involves feeding the labeled images into the model and adjusting

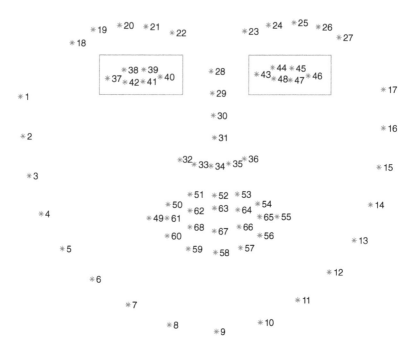

FIGURE 3.8   Facial and eye region localization.

its parameters to minimize the difference between the model's predictions and the accurate annotations. Once the model has been trained, the locating procedure shown in Figure 3.8 can automatically detect eyes in new images or videos. This procedure involves applying the trained model to each face region in the image or video and identifying the areas the model predicts contain eyes. This two-step approach can effectively localize eyes in face regions if the training dataset is carefully selected and the model is trained and evaluated thoroughly to ensure accuracy and reliability.

Facial landmarks are specific points on the face that can be detected and tracked using computer vision algorithms [63]. In the case of eye detection, these landmarks might include points around the eyes, such as the corners of the eyes and the center of the iris. The six coordinates mentioned in Figure 3.9 likely correspond to specific landmarks around each eye. By analyzing the position and movement of these landmarks over time, it may be possible to detect when the eyes are blinking or closing.

The eye aspect ratio (EAR) equation [64] mentioned in Figure 3.9 is likely a mathematical formula that uses the positions of the landmarks to calculate a ratio that reflects the shape of the eye. This ratio can then determine whether the eye is open or closed. Overall, this approach to eye blink detection using facial landmarks and the EAR equation can be helpful in real-time monitoring applications. It does not require specialized hardware and can be implemented using standard cameras or video streams. However, like any detection algorithm, it is important to thoroughly

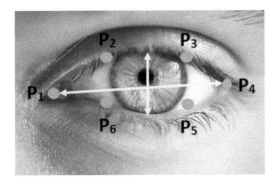

FIGURE 3.9 Demonstration of six coordinates of an eye.

evaluate its accuracy and performance in various scenarios to ensure its reliability. The following is the equation:

$$EAR = \frac{\| P_2 - P_6 \| + \| P_3 - P_5 \|}{2 \| P_1 - P_4 \|}$$

where P_1, P_2, P_3, P_4, P_5, and P_6 are facial landmark locations in two dimensions. The exact formula for calculating the EAR may vary depending on the application and the landmarks used. Still, it typically involves dividing the sum of certain landmark distances by the distance between other landmarks. The resulting ratio can then be compared with a threshold value to determine whether the eye is open or closed. Overall, the EAR is helpful for eye detection and monitoring. It can detect blinks and other eye movements in real time using standard cameras or video streams. However, it is important to carefully select and evaluate the facial landmarks used in the calculation to ensure their accuracy and reliability.

3.8.2 EYE TRACKING AND GAZE ESTIMATION

Eye tracking and gaze estimation are real-time techniques for monitoring and analyzing eye movements and positions [65]. These techniques have many applications, including HCI, VR, gaming, and medical research. Eye tracking involves using specialized hardware, such as eye-tracking cameras, to monitor the eye's movements in real time [66]. By tracking the position and movement of the eye, it is possible to analyze where a person is looking, how long they are looking at a particular point, and other information related to their visual attention. Gaze estimation is a related technique that uses computer vision algorithms to estimate where a person is looking based on the position and movement of their eyes. This technique can be used with standard cameras or video streams, making it more accessible than eye tracking in some contexts.

Eye tracking and gaze estimation rely on detecting and tracking specific eye features, such as the pupil or the iris, as they move in response to changes in visual stimuli. These features can then be used to calculate the direction and intensity of the gaze, which can be used to inform a wide range of applications and analyses.

Eye tracking and gaze estimation are powerful real-time techniques for monitoring and analyzing visual attention and eye movements. However, they require careful calibration and evaluation to ensure accuracy and reliability, particularly in complex or dynamic environments.

Gaze estimation estimates the direction of a person's line of sight or where they are looking. This can be done by using computer vision algorithms to analyze images or video streams of a person's face and eyes and then using this information to estimate the direction of their gaze. In 2D gaze estimation, the goal is to estimate the direction of the person's gaze in two dimensions, typically using a plane or screen as a reference point. This can be useful in various applications, such as studying visual attention in reading or browsing behavior or designing interfaces for HCI.

However, it is important to note that 2D gaze estimation is not the only type [67]. 3D gaze estimation involves estimating the direction of a person's gaze in three dimensions, which can be helpful in applications such as VR or robotics. Other types of gaze estimation may focus on more specific aspects of gaze behavior, such as fixations, saccades, or smooth pursuit movements. Overall, the gaze estimation model described in Figure 3.10 is an important technique for understanding visual attention and eye movements and can have a wide range of practical applications in fields such as psychology, neuroscience, HCI, and more.

3.8.3   EYE-GAZE TRACKING FRAMEWORK

An eye-gaze tracking framework monitors and analyzes a person's eye movements and gaze direction in real time. This framework typically involves using specialized hardware, such as eye-tracking cameras, and software algorithms for detecting and tracking specific eye features, such as the pupil or the iris. The eye-gaze tracking framework can be used in various applications, including HCI, VR, gaming, medical research, and more. For example, eye-gaze tracking can be used to develop more natural and intuitive interfaces for computers and mobile devices, to improve the accuracy of VR experiences, or to study visual attention and cognitive processes in

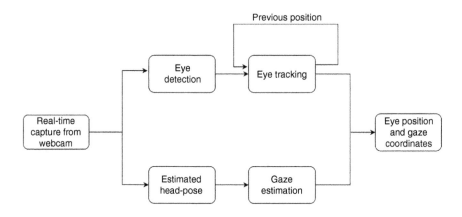

FIGURE 3.10   Eye-tracking and -gaze estimation model.

research settings. The eye-gaze tracking framework typically involves several key components, including the following:

1. Eye-tracking hardware specialized cameras or sensors that can capture high-quality images or video of the eye and its movements.
2. Calibration initialization procedures: A process for calibrating the eye-tracking system to the specific user and environment, typically involving the user following a series of prompts or stimuli.
3. Computer vision algorithms: Software algorithms to analyze the images or video captured by the eye-tracking hardware and extract specific features, such as the pupil's or iris's position and movement.
4. Gaze estimation: A process for estimating the direction of the user's gaze based on the position and movement of their eyes, typically using mathematical models and machine learning algorithms.

An eye-gaze tracking framework is powerful for studying and analyzing visual attention and eye movements in real time. However, it requires careful calibration and evaluation to ensure accuracy and reliability, particularly in complex or dynamic environments.

To use the CNN-SVM classifier to identify a person's visual focus during everyday living tasks, the system must first be trained and qualified to recognize specific visual cues or features relevant to the task. This typically involves training the CNN-SVM classifier using labeled datasets, where the system is shown examples of relevant visual cues and taught to recognize them. For example, suppose the task involves identifying and remembering specific objects in a scene. The classifier may be trained to recognize particular object categories, such as animals, vehicles, or household items.

Once the CNN-SVM classifier has been trained and qualified to recognize the relevant visual cues, it can be used in real time to identify the person's visual focus during the task, as shown in Figure 3.11. This may involve tracking the person's eye

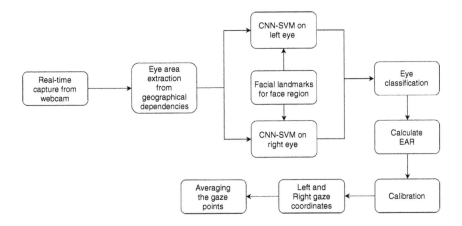

FIGURE 3.11   Implementation process of the CNN-SVM combined model.

movements, head orientation, or other physical cues to infer where their attention is focused. This approach aims to understand better how people allocate their visual attention during everyday living tasks and how this affects their ability to remember specific visual details or information. Using machine learning algorithms and computer vision techniques to identify and analyze these visual cues, researchers can gain insights into human cognition and behavior and develop new tools and technologies for supporting everyday activities and tasks.

3.9   WEBCAM-BASED EYE-GAZE RECOGNITION

Webcam-based eye-gaze recognition is a technology that uses a webcam to track the movements of a person's eyes and determine where they are looking on a computer screen or in the physical world [68]. This technology is commonly used in gaming, VR, and user interface design applications. The process of webcam-based eye-gaze recognition typically involves using vision algorithms to track the position and movement of the pupils in a real-time video feed from a webcam. This information is then used to calculate the direction of gaze and map it to a specific location on the screen or in the physical world.

Different approaches to achieving accurate eye-gaze recognition generally involve training a machine-learning model on a dataset of labeled eye images and gaze directions. The model can then predict the gaze direction of new images in real time, as shown in Figure 3.12. Webcam-based eye-gaze recognition can potentially improve the user experience in a wide range of applications, such as improving accessibility for people with disabilities, enabling more intuitive HCI, and enhancing the immersion and realism of VR environments.

3.10   QUESTIONNAIRE FOR USABILITY

The USE (Usefulness, Satisfaction, and Ease of use) questionnaire is a tool used to evaluate user experience. It consists of 30 questions and uses a 5-point Likert scale to assess three critical aspects of user experience:

- Usefulness: It measures the extent to which a system is perceived as helpful in supporting users' tasks or goals.
- Satisfaction: It measures the extent to which users are satisfied with the system's performance and how well it meets their needs.
- Ease of Use: It measures the ease of learning and using the system, including ease of navigation, clarity of instructions, and overall simplicity.

Here are some sample questions from the USE questionnaire:
Usefulness:

- To what extent did the system support your task?
- How helpful was the system in achieving your goals?
- To what extent did the system meet your expectations?

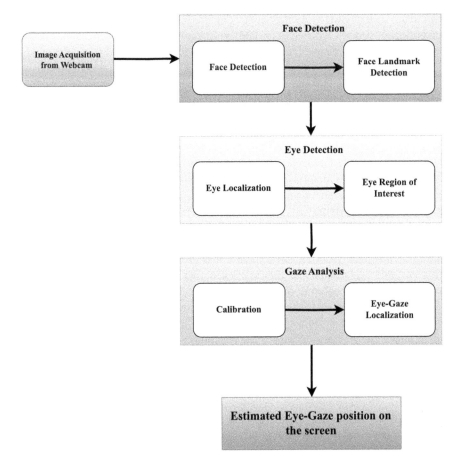

FIGURE 3.12 Webcam-based eye-gaze recognition architecture.

Satisfaction:

- How satisfied were you with the system's performance?
- How well did the system meet your needs?
- Overall, how satisfied are you with the system?

Ease of Use:

- How easy was it to learn to use the system?
- How easy was it to navigate the system?
- How easy was it to complete tasks using the system?

The USE questionnaire can be customized to suit the specific needs of the project or system being evaluated, and additional questions can be added as needed. The USE questionnaire is a flexible tool that can be adapted to fit the unique requirements of a given project or system. By adding or modifying questions, researchers can tailor the questionnaire to capture specific aspects of the user experience relevant to the evaluated system. For example, suppose the system is designed for users with a particular skill level. In that case, questions about ease of use and learning could be modified to reflect the target user's knowledge and experience. Alternatively, if the system is used for a specific task or activity, questions could be added to assess how well the system supports that activity.

It is important to note that the USE questionnaire is just one tool for evaluating user experience. It should be used with user testing, interviews, and analytics. By combining multiple methods, researchers can gain a complete understanding of users' needs and preferences and use that information to improve the design and functionality of the system.

It is great that we have a structured plan for interacting with the target users, as the questionnaire prepared in Appendix 1. This will help to gather consistent and meaningful feedback from all participants. It is also a good idea to provide clear instructions and explanations for the experiment and questionnaire so that users can understand what is expected of them and provide accurate and helpful feedback.

One thing to remember is that the USE questionnaire is just one tool for assessing user experience. It is important to also gather qualitative feedback from users through interviews or open-ended survey questions and quantitative data on system performance (e.g., the accuracy of visual attention detection). By combining multiple methods, you can gain a more comprehensive understanding of users' experiences and identify areas for improvement in the system design.

While the USE questionnaire can help assess user experience, using various methods to gather user feedback is important. This can include qualitative methods, such as user interviews or open-ended survey questions, which allow users to provide more detailed and nuanced feedback on their experiences. Qualitative feedback can help identify specific pain points or areas where the system could be improved and provide insight into how users interact with the system and why they may be experiencing difficulties.

In addition to qualitative feedback, collecting quantitative data on system performance is important. This can include metrics such as accuracy, response time, or completion rate, which can help identify areas where the system may fall short in functionality or usability. Collecting qualitative and quantitative data allows you to understand users' experiences better and identify areas where the system can be improved to meet users' needs better.

REFERENCES

1. Moladande, M. W. C. N., & Madhusanka, B. G. D. A. (2019, March). Implicit intention and activity recognition of a human using neural networks for a service robot eye. In 2019 International Research Conference on Smart Computing and Systems Engineering (SCSE) (pp. 38–43). Colombo: IEEE.
2. Cook, A. M., & Hussey, S. M. (2002). Assistive Technologies. Principles and Practice. Amsterdam: Elsevier.
3. Portet, F., Vacher, M., Golanski, C., Roux, C., & Meillon, B. (2013). Design and evaluation of a smart home voice interface for the elderly: Acceptability and objection aspects. Personal and Ubiquitous Computing, 17, 127–144.

4. Mathew, A. R., Al Hajj, A., & Al Abri, A. (2011, June). Human-computer interaction (HCI): An overview. In 2011 IEEE International Conference on Computer Science and Automation Engineering (Vol. 1, pp. 99–100). Shanghai: IEEE.

5. Sinha, G., Shahi, R., & Shankar, M. (2010, November). Human computer interaction. In 2010 3rd International Conference on Emerging Trends in Engineering and Technology (pp. 1–4). Goa: IEEE.

6. Gunarathne, L. K. P., Welihinda, D. V. D. S., Herath, H. M. K. K. M. B., & Yasakethu, S. L. P. (2023, May). EEG-Assisted EMG-Controlled Wheelchair for Improved Mobility of Paresis Patients. In 2023 IEEE IAS Global Conference on Emerging Technologies (GlobConET) (pp. 1–6). London: IEEE.

7. Drewes, H. (2010). Eye gaze tracking for human computer interaction (Doctoral dissertation, LMU).

8. Sunny, M. S. H., Zarif, M. I. I., Rulik, I., Sanjuan, J., Rahman, M. H., Ahamed, S. I.,. . . Brahmi, B. (2021). Eye-gaze control of a wheelchair mounted 6DOF assistive robot for activities of daily living. Journal of NeuroEngineering and Rehabilitation, 18(1), 1–12.

9. Rayner, K. (1977). Visual attention in reading: Eye movements reflect cognitive processes. Memory & Cognition, 5(4), 443–448.

10. Theofilou, G., Ladakis, I., Mavroidi, C., Kilintzis, V., Mirachtsis, T., Chouvarda, I., & Kouidi, E. (2022). The effects of a visual stimuli training program on reaction time, cognitive function, and fitness in young soccer players. Sensors, 22(17), 6680.

11. Evans, K. K., Horowitz, T. S., Howe, P., Pedersini, R., Reijnen, E., Pinto, Y.,. . . Wolfe, J. M. (2011). Visual attention. Wiley Interdisciplinary Reviews: Cognitive Science, 2(5), 503–514.

12. Richards, J. E. (2003). The development of visual attention and the brain. The Cognitive Neuroscience of Development, 73–98.

13. Herath, H. M. K. K. M. B., Dhanushi, R. G. D., & Madhusanka, B. G. D. A. (2022). High-performance medicine in cognitive impairment: Brain-computer interfacing for prodromal Alzheimer's disease. In Predictive Modeling in Biomedical Data Mining and Analysis (pp. 105–121). Academic Press.

14. Liu-Ambrose, T. Y., Ashe, M. C., Graf, P., Beattie, B. L., & Khan, K. M. (2008). Increased risk of falling in older community-dwelling women with mild cognitive impairment. Physical Therapy, 88(12), 1482–1491.

15. Aartsen, M. J., Van Tilburg, T., Smits, C. H., & Knipscheer, K. C. (2004). A longitudinal study of the impact of physical and cognitive decline on the personal network in old age. Journal of Social and Personal Relationships, 21(2), 249–266.

16. Mather, M. (2010). Aging and cognition. Wiley Interdisciplinary Reviews: Cognitive Science, 1(3), 346–362.

17. Landefeld, C. S. (2003). Improving health care for older persons. Annals of Internal Medicine, 139(5_Part_2), 421–424.

18. Law, M. (1993). Evaluating activities of daily living: Directions for the future. The American Journal of Occupational Therapy, 47(3), 233–237.

19. Uddin, M. Z., Khaksar, W., & Torresen, J. (2018). Ambient sensors for elderly care and independent living: A survey. Sensors, 18(7), 2027.

20. Iancu, I., & Iancu, B. (2020). Designing mobile technology for elderly. A theoretical overview. Technological Forecasting and Social Change, 155, 119977.

21. Gudur, R. R. (2012). Approaches to designing for older adults' intuitive interaction with complex devices (Doctoral dissertation, Queensland University of Technology).

22. Hirsch, T., Forlizzi, J., Hyder, E., Goetz, J., Kurtz, C., & Stroback, J. (2000, November). The ELDer project: Social, emotional, and environmental factors in the design of eldercare technologies. In Proceedings on the 2000 Conference on Universal Usability (pp. 72–79). New York: Association for Computing Machinery.

23. Donovan, N. J., & Blazer, D. (2020). Social isolation and loneliness in older adults: Review and commentary of a national academies report. The American Journal of Geriatric Psychiatry, 28(12), 1233–1244.

24. Steptoe, A., Shankar, A., Demakakos, P., & Wardle, J. (2013). Social isolation, lone-liness, and all-cause mortality in older men and women. Proceedings of the National Academy of Sciences, 110(15), 5797–5801.
25. Kurosu, M. (2011). Human centered design. In Second International Conference, HCD (pp. 9–14). Orlando, FL: Springer.
26. Rouse, W. B. (2007). People and organizations: Explorations of human-centered design. John Wiley & Sons.
27. Harte, R., Glynn, L., Rodríguez-Molinero, A., Baker, P. M., Scharf, T., Quinlan, L. R., & ÓLaighin, G. (2017). A human-centered design methodology to enhance the usability, human factors, and user experience of connected health systems: A three-phase method-ology. JMIR Human Factors, 4(1), e5443.
28. Vredenburg, K., Mao, J. Y., Smith, P. W., & Carey, T. (2002, April). A survey of user-centered design practice. In Proceedings of the SIGCHI Conference on Human Factors in Computing Systems (pp. 471–478). New York: Association for Computing Machinery.
29. Carroll, J. B. (1993). Human Cognitive Abilities: A Survey of Factor-analytic Studies (No. 1). Cambridge: Cambridge University Press.
30. Demetriou, A., Christou, C., Spanoudis, G., Platsidou, M., Fischer, K. W., & Dawson, T. L. (2002). The development of mental processing: Efficiency, working memory, and thinking. Monographs of the Society for Research in Child Development, i-167.
31. Petzold, B., Zaeh, M. F., Faerber, B., Deml, B., Egermeier, H., Schilp, J., & Clarke, S. (2004). A study on visual, auditory, and haptic feedback for assembly tasks. Presence: Teleoperators & Virtual Environments, 13(1), 16–21.
32. Xu, K., Shi, Y., Zheng, L., Zhang, J., Liu, M., Huang, H.,. . . Chen, B. (2016). 3D attention-driven depth acquisition for object identification. ACM Transactions on Graph-ics (TOG), 35(6), 1–14.
33. Henderson, J. M., Pollatsek, A., & Rayner, K. (1989). Covert visual attention and extra-foveal information use during object identification. Perception & Psychophysics, 45(3), 196–208.
34. Frintrop, S., Rome, E., & Christensen, H. I. (2010). Computational visual attention sys-tems and their cognitive foundations: A survey. ACM Transactions on Applied Percep-tion (TAP), 7(1), 1–39.
35. Duncan, J. (1998). Converging levels of analysis in the cognitive neuroscience of visual attention. Philosophical Transactions of the Royal Society of London. Series B: Biolog-ical Sciences, 353(1373), 1307–1317.
36. Spratling, M. W., & Johnson, M. H. (2004). A feedback model of visual attention. Jour-nal of cognitive neuroscience, 16(2), 219–237.
37. Zupan, J. (1994). Introduction to artificial neural network (ANN) methods: What they are and how to use them. Acta Chimica Slovenica, 41, 327–327.
38. Vitay, J., Rougier, N. P., & Alexandre, F. (2005). A distributed model of spatial visual attention. In Biomimetic Neural Learning for Intelligent Robots: Intelligent Systems, Cognitive Robotics, and Neuroscience (pp. 54–72). Berlin, Heidelberg: Springer.
39. Wang, Z., Mülling, K., Deisenroth, M. P., Ben Amor, H., Vogt, D., Schölkopf, B., & Peters, J. (2013). Probabilistic movement modeling for intention inference in human–robot interaction. The International Journal of Robotics Research, 32(7), 841–858.
40. Luo, R. C., & Mai, L. (2019, November). Human intention inference and on-line human hand motion prediction for human-robot collaboration. In 2019 IEEE/RSJ International Conference on Intelligent Robots and Systems (IROS) (pp. 5958–5964). Macau: IEEE.
41. Ravichandar, H. C., Kumar, A., & Dani, A. (2018). Gaze and motion information fusion for human intention inference. International Journal of Intelligent Robotics and Applica-tions, 2, 136–148.
42. Bicho, E., Louro, L., & Erlhagen, W. (2010). Integrating verbal and nonverbal commu-nication in a dynamic neural field architecture for human-robot interaction. Frontiers in Neurorobotics, 4, 1222.

43. Saunderson, S., & Nejat, G. (2019). How robots influence humans: A survey of nonverbal communication in social human–robot interaction. International Journal of Social Robotics, 11, 575–608.

44. Chaandar Ravichandar, H., & Dani, A. (2015, September). Human intention inference through interacting multiple model filtering. In 2015 IEEE International Conference on Multisensor Fusion and Integration for Intelligent Systems (MFI) (pp. 220–225). San Diego, CA: IEEE.

45. Horváth, L., & Rudas, I. J. (2009). Human intent representation in knowledge intensive product model. Journal of Computers, 4(10), 954–961.

46. Blakemore, S. J., & Decety, J. (2001). From the perception of action to the understanding of intention. Nature Reviews Neuroscience, 2(8), 561–567.

47. Frith, C. D., & Frith, U. (2006). The neural basis of mentalizing. Neuron, 50(4), 531–534.

48. Haynes, J. D., Sakai, K., Rees, G., Gilbert, S., Frith, C., & Passingham, R. E. (2007). Reading hidden intentions in the human brain. Current Biology, 17(4), 323–328.

49. Agarap, A. F. (2017). An architecture combining convolutional neural network (CNN) and support vector machine (SVM) for image classification. arXiv preprint. arXiv:1712.03541.

50. Nam, H., & Han, B. (2016). Learning multi-domain convolutional neural networks for visual tracking. In Proceedings of the IEEE Conference on Computer Vision and Pattern Recognition (pp. 4293–4302). Vancouver, BC: IEEE.

51. Wang, J. G., & Sung, E. (2002). Study on eye gaze estimation. IEEE Transactions on Systems, Man, and Cybernetics, Part B (Cybernetics), 32(3), 332–350.

52. Venkateswarlu, R. (2003, October). Eye gaze estimation from a single image of one eye. In Proceedings Ninth IEEE International Conference on Computer Vision (pp. 136–143). Vancouver, BC: IEEE.

53. Pathirana, P., Senarath, S., Meedeniya, D., & Jayarathna, S. (2022). Eye gaze estimation: A survey on deep learning-based approaches. Expert Systems with Applications, 199, 116894.

54. Sun, X., Liu, L., Li, C., Yin, J., Zhao, J., & Si, W. (2019). Classification for remote sensing data with improved CNN-SVM method. IEEE Access, 7, 164507–164516.

55. Shao, G., Che, M., Zhang, B., Cen, K., & Gao, W. (2010, August). A novel simple 2D model of eye gaze estimation. In 2010 Second International Conference on Intelligent Human-Machine Systems and Cybernetics (Vol. 1, pp. 300–304). Nanjing: IEEE.

56. Madhusanka, B. G. D. A., Ramadass, S., Rajagopal, P., & Herath, H. M. K. K. M. B. (2022). Concentrated gaze base interaction for decision making using human-machine interface. In Multimedia Computing Systems and Virtual Reality (pp. 257–279). CRC Press.

57. Madhusanka, B. G. D. A., Ramadass, S., Rajagopal, P., & Herath, H. M. K. K. M. B. (2022). Attention-aware recognition of activities of daily living based on eye gaze tracking. In Internet of Things for Human-Centered Design: Application to Elderly Healthcare (pp. 155–179). Singapore: Springer Nature.

58. Rathod, D., Vinay, A., Shylaja, S., & Natarajan, S. (2014). Facial landmark localization-a literature survey. International Journal of Current Engineering and Technology, 4(3), 1901–1907.

59. Ouanan, H., Ouanan, M., & Aksasse, B. (2016, October). Facial landmark localization: Past, present and future. In 2016 4th IEEE International Colloquium on Information Science and Technology (CiSt) (pp. 487–493). Tangier: IEEE.

60. Park, S., Zhang, X., Bulling, A., & Hilliges, O. (2018, June). Learning to find eye region landmarks for remote gaze estimation in unconstrained settings. In Proceedings of the 2018 ACM Symposium on Eye Tracking Research & Applications (pp. 1–10). New York: Association for Computing Machinery.

61. Huang, B., Chen, R., Zhou, Q., & Xu, W. (2020). Eye landmarks detection via weakly supervised learning. Pattern Recognition, 98, 107076.

62. George, A., & Routray, A. (2016, June). Real-time eye gaze direction classification using convolutional neural network. In 2016 International Conference on Signal Processing and Communications (SPCOM) (pp. 1–5). Bangalore: IEEE.

63. Wen, T., Ding, Z., Yao, Y., Wang, Y., & Qian, X. (2022). Picassonet: Searching adaptive architecture for efficient facial landmark localization. IEEE Transactions on Neural Networks and Learning Systems, 34(12), 10516–10527.

64. Dewi, C., Chen, R. C., Jiang, X., & Yu, H. (2022). Adjusting eye aspect ratio for strong eye blink detection based on facial landmarks. PeerJ Computer Science, 8, e943.

65. Venugopal, D., Amudha, J., & Jyotsna, C. (2016, May). Developing an application using eye tracker. In 2016 IEEE International Conference on Recent Trends in Electronics, Information & Communication Technology (RTEICT) (pp. 1518–1522). Bangalore: IEEE.

66. Majaranta, P., & Bulling, A. (2014). Eye tracking and eye-based human–computer interaction. In Advances in Physiological Computing (pp. 39–65). London: Springer London.

67. Wang, J., Zhang, G., & Shi, J. (2016). 2D gaze estimation based on pupil-glint vector using an artificial neural network. Applied Sciences, 6(6), 174.

68. Cuong, N. H., & Hoang, H. T. (2010, December). Eye-gaze detection with a single WebCAM based on geometry features extraction. In 2010 11th International Conference on Control Automation Robotics & Vision (pp. 2507–2512). Singapore: IEEE.

4 The Artificial Neural Network Approached Gaze-Based Implicit Intention Communication

The ANN is a machine-learning model that simulates how the human brain processes information. It comprises interconnected nodes or "neurons" that recognize patterns and make predictions based on input data. One area where ANNs have been applied is gaze-based implicit intention communication [1].

Gaze-based communication refers to using eye movements to convey information, such as a person's attention or intention [2, 3]. For example, looking at an object can indicate that they are interested in that object or plan to interact with it. In the context of ANNs, researchers have explored how to use eye-tracking technology to train neural networks to recognize and interpret these gaze cues [4].

One approach to gaze-based implicit intention communication using ANNs involves training the network on a dataset of eye movements and corresponding actions [1, 5, 6]. For example, the network could be trained on data collected from participants who were asked to look at different objects and perform different activities, such as reaching for the object or moving their eyes away. The network would learn to recognize patterns in the eye movements that correspond to different actions, allowing it to predict a person's intentions based on their gaze patterns.

Another approach involves using ANNs to decode the neural activity [7] associated with gaze-based communication. Researchers have used functional magnetic resonance imaging [8] to identify the brain regions involved in gaze processing and trained ANNs to recognize patterns in this neural activity. This approach has the potential to provide insights into the neural mechanisms underlying gaze-based communication and could lead to new treatments for communication disorders.

Overall, the use of ANNs in gaze-based implicit intention communication can improve our understanding of how people communicate nonverbally and could have applications in fields such as HRI, where robots could use gaze cues to understand better and respond to human intentions [9].

To use gaze-based communication in an ANN, it is necessary to establish a mapping function between the user's estimated gaze vector and the screen's points. This mapping function is critical because it allows the neural network to understand which part of the screen the user is looking at. To create this mapping function, a

DOI: 10.1201/9781003373940-4

calibration process is required. During calibration, the user is typically asked to look at a series of known points on the screen while their gaze vector is estimated [10, 11]. For example, the known points on the screen could be represented by a grid. By measuring the gaze vector at each known point, it is possible to create a mapping function that describes the relationship between the user's gaze vector and the screen's points.

Once the mapping function has been established, it can interpret the user's gaze in real time. For example, if the user looks at a particular point on the screen, the mapping function can determine which screen point corresponds to that gaze vector. The ANN can then use this information to infer the user's intentions or actions. The calibration process [12] is important for gaze-based communication in an ANN. It is necessary to ensure that the mapping function accurately reflects the relationship between the user's gaze vector and the screen's points, which is essential for an accurate interpretation of the gaze [13, 14].

To use gaze-based communication in an ANN, it is necessary to establish a mapping function between the user's estimated gaze vector and the screen's points. This mapping function is critical because it allows the neural network to understand which part of the screen the user is looking at. To create this mapping function, a calibration process is required. During calibration, the user is typically asked to look at a series of known points on the screen while their gaze vector is estimated. For example, the known points on the screen could be represented by a grid. By measuring the gaze vector at each known point, it is possible to create a mapping function that describes the relationship between the user's gaze vector and the screen's points.

Once the mapping function has been established, it can interpret the user's gaze in real time. For example, if the user looks at a particular point on the screen, the mapping function can determine which screen point corresponds to that gaze vector. The ANN can then use this information to infer the user's intentions or actions. The calibration process is important for gaze-based communication in an ANN [13, 15]. It is necessary to ensure that the mapping function accurately reflects the relationship between the user's gaze vector and the screen's points, which is essential for an accurate interpretation of the gaze.

The proposed method for eye-gaze direction estimates has several advantages, including resistance to noise, blur, and mistakes in localization. Additionally, the testing step requires less computing power than other methods, averaging 30 frames per second (fps) in a Python-based implementation using graphics processing units. In terms of the experimental setup, participants were asked to sit in front of a monitor displaying an image of a kitchen scene. At the same time, their eye movements and gaze locations were recorded. By examining various items in the scene, participants attempted to communicate their purpose to the human–computer interface.

The eye-gaze data were then analyzed using an ANN classifier to identify the user's visual attention and recognize the objects they were looking at. This method allows for interpreting the user's intentions based on their gaze patterns, which has potential applications in fields such as HRI or assistive technology. Overall, this chapter provides a comprehensive review of state of the art in eye-gaze direction estimates and presents a promising method for interpreting gaze patterns using an ANN classifier. This method could significantly improve HCI and assistive technologies for individuals with disabilities.

4.1 PROPOSED METHOD FOR GAZE ESTIMATION

The new technique for estimating the pupil's vector involves using linear and non-linear regression features to create a map function between the pupil vector and the point of gaze (PoG) [14]. This map function then determines the user's gaze direction [15]. The use of linear and nonlinear regression features is likely intensive in the accuracy and robustness of the mapping function. Linear regression is a statistical method for identifying a linear relationship between two variables, while nonlinear regression can capture more complex relationships between variables. Combining these two methods allows the mapping function to better account for the factors affecting the pupil vector and gaze direction.

Additionally, an ANN is used to establish the mapping function. ANNs are particularly well-suited to this task because they can identify complex patterns in the data and make predictions based on those patterns. An ANN also suggests that the mapping function can be trained on a large dataset, allowing it to generalize well to new users and environments.

Overall, using a robust and efficient mapping function based on linear and nonlinear regression features and an ANN will likely result in more accurate and reliable estimates of gaze direction, which could have important applications in fields such as HCI and assistive technology. The flow method for the gaze estimate is illustrated in Figure 4.1. First, a camera connected to the laptop screen collects the eye images of participants while gazing at the calibration marker on the screen.

After calibrating parameters, the image was processed using several techniques to enhance the accuracy of pupil tracking. First, bilateral filters were used to smoothen the image while preserving the edges of the image content. This will likely reduce noise in the image and make it easier to identify the pupil. Next, the histogram of the image was equalized to enhance the contrast. This technique is commonly used to increase the dynamic range of an image and improve its visual appearance. Finally, the average intensity within the pupil was approximated by filling the surrounding regions with moderate intensity. This is likely to improve the accuracy of pupil tracking by providing a more consistent and uniform intensity profile for the pupil. These techniques suggest a careful and methodical approach to image processing for pupil

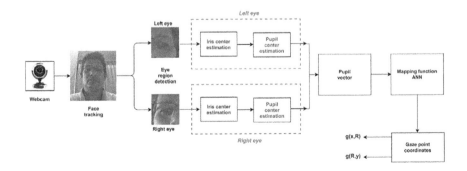

FIGURE 4.1   Flow process of gaze direction estimation.

tracking. Combining smoothing, histogram equalization, and intensity averaging techniques, the resulting pupil-tracking algorithm is likely more accurate and robust.

Global thresholding is applied after the image has been processed using bilateral filtering, histogram equalization, and intensity averaging. This involves calculating the average power within the pupil and inverting the image to highlight the pupil blob. However, there may still be other dark blobs in the binary image that need to be removed. Morphological operations are performed to distinguish the pupil region from these noisy blobs. These operations involve applying mathematical functions such as erosion and dilation to the binary image to remove unwanted blobs and refine the shape and size of the pupil region. Once the noisy blobs have been removed, the final pupil region is determined by considering the blobs' shape, size, and location. The center of gravity of this final pupil region is then calculated and used as the pupil center feature.

This thresholding, noise removal, and feature extraction process are expected in pupil tracking algorithms. By carefully considering the various features of the pupil region and using morphological operations to remove unwanted blobs, the resulting pupil-tracking algorithm is likely both accurate and robust.

The next step in the proposed method is to identify the pupillary iris boundary using a Canny edge detector and a Hough circular transformation. This involves combining profile and mask techniques to define the iris's borders for pupil detection and circular Hough transformation. The gradients on the outer iris border are vertical, and the mismatch between the pupil and iris centers and radii is responsive to threshold values. The detection accuracy is assessed once the pupillary iris boundary has been identified. The next step is calculating the pupil vector using the suggested ANN mapping function input after eliminating the iris and pupil center coordinates. This involves using a three-layer ANN to compute the mapping function between pupil vectors and related gaze positions. The three layers are the input layer, hidden layer, and output layer.

Finally, once the mapping function has been computed, the gaze points on the screen can be calculated using the mapping function. This process is common in gaze-based implicit intention communication, where the user's gaze is used to communicate their intention to the HCI. Combining techniques such as edge detection, Hough circular transformation, and ANN mapping functions, the resulting method is likely accurate and robust.

4.1.1 Visual Gaze Estimation

This section discusses the importance of hardware and user calibration in improving tracking robustness for gaze estimation under real-world conditions. User calibration is necessary to model personal parameters for bias correction of the estimates [16]. While increasing the quantity of calibration data can improve calibration quality, it can also be tedious and damage user experience. Therefore, the trade-off between the quality and convenience of user calibration has been widely studied in the literature. The section also mentions advancements in this area, such as developing better geometric eye models, more effective bias correction models, and introducing implicit calibration methods. These advancements have contributed to improving gaze tracking accuracy and user convenience. The trade-off between calibration quality and comfort for the user is an important consideration in the development of gaze estimation systems. While increasing the quantity of calibration data can improve the system's accuracy, it can also be tedious and negatively impact the user experience. Therefore, researchers have been exploring alternative approaches to calibration that balance the need for accuracy with user convenience. Some of the advancements in this area include the development of more effective bias correction models and the use of implicit calibration methods that require minimal user effort.

The proposed webcam-based eye-gaze tracking methodology consists of several steps. First, the camera and monitor setup is calibrated to establish the mapping between the user's gaze direction and the monitor's screen coordinates. This involves recording the user's gaze while they fixate on known calibration points displayed on the screen. The resulting gaze data are used to estimate the mapping function. Second, image processing techniques extract the user's eye region from the webcam video stream. This involves detecting and tracking the position of the user's pupils and iris. Third, the user's gaze direction is estimated based on the position of the pupils and iris. This involves applying the mapping function from step one to determine the user's gaze position on the screen. Finally, the estimated gaze direction controls the mouse cursor or other interactive elements on the screen. The proposed methodology may include additional steps to improve tracking accuracy and robustness, such as applying filters to reduce noise or using machine learning algorithms to improve pupil and iris detection. Additionally, the user may be required to perform calibration or training to improve the system's accuracy. The proposed webcam-based eye-gaze tracking methodology offers a low-cost and non-invasive alternative to more complex gaze-tracking systems. An overview of the method is illustrated in Figure 4.2.

The deployed webcam system is advanced for estimating gaze and detecting blinks. The system provides a comprehensive real-time solution for gaze estimation and blink detection. These systems have numerous applications, including HCI, eye-controlled devices, and assistive technologies. Integrating advanced techniques such as non-rigid face tracking, supervised face shape estimation, and eye region extraction improves the precision and reliability of the system.

4.1.1.1 Iris Detection

The iris center is identified in the ocular area after the extraction utilizing the preceding procedures [17, 18]. We begin by calculating the radius of the iris. The iris center is then located using a mix of high energy and edge strength information. We first smooth the eye area to calculate the radius using the L_0 gradient minimization technique, eliminating noisy pixels while retaining the edges. The color intensity may be used to gap approximate the iris center and ocular areas are then detected using a Canny edge detector. Eliminate weak edges; certain invalid advantages with short length and distance filters are used. That is too near or far from the iris's rough center. The random sample consensus (RANSAC) [19, 20] technique is used to estimate the parameters of the iris circle model. After applying RANSAC on the iris's

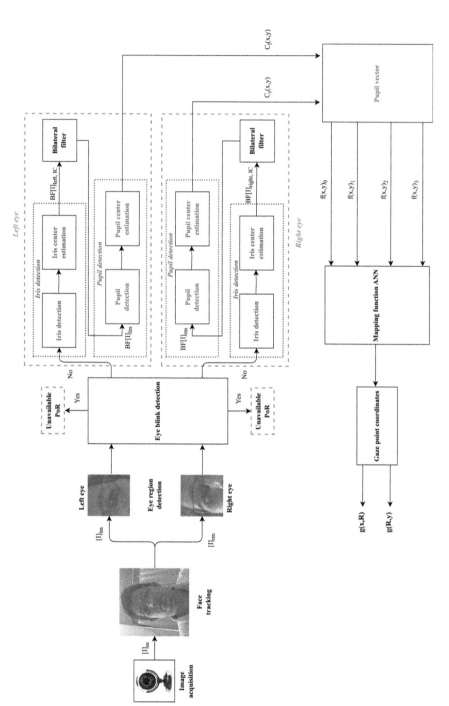

FIGURE 4.2   Overview of a camera system, which comprises gaze tracking for both eyes.

edge points, the radius r of the iris may be determined. Finally, we integrate the intensity energy and edge strength to select the location of the iris's central region. The intensity energy and the edge strength are denoted by E_1 and E_2, respectively:

$$E_1 = \Sigma(I \times S_r) \tag{4.1}$$

$$E_2 = \sqrt{g_x^2 + g_y^2} \tag{4.2}$$

where I is the eye area and the S_r is a circular window of the same radius as the iris. The g_x and g_y are horizontal and vertical pixel gradients that identify the iris center, the energy of the circles' window should be minimized, and the strength of the iris edges should be maximized. The parameter tau controls the trade-off. That is,

$$\left(x_{BF[I]_{IC}}, y_{BF[I]_{IC}}\right) = \min_{(x,y)}\left\{E_1(x,y) - \tau.\left(\int_{-\pi/5}^{+\pi/5} E_2(x,y).ds + \int_{4\pi/5}^{6\pi/5} E_2(x,y).ds\right)\right\} \tag{4.3}$$

where $\left(x_{BF[I]_{IC}}, y_{BF[I]_{IC}}\right)$ is the iris center's estimate coordinate, and the integral intervals are the iris edge ranges that do not overlap the eyelids.

A dark-pupil-based approach rather than a bright-pupil-based one is followed for pupil center detection due to its improved robustness to illumination and eye type variations [21]. Bilateral filtering [22] is performed on the input eye region with the dark pupil to smooth the pupil while keeping the pupil to the iris sharp using equation (4.3). Bilateral filtering also uses the space of a Gaussian filter to treat a pixel difference function as another Gaussian filter [23, 24]. The Gaussian function ensures that only adjacent pixels are regarded as blurring. On the other hand, the Gaussian intensity difference function provides only pixels with comparable intensity with the center pixel that is a blur. It conserves the edges because the pixels near the edges exhibit a substantial fluctuation in intensity. The essential point of bilateral filtering is that the two pixels are close if they occupy adjacent spatial positions and are comparable in the photometric range. The disadvantage of these bilateral filtering characteristics is addressed by several methods, such as meaning blur, Gaussian blur, and median blur, as they may maintain edges on par [25]:

$$BF[I]_p = \frac{1}{W_p}\sum_{q\in s} G_{\sigma s}(\| p - q \|)G_{\sigma r}(I_p - I_q)I_q \tag{4.4}$$

where W_p is a normalization factor,

$$W_p = \sum_{q\in s} G_{\sigma s}(\| p - q \|)G_{\sigma r}(I_p - I_q)I_q \tag{4.5}$$

Equations (4.4) and (4.5) are used for the bilateral filter, where p is the target pixel, q is one pixel around the target pixel, I_p is the color of the target pixel, I_q is the color of a pixel around the target pixel, s is the pixel group around the target pixel, $G_{\sigma s}$ is the weighted pixels according to the distance, and $G_{\sigma r}$ is the weighted pixels according to pixel color difference.

4.1.1.2   Pupil Detection

After calibrating parameters, we used bilateral filters to smoothen the image and preserve the edges of the image content of $BF[I]_{(x,y)}$ that was suitable for retaining the pupil's features. Then, equalize the histogram to enhance the contrast. Then, approximate the average intensity within the pupil by the surrounding regions by filling them with moderate intensity [26]. Then, apply global thresholding by considering the average power within the pupil and inverting the image to highlight the pupil blob. Nonetheless, a few other blobs, as dark as the pupil region, such as eyelashes, eyelids, and shades, remain in the binary image [27, 28]. To distinguish the actual pupil region from the noisy blobs, morphological operations are performed for noise removal. The final pupil is determined among the remaining candidate blobs by considering the blobs' shape, size, and location. Its center of gravity is then used as the pupil center feature [29].

A Canny edge sensor and circular Hough transform are the determining limits of the pupil iris [30, 31]. The profile and mask fusion methods are utilized to identify pupil detection, and circular Hough transforms iris boundaries, which means that detecting canny borders is employed to create an edge map. The gradients of the external iris border are skewed in the vertical direction. Depending on the threshold level, the variations between pupils, iris centers, and radii have complied. Then the accurate detection is evaluated. For example, when the thresholds are T_1, the points T_2 are used to represent the pupil difference of the iris center in the X direction, while the threshold value T_2 is used to represent the radius differences between pupils and the iris center differences in the Y direction followed by T_3 and T_4 as shown in Figure 4.3.

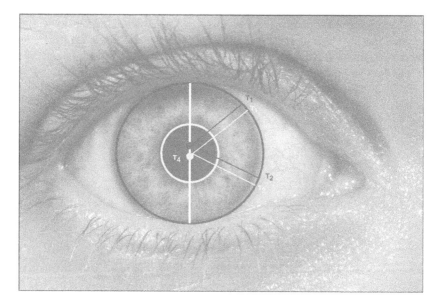

FIGURE 4.3   Both iris and pupil center determination.

Determine the center of the pupil by X_c and Y_c, respectively:

$$x_c = x_{c-iris} - x_{c-pupil} \qquad (4.6)$$

$$y_c = y_{c-iris} - y_{c-pupil} \qquad (4.7)$$

where $(x_{c-iris}, y_{c-iris}) = BF[I]_{(x,y)}$ which describes iris center estimation coordinates.

Also, $x_c < T_1$, in the x-direction, the pupil and iris center thresholds are different. Then, the system can detect the user's gaze moving in either the left or right direction, respectively. Then, $y_c < T_2$, in the y-direction, the pupil and iris center thresholds are different. Then, the system can detect the user's gaze moving in either up or down trend, respectively. If $T_4 < R_d < T_3$, the correct center of the eye is detected, where R_d is the radius difference between the iris and the pupil center.

Furthermore, the masking technique will be implemented to determine the pupil's radius, as shown in Figure 4.4.

By averaging both R_1 and R_2, the radius of the pupil labeled as R can be computed where the radius R_1 is determined by calculating the difference between x_{max} and x_{min} followed by division by two using equation (4.8):

$$R_1 = \frac{x_{max} - x_{min}}{2} \qquad (4.8)$$

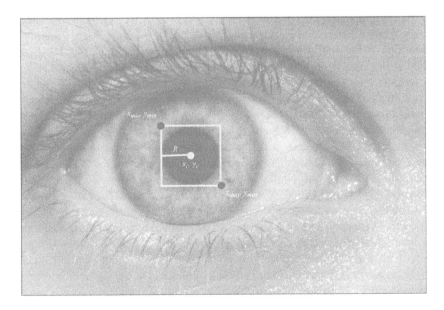

FIGURE 4.4 Pupil detection based on masking.

The same method is used to compute the value of radius R_2 as in the following equation:

$$R_2 = \frac{y_{max} - y_{min}}{2} \qquad (4.9)$$

Finally, the pupil radius denoted by R is computed using equation (4.10), while pupil center estimation coordinates represented by $C(x_c, y_c)$ are determined based on equation (4.11), respectively:

$$R = \frac{R_1 + R_2}{2} \qquad (4.10)$$

$$C = x_{min} + R, y_{min} + R \qquad (4.11)$$

A 2D gaze estimation technique based on pupil vector is presented in this study using the corresponding pupil center estimation coordinates obtained from equation (4.11) for the left and right eyes. The mapping function between pupil vector and gaze point coordinates is solved using an enhanced ANN, and the gaze direction of $g(x, R)$ and $g(y, R)$.

4.1.2 GAZE POINT ESTIMATION BASED ON NEURAL NETWORKS

The neural network was used to build the mapping relations $C_l(x, y)$ and $C_r(x, y)$ representing the pupil estimation coordinates of both left and right eyes to estimate the left and right visual axes and gaze point coordinates [32]. NN with one hidden layer was chosen because of its advanced capability of modeling highly nonlinear relationships. In this study, the pupil positions (x and y components) of both eyes are selected as the input feature for estimating each eye's gaze point coordinates.

Before the NNs can perform the estimation, they must be trained with the data collected in a calibration process. The hidden layer in the NN model is an essential component that can significantly affect the estimation of the gaze vector. To investigate its effect and find a better NN configuration, hidden layers with different hidden units were tested. The changes in the hidden units first affect the estimation of the gaze vector, which eventually affects the estimation accuracy of the 2D gaze. Thus, for the optimal analysis, the number of hidden units can be chosen as 5. Though the error of the gaze vector increases, it does not affect the final 2D gaze estimation because of the gaze vector method characteristic that when the gaze vector has a small error. The enhanced NN scheme structure, including an input layer, a hidden layer, and an output layer, is shown in Figure 4.5. The NN input defines elements input to both eyes' pupil vectors. Gaze point coordinates output elements should be specified as the NN output. There are 4, 2, and 5 nodes, correspondingly input, output, and hidden layers.

Video-based vision tracking systems are included in a camera with a user interface for user eye view tracks [33, 34]. Figure 4.6 shows the typical setup for eye-gaze

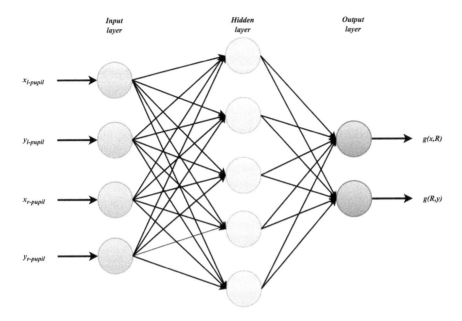

FIGURE 4.5   Scheme framework of the three-layer NN.

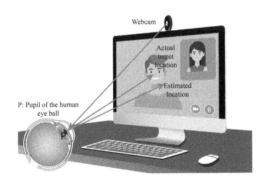

FIGURE 4.6   Schematic diagram of a typical gaze-tracking system.

monitoring. The user calibration, visual, and eye videos are distinct stages of passive video-based eye tracking, visual recognition, and mapping to the screen's gaze
coordinates. The direction of the eye is determined based on both the pupil and
the iris center. Gaze estimation is the technique through which a person's 2D view
line may be estimated or tracked mostly while seeing [35]. It computes the relative
gaze motion between the pupil center and the iris position. The gaze-tracking user
interface may be active or passive, individual or multi-modal. The user's gaze may
be detected for a dynamic user interface to be activated. Gaze data may be used as
some input. An interface without a command is passive in which eye-gaze data are

collected to understand users' interests and attention. The gaze is the single variable for entries for single-mode eye-tracking interfaces. In contrast, a multi-modal input combines mouse, keyboard, touch, or blink input with gaze input [36].

4.2 CALIBRATION

The user is given a series of targets dispersed over the front calibration, as illustrated in Figure 4.7, and the user is requested to gaze at them for some time. The webcam collects the different eye locations of each destination point, and then the tracker learns this mapping function by mapping it to the relevant eye coordinates [37]. The number of target points, the user time for each dot, and the mapping method employed thus vary in the calibration procedures.

Calculating at least 3, 6, and 10 polynomials is necessary if a first, second, and third linear polynomial is used for calibration, meaning a minimum of 3, 6, and 10 calibration markers are required. If too many calibration markers are necessary, unimportant inputs may be deleted according to the primary component analysis to decrease the number of coefficients for polynomial resolution. Generally, four and five calibration target point models are most often used for calculating the first order based on an overall assessment of the real-time quality and precision of the gaze monitoring system. By contrast, six- and nine-target point calibration models have often been used to calculate second order. This research thus examines the mapping function model of nine-target calibration locations. Then, the participants were instructed to calibrate the laptop screen by looking at the nine target calibration points until each progress percentage bar was filled, as shown in Figure 4.8. Once the progress bar gets filled, the blue color dot is displayed.

4.2.1 ESTIMATION OF GAZE TRACKING ACCURACY

Visual stimulation in a set of objectives or scenarios is offered when a user looks at a user interface in a typical visual monitoring operation on a computer screen.

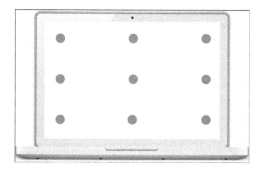

FIGURE 4.7   Calibration screen with nine target points.

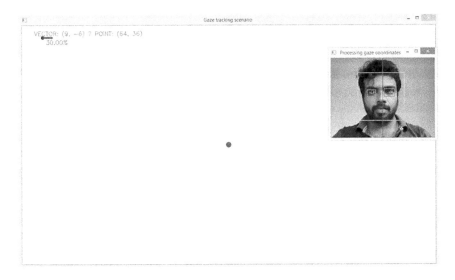

FIGURE 4.8   Eye-gaze calibrate the laptop screen by looking at the nine target points.

The accuracy of the gaze tracking procedure is evaluated as an average difference between the natural stimulus and the gaze location. Concerning the gaze, precision tracking is assessed with pixel distance and distance. The computations given in the following are these accuracy estimates.

Calibration techniques are designed to aid the systems incorrectly calculating the PoG. Therefore, a decision about the number of calibration points is critical. An effective calibration algorithm must have as many numbers as possible of calibration points, making the user familiar with the system. On the other hand, it should also be simple enough to avoid causing trouble to the user. It may be helpful to determine the eye area utilized to scan the laptop screen behind the conception of a calibration method. In accessible mode, the user may remain at a corner point for an indefinite length of time. This concept enables the system to minimize mistakes caused by the miscalibration of the gaze. Single computations are given for brevity; the same equation applies to the left and right eyes. PoG_{x-left}, PoG_{y-left}, $PoG_{x-right}$, and $PoG_{y-right}$ are the measured x, y coordinates of the left and right eye's PoG. The mean gaze coordinates considering both eyes are PoG_x and PoG_y which are the distance of the eye from the screen in equations (4.12) and (4.13):

Gaze point coordinates:

$$PoG_x = \frac{PoG_{x-left} + PoG_{x-right}}{2} \tag{4.12}$$

$$PoG_y = \frac{PoG_{y-left} + PoG_{y-right}}{2} \tag{4.13}$$

4.2.2 EYE-GAZE ESTIMATION ALGORITHM

The vector between the iris and pupil centers is mapped using a polynomial transformation function or a geometric eye model utilizing a regression-based technique to match the gaze locations on the frontal screen [38]. The 2D regression is used to evaluate the direction of the gaze, which is given afterward. The pupil vector is first computed utilizing the pupil and the iris center [39]. The second linear gaze mapping function is in equation (4.14) and pupil vector (4.15):

$$x_c = a_0 + \sum_{p=1}^{N} \times \sum_{i=0}^{p} a_{(i,p)} X_e^{p-1} Y_e^i \tag{4.14}$$

$$y_c = b_0 + \sum_{p=1}^{N} \times \sum_{i=0}^{p} b_{(i,p)} X_e^{p-1} Y_e^i \tag{4.15}$$

where $i = 1,2,3,\ldots,N$, N is the number of calibration points, (x_c, y_c) is the coordinate of gaze calibration markers on-screen coordinate system, and (X_e, Y_e) is the coordinate of pupil vector on the image coordinate system. As conventional linear methods, least squares are utilized to solve the gaze mapping function shown in equations (4.14) and (4.15). In addition, the polynomial is optimized through calibration in which a user is asked to gaze at specific fixed points on the frontal screen.

The order and coefficients are then chosen to minimize the mean squared difference (ε) between the estimated and actual screen coordinates (4.16):

$$\varepsilon = \left(x_c - Ma\right)^T \left(x_c - Ma\right) + \left(y_c - Mb\right)^T \left(y_c - Mb\right) \tag{4.16}$$

where a and b are the coefficient vectors and M is the transformation matrix given by

$$a^T = \begin{bmatrix} a_0 & a_1 & \cdots & a_m \end{bmatrix} \tag{4.17}$$

$$b^T = \begin{bmatrix} b_0 & b_1 & \cdots & b_m \end{bmatrix} \tag{4.18}$$

$$M = \begin{bmatrix} 1 & X_{e1} & Y_{e1} & \cdots & X_{e1}^n & \cdots & X_{e1}^{n-i} Y_{e1}^i & \cdots & Y_{e1}^n \\ 1 & X_{e2} & Y_{e2} & \cdots & X_{e2}^n & \cdots & X_{e2}^{n-i} Y_{e2}^i & \cdots & Y_{e2}^n \\ \vdots & \vdots & \vdots & \cdots & \vdots & \cdots & \vdots & \cdots & \vdots \\ 1 & X_{eN} & Y_{eN} & \cdots & X_{eN}^n & \cdots & X_{eN}^{n-i} Y_{eN}^i & \cdots & Y_{eN}^n \end{bmatrix} \tag{4.19}$$

where M is the transformation matrix, m is the number of coefficients, and N represents the calibration points. The coefficients can be obtained by inverting the matrix, M, as follows:

$$a = M^{-1} x_c, b = M^{-1} y_c \tag{4.20}$$

This chapter uses a nine-point calibration [40] $(N = 9)$ routine and second-order polynomial transformation. The overall accuracy of the eye appearance is based on the calibration target and mapping function configuration. In this case, the components in the higher-order mapping function are utilized to rectify inaccuracies in the anticipated gaze direction. The higher the rank of the polynomial, the more accurate the calculation. However, the number of polynomial coefficients that can be resolved may also be increased.

In addition, the number of calibration markers has also risen. Calibration time is extended, and the high calibration process also increases the user burden. Users are sensitive to tiredness, which reduces calibration accuracy. In addition, you increase the mapping accuracy and accurately evaluate the direction of the user's gaze. A mapping function between pupil vectors and display calibration points is resolved with the ANN based on direct minimum square regression.

The steepest descending gradients approach is the NN training method for mapping functions in equations (4.14) and (4.15). First, creating a link between the hidden and output layers is necessary. Next, the minimal direct solution restriction for square regression defines the cost of error and the continuous learning rule for NN. According to the gaze estimate, the Euclid standard is selected to get a low-cost function as an error-fixing criterion for a minimal square regression, as stated in equation (4.16).

4.2.3   EYE-GAZE DIRECTION CLASSIFICATION

To evaluate the performance of the developed algorithms, we have created a dedicated, novel test framework. It works on real-time test sequences and can measure the difference between the actual place where the user is looking and the system's estimation. The test sequences are classified as "blinking," "looking at the center," "looking at the left direction," and "looking at the right" by looking at the screen. The researchers propose to use two stages: one with a motionless head and one with head movements. Both settings can be identified using the facial feature detection algorithm. The method that uses desktop environments depends on one or multiple cameras fixed in position and thus does not need to be attached to the user, allowing for a non-intrusive tracking of the user's gaze. On the other hand, since the camera's position is fixed and the user's relation to the camera is innately unknown, the method needs somehow to estimate the position of the user's eyes.

The way of solving this problem is to detect the user's face region. By doing this, the face region can be searched to find and extract the eye region. Since the face region needs to be detected, another problem arises head movement. Either method must assume that the user does not move the head during calibration and estimation. The technique needs to somehow compensate for such action in its gaze estimation. From this, higher demands are placed on the user's interaction with the program, or a more complex implementation is needed. This is the trade-off compared with the expensive and intrusive equipment that head-mounted environments entail. The system's evaluation includes two hardware pieces, a web camera for producing the image stream and a computer to run the system. The camera has a resolution of 1,280×720 pixels and a 30 frames per second frame rate. The camera is installed on the computer's monitor and at its horizontal center.

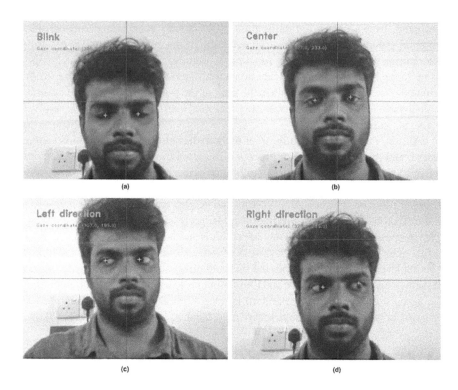

FIGURE 4.9 (a) Test sequence of "blinking," (b) test sequence of "looking at the center," (c) test sequence of "looking at the left direction," and (d) test sequence of "looking at the right direction."

Figure 4.9(a) depicts the "blinking" evaluation series. Blinking an eye is a human eye's rapid closure and reopening. Each person's blinking behavior is slightly different. The blink size, the intensity of the gaze closes/opens, and the degree of gripping the eye vary. EAR monitoring aims to determine whether a blink of an eye occurs. The test sequence of "looking at the center" is shown in Figure 4.9(b). The optimum field of view of the gaze direct to looking at the center is 5°, at which the user's eyes focus correctly. The test sequence of "looking at left" is shown in Figure 4.9(c). The optimum field of view of the gaze direct to the left direction is 25° from the center. The test sequence of "looking at the right" is shown in Figure 4.9(d). The optimum field of view of the gaze directed to looking in the right direction is 25° from the center.

REFERENCES

1. Li, S., & Zhang, X. (2017). Implicit intention communication in human–robot interaction through visual behavior studies. IEEE Transactions on Human-Machine Systems, 47(4), 437–448.
2. Yin, J., Sun, J., Li, J., & Liu, K. (2022). An Effective Gaze-Based Authentication Method with the Spatiotemporal Feature of Eye Movement. Sensors, 22(8), 3002.

3. Madhusanka, B. G. D. A., Ramadass, S., Rajagopal, P., & Herath, H. M. K. K. M. B. (2022). Attention-aware recognition of activities of daily living based on eye gaze tracking. In Internet of Things for Human-Centered Design: Application to Elderly Healthcare (pp. 155–179). Singapore: Springer Nature.

4. Madhusanka, B. G. D. A., Ramadass, S., Rajagopal, P., & Herath, H. M. K. K. M. B. (2022). Biofeedback method for human-computer interaction to improve elder caring: Eye-gaze tracking. In Predictive Modeling in Biomedical Data Mining and Analysis (pp. 137–156). Academic Press.

5. Pettersson, J., & Falkman, P. (2023). Comparison of LSTM, Transformers, and MLP-mixer neural networks for gaze based human intention prediction. Frontiers in Neurorobotics, 17, 1157957.

6. Skodras, E., Kanas, V. G., & Fakotakis, N. (2015). On visual gaze tracking based on a single low cost camera. Signal Processing: Image Communication, 36, 29–42.

7. Aghagolzadeh, M., & Oweiss, K. (2009). Compressed and distributed sensing of neuronal activity for real time spike train decoding. IEEE Transactions on Neural Systems and Rehabilitation Engineering, 17(2), 116–127.

8. Matthews, P. M., & Jezzard, P. (2004). Functional magnetic resonance imaging. Journal of Neurology, Neurosurgery & Psychiatry, 75(1), 6–12.

9. Madhusanka, B. G. D. A., Ramadass, S., Premkumar, R., & Herath, H. M. K. K. M. B. (2022). Concentrated gaze base interaction for decision making using human-machine interface. Multimedia Computing Systems and Virtual Reality, 257–279.

10. Zhu, Z., Ji, Q., & Bennett, K. P. (2006, August). Nonlinear eye gaze mapping function estimation via support vector regression. In 18th International Conference on Pattern Recognition (ICPR'06) (Vol. 1, pp. 1132–1135). Hong Kong: IEEE.

11. Zhang, C., Chi, J., Zhang, Z., Gao, X., Hu, T., & Wang, Z. (2011). Gaze estimation in a gaze tracking system. Science China Information Sciences, 54, 2295–2306.

12. Kondou, Y., & Ebisawa, Y. (2008, July). Easy eye-gaze calibration using a moving visual target in the head-free remote eye-gaze detection system. In 2008 IEEE Conference on Virtual Environments, Human-Computer Interfaces and Measurement Systems (pp. 145–150). Istanbul: IEEE.

13. Modi, N., & Singh, J. (2022). Real-time camera-based eye gaze tracking using convolutional neural network: A case study on social media website. Virtual Reality, 26(4), 1489–1506.

14. Zhang, X., Sugano, Y., & Bulling, A. (2019, May). Evaluation of appearance-based methods and implications for gaze-based applications. In Proceedings of the 2019 CHI Conference on Human Factors in Computing Systems (pp. 1–13). New York: Association for Computing Machinery.

15. Sheela, S. V., & Vijaya, P. A. (2011). Mapping functions in gaze tracking. International Journal of Computer Applications, 26(3), 36–42.

16. Valenti, R., Staiano, J., Sebe, N., & Gevers, T. (2009). Webcam-based visual gaze estimation. In Image Analysis and Processing–ICIAP 2009: 15th International Conference Vietri sul Mare, Italy, September 8–11, 2009 Proceedings 15 (pp. 662–671). Berlin, Heidelberg: Springer.

17. Kawaguchi, T., & Rizon, M. (2003). Iris detection using intensity and edge information. Pattern Recognition, 36(2), 549–562.

18. Mäenpää, T. (2005, October). An iterative algorithm for fast iris detection. In International Workshop on Biometric Person Authentication (pp. 127–134). Berlin, Heidelberg: Springer.

19. Fischler, M. A., & Bolles, R. C. (1981). Random sample consensus: A paradigm for model fitting with applications to image analysis and automated cartography. Communications of the ACM, 24(6), 381–395.

20. Lee, S., Jeong, J., Kim, N., Shin, M., & Kim, S. (2022). Improving performance of the human pupil orbit model (HPOM) estimation method for eye-gaze tracking. Sensors, 22(23), 9398.

21. Arar, N. M. (2017). Robust eye tracking based on adaptive fusion of multiple cameras (No. THESIS). EPFL.

22. Fleishman, S., Drori, I., & Cohen-Or, D. (2003). Bilateral mesh denoising. In ACM SIG-GRAPH 2003 Papers (pp. 950–953). New York: Association for Computing Machinery.

23. Xiao, J., Cheng, H., Sawhney, H., Rao, C., & Isnardi, M. (2006). Bilateral filtering-based optical flow estimation with occlusion detection. In Computer Vision–ECCV 2006: 9th European Conference on Computer Vision, Graz, Austria, May 7–13, 2006. Proceedings, Part I 9 (pp. 211–224). Berlin, Heidelberg: Springer.

24. Yoshizawa, S., Belyaev, A., & Yokota, H. (2010, March). Fast gauss bilateral filtering. In Computer Graphics Forum (Vol. 29, No. 1, pp. 60–74). Oxford, UK: Blackwell Publishing Ltd.

25. Hale, D. (2011, September). Structure-oriented bilateral filtering of seismic images. In SEG International Exposition and Annual Meeting (pp. SEG-2011). SEG.

26. Morimoto, C. H., Koons, D., Amir, A., & Flickner, M. (2000). Pupil detection and tracking using multiple light sources. Image and Vision Computing, 18(4), 331–335.

27. Min-Allah, N., Jan, F., & Alrashed, S. (2021). Pupil detection schemes in human eye: A review. Multimedia Systems, 27(4), 753–777.

28. Ebisawa, Y. (1998). Improved video-based eye-gaze detection method. IEEE Transactions on Instrumentation and Measurement, 47(4), 948–955.

29. Madhusanka, B. G. D. A., & Ramadass, S. (2021). Implicit intention communication for activities of daily living of elder/disabled people to improve well-being. IoT in Healthcare and Ambient Assisted Living, 325–342.

30. Singh, N., Gandhi, D., & Singh, K. P. (2011). Iris recognition system using a canny edge detection and a circular Hough transform. International Journal of Advances in Engineering & Technology, 1(2), 221.

31. Caya, M. V., Padilla, D., Ombay, G., & Hernandez, A. J. (2019, November). Detection and counting of red blood cells in human urine using canny edge detection and circle Hough transform algorithms. In 2019 IEEE 11th International Conference on Humanoid, Nanotechnology, Information Technology, Communication and Control, Environment, and Management (HNICEM) (pp. 1–5). Laoag: IEEE.

32. Wang, J., Zhang, G., & Shi, J. (2016). 2D gaze estimation based on pupil-glint vector using an artificial neural network. Applied Sciences, 6(6), 174.

33. Pentland, A. (2000). Perceptual user interfaces: Perceptual intelligence. Communications of the ACM, 43(3), 35–44.

34. Grauman, K., Betke, M., Lombardi, J., Gips, J., & Bradski, G. R. (2003). Communication via eye blinks and eyebrow raises: Video-based human-computer interfaces. Universal Access in the Information Society, 2, 359–373.

35. Hansen, D. W., & Ji, Q. (2009). In the eye of the beholder: A survey of models for eyes and gaze. IEEE Transactions on Pattern Analysis and Machine Intelligence, 32(3), 478–500.

36. Halwani, Y. (2017). An investigation of multi-modal gaze-supported zoom and pan interactions in ultrasound machines (Doctoral dissertation, University of British Columbia).

37. Prabhakar, G., Ramakrishnan, A., Madan, M., Murthy, L. R. D., Sharma, V. K., Deshmukh, S., & Biswas, P. (2020). Interactive gaze and finger controlled HUD for cars. Journal on Multimodal User Interfaces, 14, 101–121.

38. Wang, J. G., & Sung, E. (2002). Study on eye gaze estimation. IEEE Transactions on Systems, Man, and Cybernetics, Part B (Cybernetics), 32(3), 332–350.

39. Sesma, L., Villanueva, A., & Cabeza, R. (2012, March). Evaluation of pupil center-eye corner vector for gaze estimation using a web cam. In Proceedings of the Symposium on Eye Tracking Research and Applications (pp. 217–220). New York: Association for Computing Machinery.

40. Ho, H. F. (2014, May). Low cost and better accuracy eye tracker. In 2014 International Symposium on Next-Generation Electronics (ISNE) (pp. 1–2). Kwei-Shan Tao-Yuan: IEEE.

5 Gaze-Based Tracking Applications for the Assisted Living of Elderly People

This study proposes a new method for estimating the pupil's vector using linear and non-linear regression features. Determine the gaze direction by solving the map function between the pupil vector and the PoG. An ANN [1] that is reliable and efficient has been created. As a multidisciplinary field [2], eye-gaze estimation has attracted academics, industry, and general users over the past few decades due to the availability of computer hardware and software resources and increased demand for HCI technology. The results assess that the human eye's focus location on display using the head is not fixed. It maps gaze locations and fixation targets from one plane to the next. Additionally, a new 2D gazing technique based on the pupil vector allows for explicitly calibrating the gaze direction's mobility in two dimensions.

As described in Chapter 4, the proposed gaze estimation framework starts with face tracking on the captured frames. They extract eye regions and perform eye-gaze estimation—the resolution of the color stream set to $1280\, pixels \times 720\, pixels$. Display camera calibration is achieved with the method proposed in Chapter 4, where only a thread is utilized to estimate the nine-screen calibration coordinates in the camera coordinates system. Due to low-resolution color images, 2D gaze detection is a challenge, and this research expects more advanced techniques to be developed to improve the 2D feature detection accuracy [3]. Besides these global operations to reduce noise and remove outliers [4, 5], both iris and pupil centers are estimated using the bilateral filtering method during calibration [6–8]. As the system knows ground-truth gaze points during calibration, it finds inliers to estimate subject-dependent eye parameters better [9, 10]. The webcam is focused on human eyes to improve feature detection. Also, the webcam-based gaze-tracking system can capture the upper body of subjects more likely to capture the image of two eyes. The experiments performed the exact personal calibration and gaze estimation procedure for the left and right eyes. The final PoG is the average of the PoG from the left and right eyes. Also, this applies to cases where results from two eyes are outliers.

At the theoretical and methodological levels, there have been many discussions of how to improve the ergonomics and interaction design for the elderly; at the cognitive level, there have been many reviews of the effects of aging on human factors; and at the experimental and research groups, there have been many projects focusing on novel interaction paradigms and multiple devices. It is well known that it is advantageous to maintain our mental, social, and physical acuity as we age. With the help of digital technology, this is doable. However, everything changes when products and services targeted at older people must be better designed, especially now that computer interaction is no longer confined to a desktop. Computers are so commonplace in modern life that one author said, "We carry them, wear them, and may even have them implanted inside us." Ironically, older adults may most experience the adverse effects of poorly designed digital products and interfaces. Even though older adults may not have grown up with technology at their fingertips like today's children, they frequently have a wealth of professional and personal experience with it.

Many studies on the relationship between age and technology use have examined usability, user experience, accessibility, and adoption. The goals of these research projects are usage frequency, performance, efficiency, and precision. Many types of research suggest that many older people need assistance using modern consumer devices due to their functionality and interface design complexity.

This chapter examines how an aging population might benefit from the sensory benefit of eye-gaze contact with digital technology. The undersigned are specialists in interaction design and human factors and are eager to learn more about enhancing the elderly user experience through eye-gaze design. In more detail, the authors will concentrate on a deliberate and well-thought-out design approach influenced by participatory, user-centered, and critical design practices.

5.1   DIVERSITY AND TYPES OF EYE-TRACKING APPLICATIONS

A vast range of eye-tracking applications may be categorized into two major categories: Diagnostic and interactive. The eye tracker offers objective and quantifiable proof of the user's visual and (overt) attentional processes for diagnostic purposes [11–15]. The eye tracker is a potent input device that various visually mediated applications may use as an interface modality.

In its diagnostic function, eye movements are recorded to determine the user's attentional patterns in response to specific stimuli [16]. The non-intrusive use of eye-tracking technology [17] distinguishes diagnostic applications. In some circumstances, concealing the eye tracker from prospective subjects may be beneficial [18]. In addition, the stimulus may not need to alter or respond to the viewer's attention. In this situation, the eye tracker collects eye movements for offline, post-experiment evaluation of the experiment participant's gaze. Thus, eye movement data may objectively confirm the viewer's point of regard or explicit locus of attention. For instance, studies that test the look of some part of a display, such as the placement of an advertising banner on a Web page, may be strengthened by objective proof of the user's attention falling on (or missing) the banner in question. Standard statistical metrics may include the number of fixations over the banner during a five-minute "Web surfing" session. Diagnostic eye-tracking methods apply to (but are not limited to) psychology (including psychophysics), marketing/advertising, human factors, and ergonomics.

Equipped with an eye tracker as an input device, an interactive system is intended to react to the user's gaze or engage with them [19, 20]. Therefore, it is assumed that interactive apps would respond somehow to the user's sight. Such interactive systems may be classified as either selective or gaze-dependent. The latter may be further distinguished in display processing, as seen in Figure 2.2. The prototypical interactive eye-tracking application employs the user's gaze as a pointing device [21]. This form of ocular contact may be seen as one of a series of multimodal input tactics from the system's perspective; for people with quadriplegia, a system that relies simply on gaze as input is an essential communication tool. The eyeballs are used to place a pointer over a gigantic projected keyboard. Multiparty computer-supported collaborative work systems have also investigated the use of gaze to assist communication [22, 23]. In addition to being used as a pointing device, information about the user's gaze may be utilized to modify the display to increase rendering performance, as may be necessary when generating complicated virtual worlds. The use of interactive eye-tracking systems is not limited to the domains of HCI [24], visual displays [25], and computer graphics [26].

5.2   NATURAL TASKS

Psychophysical testing has yielded valuable factual information (e.g., spatial acuity, contrast sensitivity function). Typically, these investigations depend on showing simple stimuli, such as sine wave gratings, horizontal and vertical bars, and so on. Simplicity critiques these artificial stimuli, despite their centrality to developing ideas such as feature integration. As mentioned, visual search experiments are increasing to include more complex stimuli, such as natural landscapes [27]. However, observing images displayed on a laboratory monitor still represents an artificial activity. Recent improvements in wearable and virtual displays now provide the gathering of eye movements under more natural circumstances, often incorporating unrestricted eye, head, and hand motions [28–31].

Land [32] and Land et al. [33] reported on significant work in this area. The first research attempted to examine the pattern of fixations during a well-learned job in a natural context (making tea) and to categorize the monitoring activities that the eyes do. According to this research, even ordinary automated tasks need a surprising degree of continual supervision. A head-mounted eye-movement video camera was utilized to offer a constant view of the scene ahead, with a dot denoting the foveal orientation to within 1°. The foveal orientation was usually near the controlled item, and relatively few fixations were unrelated to the activity. Approximately one-third of all fixations on objects can be attributed to one of four monitoring functions: locating objects used later in the process, directing the hand or object in hand to a new location, guiding the approach of one object to another (e.g., kettle and lid), and monitoring the state of some variable (e.g., water level). Land et al. [33] find that even though tea-making acts are "automated" and entail no cognitive input, the eyes attentively watch every process step. This form of unconscious focus must be a typical occurrence in daily life.

Examining a comparable natural activity [34], some researchers [35, 36] investigated the relationship between eye and hand movements during prolonged meal preparation activities. The article contrasts brewing tea with making peanut butter and jelly sandwiches. In both instances, the position of the foveal gaze was constantly measured using a head-mounted eye tracker with an accuracy of around 1, while the head was free to move. In the tea-making research [35], the three individuals had to travel about the room to find the necessary items; in the sandwich-making study, the seven subjects were seated at a table. Typically, the eyes reach the next item in the sequence before any evidence of manipulation, demonstrating that eye movements are designed into the motor pattern and lead to each action. Throughout an activity, the eyes are often fixed on a single object.

Nonetheless, they often moved on to the next item in the sequence before completing the previous activity. The functions of individual fixations were comparable with those of the tea-making job. Land et al. [33] believe that, at the outset of each activity, the oculomotor system receives the identification of the needed objects, information about their position, and instructions for the kind of monitoring required throughout the action. During this kind of activity, many eye movements are directed toward task-relevant objects; as a result, their regulation is predominantly top-down, and intrinsic salience has minimal effect. The eyes give information on an "as required" basis; although the relevant eye movements often predate the motor actions, they mediate by a fraction of a second. Eye movements are thus at the forefront of each action plan, not just reactions to circumstances. Land et al. [33] conclude that their research does not support that the visual system creates a detailed representation of the environment and then works based on this model. Most of the information is acquired from the scene as required.

Researchers can study different parts of human behavior in a controlled and changeable setting using virtual settings. By changing the virtual environment at specific points during the task, researchers can see how people react and respond to different situations [37]. This method can help determine what is happening under the surface, test other ideas, and learn more about the observed behavior. In a virtual environment where subjects replicate toy models, the authors demonstrate that individuals employ regularities in the spatial structure to govern eye movement targeting [38]. Other trials in a virtual world with haptic feedback [39] show that even basic visual features, such as size, are not continually accessible or processed automatically by the visual system but are dynamically acquired and discarded based on the needs of the present job.

5.3   RESULTS OF THE EYE-GAZE DIRECTION CLASSIFICATION

To evaluate the eye-gaze performance, we recorded a set of videos with 10 participants. For each frame of those videos, the correct gaze direction was human-labeled. A total of 10 videos were recorded, with different lighting conditions, using glasses or not, and in other positions concerning a laptop webcam. These people were instructed to start capturing the video by looking at the screen's center, directing their gaze to the left and right, and finally blinking their eyes. The captured videos have 6,000 frames classified concerning the eye-gaze direction, with 20 seconds for each participant, with an average processing rate of 30 fps. The distribution of each movement of gaze is described in Table 5.1. Aiming for a quantitative evaluation of qualitative aspects of the images, we tested the algorithm's performance in different image conditions, such as Figures 4.9(a) to 4.9(d).

TABLE 5.1

Distribution of Each Direction of Gaze

Gaze direction	Approximate no. of frames
Center	1,500
Left	1,350
Right	1,350
Blink	1,500

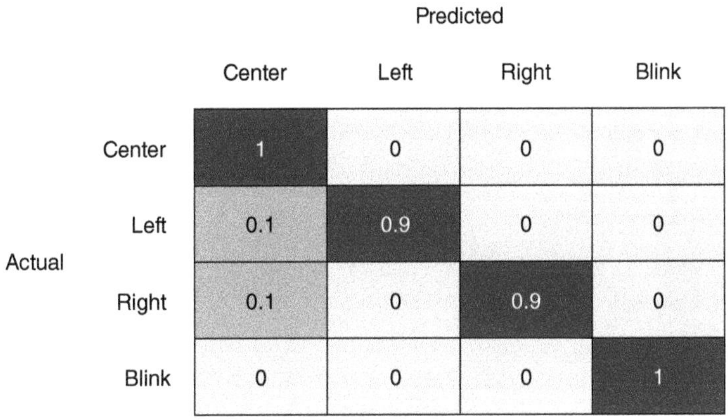

Predicted

		Center	Left	Right	Blink
	Center	1	0	0	0
	Left	0.1	0.9	0	0
Actual	Right	0.1	0	0.9	0
	Blink	0	0	0	1

FIGURE 5.1   Confusion matrix for the gaze direction.

One detailed inference performance of the observable results that intention to the "gaze direction" is illustrated as a confusion matrix shown in Figure 5.1. The horizontal axis is the predicted intention, and the vertical axis is the actual intention. The precision and accuracy for each type of intention to the objects are summarized in Table 5.2. The precision of the intention to "gaze direction to center" was inferred in 1.0 cases, and the accuracy of the intention to "gaze direction to the left" was implied in 0.9 cases. The precision of the intention to "gaze direction to the right" was inferred in 0.9 cases. Finally, the precision of the intention to "gaze to blink" was figured in 1.0 cases. The overall accuracy rate was 0.91. Notably, 0.09 of the error occurs for the intention to the eye-gaze variation. With fewer dominant eye-gaze variations, it is more challenging to characterize the intention from the object aspect. The CNN-SVM model has less tolerance for the mistakes of the attention detection classifier.

The mean accuracy and precision for each type of intention are men in Figure 5.2. Furthermore, the mean accuracy of the intention to "gaze direction to center" was inferred in 0.95 cases. The mean accuracy of the intention to "gaze direction to the left" was inferred in 0.97 cases. The mean accuracy of the intention to "gaze direction to the right" was inferred in 0.97 cases. Finally, the mean accuracy of the intention to "gaze to blink" was inferred in 1.0 cases.

TABLE 5.2
Accuracy and Precision of Intention to Each Gaze Direction

Gaze direction	Accuracy	Precision
Center	0.95	1
Left	0.97	0.9
Right	0.97	0.9
Blink	1	1

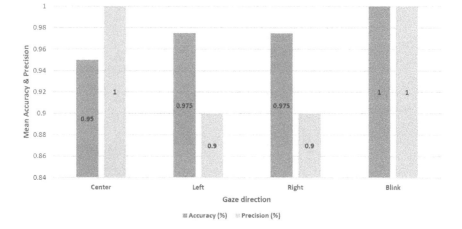

FIGURE 5.2   Mean accuracy and precision for each intention.

5.4   PERCEPTION OF HUMAN INTENTIONS

The way to deduce the user's intention may be to indirectly convey the intended goal, for example, via nonverbal instructions [40, 41]. However, if implicated user contact is needed, it may result in successful cooperation. People anticipate the intents of others exceptionally well, showing that nonverbal communication may contain inference intentions. This chapter investigates how older people's desire to convey nonverbal signs and indirect indications that the user implicitly gives while carrying out activities for quicker and natural engagement may be used. This research offers instructions to control the eye and analyze the user's intention to deduce everyday tasks. The suggested technique of this study is the SVM classification to inform the identification of human intents. An assessment examines inferred intention and is generally performed alone in domestic cases. A questionnaire based on contextual factors is utilized for intention recognition. The caregivers then decide or diagnose based on a technique for identifying intentions.

Four deliberate items have been empirically detected in the kitchen scenario. These four items have been deliberately created as *teacups*, *water glasses*, *juice glasses*, and *soup bowls.* The simulated kitchen scene included all handling objects. In this investigation, visual attention and purpose, essential components of the national situation, were detected. The house scenario is modeled on the user feedback scene picture, as illustrated in Figure 3.3.

Then, we recorded videos with 30 participants to evaluate the eye-gaze performance. For each frame of those videos, the correct gaze direction was considered human. Thus, 30 videos were recorded, with different lighting conditions, using glasses or not, and in other positions about a laptop webcam. First, the participants were instructed to calibrate the laptop screen by looking at the nine target calibration points, as shown in Figure 5.3. Then, participants were instructed to start capturing the video by looking at the "teacup," "glass of water," "glass of juice," and finally, "bowl of soup" in their eyes, respectively.

The visualization of the intentional and intentional gazes shows different eye-gaze properties. The intended eye-look characteristics are provided to display items in the cooking situation. A person's gaze lives more extended during the intentional gaze than the deliberate gaze depicted in Figure 5.5 and focuses more on gaze distribution. Consider, in this experiment, that the time to stay is five seconds longer. The investigation then utilized the SVM classification to identify the participants' visual attention. The user intention is displayed at the top of the screen, where it dwells relatively longer than five seconds. Figure 5.4(a) describes the user intention to "teacup"; the intention to "glass of water" is illustrated in Figure 5.4(b). Next, the user intention identified as "glass of juice" is described in Figure 5.4(c). Finally, user intention to the "bowl of soup" is illustrated in Figure 5.4(d).

The recorded videos are divided among 30 participants with an average processing rate of 30 frames per second regarding their glance at items in the kitchen scenario, with around 20 seconds for each participant. The system used the camera

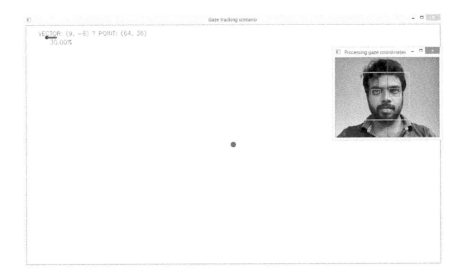

FIGURE 5.3 Calibration screen.

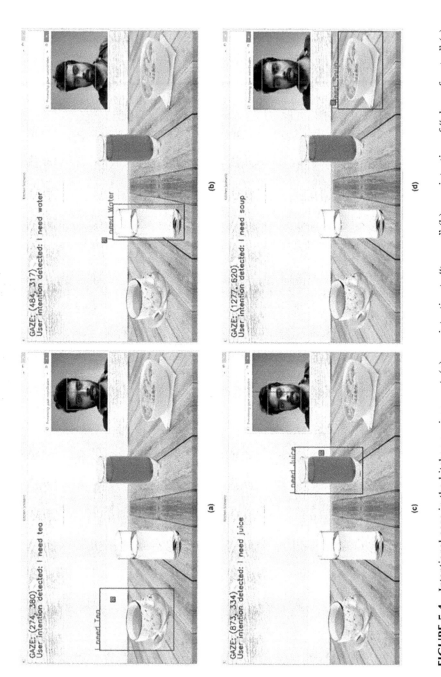

FIGURE 5.4 Intentional gaze in the kitchen environment, (a) user intention to "teacup," (b) user intention of "glass of water," (c) user intention identified as "glass of juice," and (d) user intention to the "bowl of soup."

TABLE 5.3
SVM Classifier for Object Intention Detection

Training dataset	Positive classification (%)	Negative classification (%)
Positive training data	82.3	17.7
Negative training data	15.2	84.8

under indoor illumination settings throughout this trial. At first, the individual's face was not lit by light from the top or upper corners.

The SVM classifier training gathered 95 sets of positive training data and 70 negative training datasets. These training datasets were utilized for training the classifier, and the total success rate for training was 80.67%. Table 5.3 summarizes more specific training performance.

Real attention tends to be less efficient than false detections. The classifier was developed. In the experiment, the SVM classifier is then utilized to identify the visual attention of each participant. The SVM classifier identifies user intention in this experiment, using gazing data pre-labeled based on visual attentiveness and user eye gaze closer to the chosen item. Two criteria have been used for performance assessment: Accurate detection rate and fake rate. The positive grading rate for the positive training dataset is 82.3%, whereas the negative grading rate is 17.7%. The positive grade rate in the negative training dataset is 15.2%, and the negative grade rate is 84.8% correctly identified. In the kitchen scenario, the performance of the SVM attention classifier differed considerably across four distinct subjects. The findings showed that the SVM classifier and the chosen eye-gaze characteristics could identify users' visual attention during normal visual activities.

5.5   VISUAL OBJECT INTENTION

Identify a user intention for a kitchen scenario; four intended items have been chosen and input individually into the SVM model for correlation training. Figure 5.5 shows an example of the accuracy of each kind of purpose-depicted item. Every purpose of the 30 participants in the kitchen scenario is shown in the correlation diagram. While some individuals may have seen various things for intention, most participants viewed familiar objects broadly. Most participants have, for example, adequately chosen the purpose of "water glass."

Object intention to the "teacup" refers to a linear regression analysis revealing a linear relationship. The coefficient of determination, R^2, is about 0.0814, which means that this equation explains 8.14% of the changeability in object intention. Also, this indicates a negative linear relationship of object intention to the "teacup." Then, object intention to the "glass of water" refers to a linear regression analysis of these data, revealing a linear relationship. The coefficient of determination, R^2, is about 0.0948, which means that this equation explains 9.48% of the changeability in object intention. Furthermore, this indicates a positive linear relationship of object

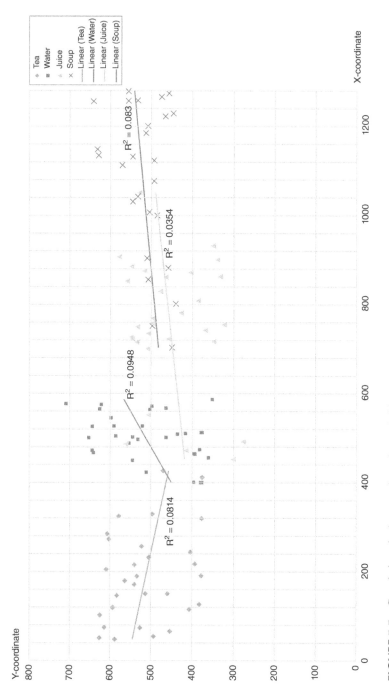

FIGURE 5.5 Correlation plot between intention and objects.

intention to the "glass of water." Next, object intention to the "glass of juice" refers to a linear regression analysis revealing a linear relationship. The coefficient of determination, R^2, is about 0.083, which means that this equation explains 8.3% of the changeability in object intention. Then, this indicates a positive linear relationship of object intention to the "glass of juice." Finally, object intention to the "bowl of soup" refers to a linear regression analysis revealing a linear relationship. The coefficient of determination, R^2, is about 0.0354, which means that this equation explains 3.54% of the changeability in object intention. Finally, this indicates a positive linear relationship of object intention to the "bowl of soup."

One detailed inference performance of the intention to the objects in the kitchen scenario is illustrated as a confusion matrix shown in Figure 5.6. Again, the horizontal axis is the predicted intention, and the vertical axis is the actual intention.

The precision and accuracy for each type of intention to the objects are summarized in Table 5.4. The precision of the intention to "teacup" was inferred in 0.93 of the cases. The precision of the intention to "glass of water" was inferred in 0.97 of the cases. The precision of the intention to "glass of juice" was inferred in 0.80 of the cases. Finally, the precision of the intention to "bowl of soup" was inferred in 0.77 cases. The overall accuracy rate was 86.7%. Notably, 13.3% of the error occurs due to the object variation in the kitchen scenario. With fewer dominant eye-gaze variations,

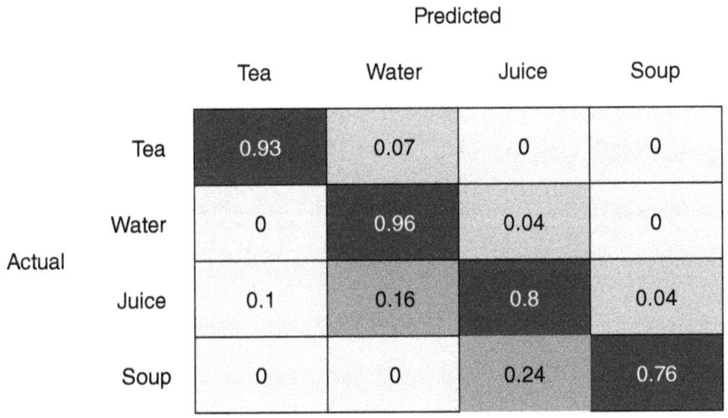

Predicted

		Tea	Water	Juice	Soup
	Tea	0.93	0.07	0	0
	Water	0	0.96	0.04	0
Actual	Juice	0.1	0.16	0.8	0.04
	Soup	0	0	0.24	0.76

FIGURE 5.6 Confusion matrix for the intention of the objects in the kitchen scenario.

TABLE 5.4
Accuracy and Precision of Intention to Each Object

Gaze intention	Accuracy (%)	Precision
Teacup	97.5	0.93
Glass of water	93.33	0.97
Glass of juice	89.17	0.80
Bowl of soup	93.33	0.77

it is more challenging to characterize the intention from the object aspect. The SVM model has less tolerance for the mistakes of the attention detection classifier.

5.6   USABILITY EVALUATION OF USE QUESTIONNAIRE

For all 30 questions, increasing raw scores were computed and then converted to percentages. The overall result of the USE questionnaire is summarized in Appendix 2, and the items that appeared across tests for the four factors are listed in Table 5.5. Also, the raw scores for each of the 30 participants were converted to normative Minnesota Satisfaction Questionnaire (MSQ) percentages shown.

Increasing raw scores were computed and converted to MSQ normative percentiles for all eight "Usefulness" questions. Table 5.5 shows the overall results for all "Usefulness" questions. The raw scores for every 30 participants were converted to MSQ normative percentile, as demonstrated in Figure 5.7. Of the participants, 4.17% had dissatisfaction, 2.91% had dissatisfaction, 13.33% had undecided, 37.5% had satisfaction, and 42.09% had high satisfaction.

TABLE 5.5
USE Results

		Likert scale				
Dimension	Cronbach's alpha (α)	Strongly disagree (%)	Disagree (%)	Undecided (%)	Agree (%)	Strongly agree (%)
Usefulness	0.93	4.17%	2.91%	13.33%	37.5%	42.09%
Ease of use	0.95	4.84%	8.78%	13.33%	34.27%	38.78%
Ease of learning	0.9	5.83%	5.84%	3.33%	40%	45%
Satisfaction	0.91	6.2%	6.67%	12.38%	32.38%	42.37%

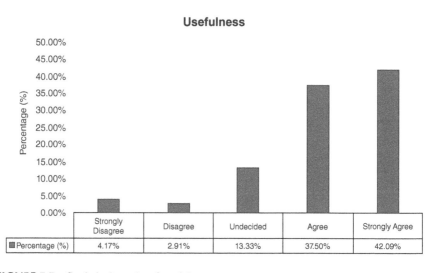

FIGURE 5.7   Statistical results of usefulness.

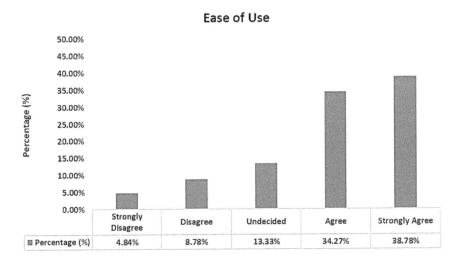

FIGURE 5.8 Statistical results of "Ease of Use."

For all 11 "Ease of Use" questions, increasing raw scores were computed and converted to MSQ normative percentiles. Table 5.5 shows the overall results for all "Ease of Use" questions. The raw scores for every 30 participants were converted to MSQ normative percentile, as demonstrated in Figure 5.8. Of the participants, 4.84% had very dissatisfaction, 8.78% had dissatisfaction, 13.33% had undecided, 34.27% had satisfaction, and 38.78% had high satisfaction.

Increasing raw scores were computed and converted to MSQ normative percentiles for all 11 "Ease of Learning" questions. Table 5.5 shows the overall results for all "Ease of Learning" questions. The raw scores for every 30 participants were converted to MSQ normative percentile, as demonstrated in Figure 5.9. Of the participants, 5.83% had very dissatisfaction, 5.84% had dissatisfaction, 3.33% has undecided, 40% had satisfaction, and 45% had high satisfaction.

Increasing raw scores were computed and converted to MSQ normative percentiles for all seven "Satisfaction" questions. Table 5.5 shows the overall results for all "Satisfaction" questions. The raw scores for every 30 participants were converted to the MSQ normative percentile, as shown in Figure 5.10. Of the participants, 6.2% had very dissatisfaction, 6.67% had dissatisfaction, 12.38% has undecided, 32.38% had satisfaction, and 42.37% had high satisfaction.

A typical camera was used to perform an algorithm assessment with 30 people. The accuracy and intention of each object are described in Table 5.4. The USE questionnaire had a reaction rate of 100%. The results of the respondents are described in Table 5.5. This study aims to show possible uses in elderly care in non-wearable technology. In the kitchen scenario, four objects were recognized from an elderly viewpoint. This technology can improve the quality of life of older people and lower the stress on care and operating costs. In addition, the suggested method is best suited for people with hearing loss, which may substantially impact all developmental domains, including language, knowledge, society, emotion, and behavior. Because of these possible developmental delays, people who are deaf or hard to hear are more likely than their typically developing counterparts to have mental health issues.

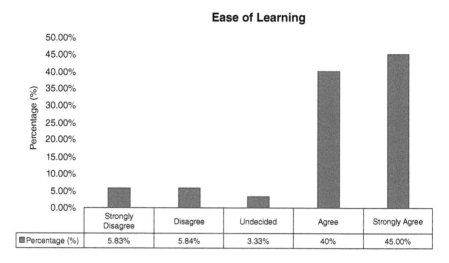

FIGURE 5.9   Statistical results of "Ease of Learning."

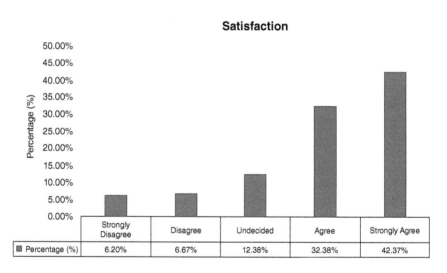

FIGURE 5.10   Statistical results of "Satisfaction."

REFERENCES

1. Morimoto, C. H., & Mimica, M. R. (2005). Eye gaze tracking techniques for interactive applications. Computer Vision and Image Understanding, 98(1), 4–24.
2. Erol, A., Bebis, G., Nicolescu, M., Boyle, R. D., & Twombly, X. (2007). Vision-based hand pose estimation: A review. Computer Vision and Image Understanding, 108(1–2), 52–73.
3. Sanjeewa, E. D. G., Herath, K. K. L., Madhusanka, B. G. D. A., Priyankara, H. D. N. S., & Herath, H. M. K. K. M. B. (2021). Understanding the hand gesture command to visual attention model for mobile robot navigation: service robots in domestic environment. In Cognitive Computing for Human-Robot Interaction (pp. 287–310). Academic Press.

4. Ahlstrom, C., Victor, T., Wege, C., & Steinmetz, E. (2011). Processing of eye/head-tracking data in large-scale naturalistic driving data sets. IEEE Transactions on Intelligent Transportation Systems, 13(2), 553–564.

5. Li, D., Babcock, J., & Parkhurst, D. J. (2006, March). openEyes: A low-cost head-mounted eye-tracking solution. In Proceedings of the 2006 Symposium on Eye Tracking Research & Applications (pp. 95–100). New York: Association for Computing Machinery.

6. Chen, Y. M., & Bajic, I. V. (2009). Motion vector outlier rejection cascade for global motion estimation. IEEE Signal Processing Letters, 17(2), 197–200.

7. Liu, J., Chi, J., Lu, N., Yang, Z., & Wang, Z. (2019). Iris feature-based 3-D gaze estimation method using a one-camera-one-light-source system. IEEE Transactions on Instrumentation and Measurement, 69(7), 4940–4954.

8. Madhusanka, B. G. D. A., Ramadass, S., Rajagopal, P., & Herath, H. M. K. K. M. B. (2022). Attention-aware recognition of activities of daily living based on eye gaze tracking. In Internet of Things for Human-Centered Design: Application to Elderly Healthcare (pp. 155–179). Singapore: Springer Nature.

9. Drewes, J., Masson, G. S., & Montagnini, A. (2012, March). Shifts in reported gaze position due to changes in pupil size: Ground truth and compensation. In Proceedings of the Symposium on Eye Tracking Research and Applications (pp. 209–212). New York: Association for Computing Machinery.

10. Wen, Q., Bradley, D., Beeler, T., Park, S., Hilliges, O., Yong, J., & Xu, F. (2020, May). Accurate real-time 3D gaze tracking using a lightweight eyeball calibration. In Computer Graphics Forum (Vol. 39, No. 2, pp. 475–485). Oxford: Blackwell Publishing Ltd.

11. Duchowski, A., & Duchowski, A. (2007). Eye tracking techniques. Eye tracking methodology: Theory and practice, 51–59.

12. Khan, M. Q., & Lee, S. (2019). Gaze and eye tracking: Techniques and applications in ADAS. Sensors, 19(24), 5540.

13. Singh, H., & Singh, J. (2012). Human eye tracking and related issues: A review. International Journal of Scientific and Research Publications, 2(9), 1–9.

14. Blascheck, T., Kurzhals, K., Raschke, M., Burch, M., Weiskopf, D., & Ertl, T. (2014, June). State-of-the-art of visualization for eye tracking data. In Eurovis (stars) (p. 29).

15. Sharafi, Z., Shaffer, T., Sharif, B., & Guéhéneuc, Y. G. (2015, December). Eye-tracking metrics in software engineering. In 2015 Asia-Pacific Software Engineering Conference (APSEC) (pp. 96–103). New Delhi: IEEE.

16. Chen, N. T., Clarke, P. J., MacLeod, C., & Guastella, A. J. (2012). Biased attentional processing of positive stimuli in social anxiety disorder: An eye movement study. Cognitive Behaviour Therapy, 41(2), 96–107.

17. Kunka, B., & Kostek, B. (2009, September). Non-intrusive infrared-free eye tracking method. In Signal Processing Algorithms, Architectures, Arrangements, and Applications SPA 2009 (pp. 105–109). IEEE.

18. Krafka, K., Khosla, A., Kellnhofer, P., Kannan, H., Bhandarkar, S., Matusik, W., & Torralba, A. (2016). Eye tracking for everyone. In Proceedings of the IEEE Conference on Computer Vision and Pattern Recognition (pp. 2176–2184). Las Vegas, NV: IEEE.

19. Ware, C., & Mikaelian, H. H. (1986, May). An evaluation of an eye tracker as a device for computer input2. In Proceedings of the SIGCHI/GI Conference on Human Factors in Computing Systems and Graphics Interface (pp. 183–188). New York: Association for Computing Machinery.

20. Venugopal, D., Amudha, J., & Jyotsna, C. (2016, May). Developing an application using eye tracker. In 2016 IEEE International Conference on Recent Trends in Electronics, Information & Communication Technology (RTEICT) (pp. 1518–1522). Bangalore: IEEE.

21. Duchowski, A. T. (2002). A breadth-first survey of eye-tracking applications. Behavior Research Methods, Instruments, & Computers, 34(4), 455–470.

22. Vertegaal, R. (1999, May). The GAZE groupware system: Mediating joint attention in multiparty communication and collaboration. In Proceedings of the SIGCHI Conference on Human Factors in Computing Systems (pp. 294–301). New York: Association for Computing Machinery.

23. Madhusanka, B. G. D. A., Ramadass, S., Rajagopal, P., & Herath, H. M. K. K. M. B. (2022). Biofeedback method for human-computer interaction to improve elder caring: Eye-gaze tracking. In Predictive Modeling in Biomedical Data Mining and Analysis (pp. 137–156). Academic Press.

24. Herath, H. M. K. K. M. B., & de Mel, W. R. (2021). Controlling an anatomical robot hand using the brain-computer interface based on motor imagery. Advances in Human-Computer Interaction, 2021, 1–15.

25. Madhusanka, B. G. D. A., & Ramadass, S. (2021). Implicit intention communication for activities of daily living of elder/disabled people to improve well-being. IoT in Healthcare and Ambient Assisted Living, 325–342.

26. Madhusanka, B. G. D. A., Ramadass, S., Premkumar, R., & Herath, H. M. K. K. M. B. (2022). Concentrated gaze base interaction for decision making using human-machine interface. Multimedia Computing Systems and Virtual Reality, 257–279.

27. Duncan, J., & Humphreys, G. W. (1989). Visual search and stimulus similarity. Psychological Review, 96(3), 433.

28. Park, H. M., Lee, S. H., & Choi, J. S. (2008, September). Wearable augmented reality system using gaze interaction. In 2008 7th IEEE/ACM International Symposium on Mixed and Augmented Reality (pp. 175–176). Cambridge: IEEE.

29. Cho, C. W., Lee, J. W., Shin, K. Y., Lee, E. C., Park, K. R., Lee, H., & Cha, J. (2012). Gaze detection by wearable eye-tracking and NIR LED-based head-tracking device based on SVR. ETRI Journal, 34(4), 542–552.

30. Rantanen, V., Vanhala, T., Tuisku, O., Niemenlehto, P. H., Verho, J., Surakka, V.,,. . . Lekkala, J. (2011). A wearable, wireless gaze tracker with integrated selection command source for human-computer interaction. IEEE Transactions on Information Technology in BioMedicine, 15(5), 795–801.

31. Stengel, M., Grogorick, S., Eisemann, M., Eisemann, E., & Magnor, M. A. (2015, October). An affordable solution for binocular eye tracking and calibration in head-mounted displays. In Proceedings of the 23rd ACM International Conference on Multimedia (pp. 15–24). New York: Association for Computing Machinery.

32. Land, M. F. (2004). The coordination of rotations of the eyes, head and trunk in saccadic turns produced in natural situations. Experimental Brain Research, 159, 151–160.

33. Land, M. F., & Hayhoe, M. (2001). In what ways do eye movements contribute to everyday activities? Vision Research, 41(25–26), 3559–3565.

34. Filik, R., Leuthold, H., Wallington, K., & Page, J. (2014). Testing theories of irony processing using eye-tracking and ERPs. Journal of Experimental Psychology: Learning, Memory, and Cognition, 40(3), 811.

35. Yu, C., Schermerhorn, P., & Scheutz, M. (2012). Adaptive eye gaze patterns in interactions with human and artificial agents. ACM Transactions on Interactive Intelligent Systems (TiiS), 1(2), 1–25.

36. Pelz, J., Hayhoe, M., & Loeber, R. (2001). The coordination of eye, head, and hand movements in a natural task. Experimental Brain Research, 139, 266–277.

37. Ugwitz, P., Kvarda, O., Juříková, Z., Šašinka, Č., & Tamm, S. (2022). Eye-tracking in interactive virtual environments: Implementation and evaluation. Applied Sciences, 12(3), 1027.

38. Wiebe, E. N., Minogue, J., Jones, M. G., Cowley, J., & Krebs, D. (2009). Haptic feedback and students' learning about levers: Unraveling the effect of simulated touch. Computers & Education, 53(3), 667–676.
39. Kangas, J., Rantala, J., Majaranta, P., Isokoski, P., & Raisamo, R. (2014, March). Haptic feedback to gaze events. In Proceedings of the Symposium on Eye Tracking Research and Applications (pp. 11–18). New York: Association for Computing Machinery.
40. Fanning, P. A., Hocking, D. R., Dissanayake, C., & Vivanti, G. (2018). Delineation of a spatial working memory profile using a non-verbal eye-tracking paradigm in young children with autism and Williams syndrome. Child Neuropsychology, 24(4), 469–489.
41. Cholewa, N., Wołk, K., & Wołk, R. (2018). Precise eye-tracking technology in medical communicator prototype. Procedia Computer Science, 138, 264–271.

6 The Challenges of Identifying Daily Living Activities Through Visual Behavior

Identifying daily living activities through visual behavior can be a challenging task due to several reasons [1, 2], including the following:

1. Complexity of activities: Daily living activities can involve multiple steps, making it difficult to identify them solely through visual behavior. For example, meal preparation may involve several steps, including selecting ingredients, chopping vegetables, and cooking on a stove. Each step may involve different visual cues that must be accurately identified to understand the overall activity [1].
2. Variability in activities: Different people may perform the same act differently, challenging identifying them through visual behavior. For example, a meal's preparation may vary depending on culture, personal preferences, or dietary restrictions.
3. Environmental factors: The environment in which an activity takes place can also affect its visual cues. For example, preparing a meal in a dimly lit kitchen may make it harder to identify visual cues accurately.
4. Limited availability of data: There is limited availability of data that can be used to train algorithms to accurately identify daily living activities through visual behavior. Collecting and annotating large datasets of activities is time-consuming and expensive.
5. Privacy concerns: Identifying daily activities through visual behavior may raise privacy concerns, as it involves capturing and analyzing people's movements and actions in their homes.

Despite these challenges, recent advances in computer vision and machine learning have made it possible to develop algorithms that can accurately identify daily living activities through visual behavior [3–5]. However, further research is needed to address these challenges and develop more robust and accurate methods for activity recognition.

Variability in the appearance of activities is another challenge to identifying daily living activities through visual behavior [6]. People may perform the same activity differently, using different objects or tools or following different steps. For example,

 DOI: 10.1201/9781003373940-6

two people preparing a meal may use different ingredients, cook in different pots or pans, or use different techniques for chopping vegetables. This variability can make developing computer vision algorithms that accurately recognize activities across individuals and contexts complex [7, 8].

To address this challenge, researchers can use techniques such as data augmentation, which involves creating variations of the same activity by changing certain features, such as the objects used or the environment in which the activity occurs [9]. This can help improve the generalization of algorithms and make them more robust to variability in the appearance of activities. Another approach is to develop personalized activity recognition models trained on data from a specific individual that can adapt to their unique movements. However, this approach requires collecting large amounts of data from each individual, which can be time-consuming and expensive.

The complexity of visual information can vary depending on various factors, such as the number of objects in the scene, their size and shape, the level of detail required, and the complexity of their relationships with other objects. For example, a simple image with only a few objects that are easy to distinguish and have clear boundaries will be less complex than an image with a cluttered background, overlapping objects, and intricate details. Furthermore, the complexity of visual information can be influenced by the observer's perception and cognitive abilities. For instance, a highly trained artist may be able to discern subtle differences and nuances in an image that an untrained individual may not even notice. Overall, the complexity of visual information is a multi-faceted concept that depends on various factors, including the characteristics of the image and the observer's cognitive and perceptual abilities [10–13].

Ambiguity in visual cues refers to situations where the visual information presented to an observer can be interpreted in multiple ways, leading to confusion or uncertainty about what is perceived. There are several reasons why ambiguity can occur in visual cues. One common reason is when the visual information is incomplete or lacks detail, making it difficult to determine what is being seen. Another reason is when there are multiple possible interpretations of the visual information, such as when viewing an optical illusion [14, 15].

Ambiguity can also arise when the visual information conflicts with other sensory information or prior expectations [16]. For example, visual information may suggest that an object is close, but other sensory cues (such as touch) may suggest that it is far away. Ambiguity in visual cues can be problematic in certain situations, such as tasks requiring accurate perception, decision-making, or action. However, it can also be helpful for creative thinking and problem-solving, prompting individuals to consider multiple interpretations and possibilities.

Limited data availability for daily living activities can refer to situations where there needs to be more information or data about an individual's daily activities and routines, such as their movements, behaviors, and interactions with their environment. This can occur for several reasons, such as the absence of monitoring devices or sensors, privacy concerns, or limitations in data collection methods. For example, monitoring an individual's activities in a private setting such as their home may be challenging, where they may need to be more comfortable installing cameras or sensors.

Limited data availability for daily living activities can have several implications [17]. For example, it may limit our ability to develop accurate models of human behavior or to understand the factors that influence it. It can also determine the effectiveness of interventions or treatments that rely on monitoring an individual's activities, such as elderly or disabled individuals who require assistance with daily living activities. To address this issue, researchers are developing new technologies and methods for monitoring and collecting data on daily living activities, such as wearable sensors, mobile apps, and other forms of assistive technology. However, privacy and ethical considerations must be carefully considered when implementing such technologies.

Privacy concerns for daily living activities refer to the potential risks and implications of monitoring an individual's activities, behaviors, and movements in their daily life [18]. Technology such as cameras, sensors, and wearable devices can provide valuable insights into an individual's daily activities and raise significant privacy concerns [19–21]. Some of the privacy concerns related to monitoring daily living activities include the following:

1. Invasion of privacy: Individuals may feel that monitoring their daily activities is intrusive and violates privacy.
2. Stigmatization: Monitoring may lead to stigmatization, particularly if the data is to stereotype or discriminate against certain groups of people.
3. Misuse of data: Data collected about an individual's daily activities may be misused, for example, by employers or insurance companies, to discriminate against individuals based on their life behavior.
4. Security risks: Collecting and storing data on an individual's daily activities may pose security risks, particularly if the data are sensitive or personal.

To address these privacy concerns, it is essential to establish clear guidelines and protocols for collecting, using, and storing data related to daily living activities. These guidelines should consider the individual's right to privacy, informed consent, and the potential risks and benefits of monitoring [22]. It is also important to ensure that the data collected are protected and used only for its intended purpose and that individuals have control over their data and how they are used.

Daily living activities' real-time and dynamic nature can pose significant challenges for real-time tracking and recognizing activities [23]. This is because daily living activities are constantly changing and may occur rapidly and unpredictably, making it difficult to capture and process the data in real time. Some of the challenges associated with tracking and recognizing daily living activities in real time include the following:

1. Variability: Daily living activities can vary significantly from person to person and from day to day, making it challenging to develop a universal system for tracking and recognition.
2. Contextual factors: Daily living activities are heavily influenced by contextual factors such as the environment, social interactions, and cultural norms, which can be challenging to capture and interpret in real time.
3. Sensor limitations: Many current sensors and monitoring devices have limitations in terms of their accuracy, range, and reliability, which can make it challenging to capture and process data in real time.

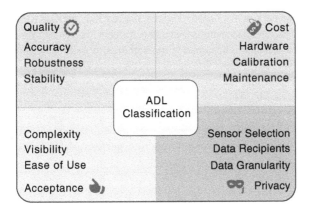

FIGURE 6.1   The challenges in ADL classification.

Researchers [24–30] are developing new real-time technologies and methods for tracking and recognizing daily activities to address these challenges. These include using machine learning algorithms and artificial intelligence to analyze data from sensors and monitoring devices, as well as the development of more advanced and versatile sensors and monitoring devices that can capture a broader range of data. Additionally, ongoing research is focused on improving the accuracy and reliability of these technologies to ensure that they can effectively track and recognize daily living activities in real time.

Figure 6.1 is likely a visual representation of the challenges that must be addressed for an ADL categorization system to be usable. By addressing these challenges, a categorization system for ADLs can be developed that is realistic, usable, and effective in providing valuable insights into an individual's daily activities and behaviors.

6.1   STATE OF THE ART IN SENSOR TECHNOLOGY TO ASSESS ADLs

Sensor technology has advanced significantly in recent years and has the potential to revolutionize the way we consider ADLs [31–33]. Here are some of the state-of-the-art sensor technologies used to determine ADLs:

1. Wearable sensors: These can be worn on the body, such as on the wrist or ankle, and can track a person's movements and activity levels. They can detect different movements, such as walking, running, and standing up, and provide insights into a person's physical activity and mobility [34, 35].
2. Ambient sensors: These are set in the environment, such as in a person's home or workplace, and can detect activity and movement in that space. They can detect different activities, such as cooking, cleaning, and using electronic devices, and provide insights into a person's daily routine and behaviors [36, 37].
3. Smart home technology includes a range of sensor-based systems and devices that can be integrated into a person's home to monitor their activity and support their independence. These systems can consist of sensors that

detect when a person has fallen, devices that remind a person to take medication, and smart home assistants that can respond to voice commands [38, 39].

4. Video-based sensors: These use video cameras to monitor a person's activity and movements. They can detect different activities, such as walking, sitting, and standing, and provide insights into a person's physical abilities and limitations [40, 41].

5. BCIs: These devices allow people to control computers or other devices using their brainwaves. They can be used to help people with physical disabilities to control their environment and perform daily tasks more efficiently [42–45].

Overall, state-of-the-art sensor technology for assessing ADLs is rapidly evolving, and innovations are constantly being developed. These technologies can improve the quality of life for people with disabilities and other health conditions by providing more accurate and detailed information about their daily activities and needs.

State of the art in sensor technology for assessing ADLs includes a variety of sensors that can capture visual, depth, motion, and audio information. These sensors can recognize and track ADLs in various settings, such as the home, workplace, and healthcare facilities. Here are some examples of these sensors:

1. Visual sensors: These sensors use cameras to capture images and videos of a person's surroundings. They can recognize objects and people in the environment and detect various movements and actions [40].

2. Depth sensors: These sensors use infrared light to create a 3D map of the environment, which can be used to detect the distance between objects and people. They can recognize different postures and movements, such as sitting, standing, and walking [40, 41].

3. Motion sensors use accelerometers and gyroscopes to detect movement and orientation. They can track a person's physical activity and monitor changes in posture and balance.

4. Audio sensors: These sensors use microphones to capture sound and can be used to detect different types of activities and events, such as talking, coughing, and opening/closing doors.

Combining these different types of sensors makes it possible to create a comprehensive picture of a person's ADLs and monitor changes over time. This can be especially useful in healthcare settings, where tracking a person's progress and identifying potential health issues is important.

Accurate and dependable sensor data are crucial for monitoring and classifying ADLs. The effectiveness of a sensor for ADL classification depends on several factors, including the type of sensor used, the placement of the sensor, and the quality of the sensor data. Several sensor types have been tested for ADL categorization, including accelerometers, gyroscopes, pressure sensors, and cameras. Each type of sensor has its strengths and weaknesses, and the choice of the sensor depends on the application's specific needs [46, 47].

The performance of an ADL monitoring system depends not only on the choice of the sensor but also on the system topology and the algorithms used for classification. Machine learning techniques, such as neural networks, decision trees, and SVMs, are commonly used for ADL classification tasks. Overall, accurate and dependable sensor data and effective system topology and classification algorithms are essential for successful ADL monitoring and categorization.

There are two basic types of sensors: Wearable and non-wearable [48]. Wearable sensors are typically attached directly to a person or their clothing to measure various physiological parameters, including motion characteristics, location, pulse rate, body temperature, blood pressure, and other important metrics. Some examples of wearable sensors include bracelet sensors, heart rate monitors, smartwatches, and fitness trackers. These sensors are often used to monitor physical activity, track fitness goals, and assess overall health.

On the other hand, non-wearable sensors are typically stationary and measure environmental factors such as temperature, humidity, and air quality. Examples of non-wearable sensors include temperature, light, and motion sensors placed in the environment to monitor changes [49]. Both wearable and non-wearable sensors have advantages and disadvantages, and the choice of the sensor depends on the application's specific needs. However, wearable sensors are often preferred for ADL monitoring and classification tasks as they provide more accurate and detailed information about a person's physical activity and physiological status.

Video-based systems are another ADL monitoring system where a camera is placed in a designated area inside a residence to detect human movement and other activities [50, 51]. These systems use computer vision algorithms to analyze video data and classify different ADLs. Video-based systems have several advantages over other sensor-based systems. For example, they can provide more detailed information about a person's movements and actions, including their posture, gestures, and facial expressions. They can also monitor multiple people simultaneously and detect subtle changes in activity patterns that other sensors may miss.

However, video-based systems also have some disadvantages [52]. For example, they may raise privacy concerns, as they can capture sensitive information about a person's behavior and activities. They also require more processing power and storage space than other types of sensors, making them more expensive and challenging to deploy. Overall, video-based systems can effectively monitor and classify ADL systems. Still, they must be used responsibly and ethically to protect the privacy and autonomy of the monitored individuals.

Privacy is a significant concern when using video-based ADL monitoring systems, and cameras can be intrusive and may compromise the privacy of the individual being monitored. A low-resolution heat sensor has been proposed as an alternative to a standard video camera for ADL monitoring. Heat or thermal sensors use infrared radiation to detect heat emitted by objects in their field of view. This technology can detect movement and track the presence of people in a room without capturing visual images that could invade privacy [53].

A low-resolution heat sensor instead of a traditional video camera may capture the same activity data without invading the user's privacy [54]. However, the sensor's effectiveness depends on the sensor's resolution and the distance between the sensor and the person being monitored. Overall, using low-resolution heat sensors may provide a useful compromise between ADL monitoring and preserving privacy. However, it is important to ensure that the sensor is used ethically and responsibly to protect the privacy and autonomy of the monitored individual.

Several sensors can identify human activity for ADL monitoring and classification. The choice of the sensor depends on the application's specific needs and the type of activities being monitored. Some standard sensors used for human activity detection include the following:

1. Accelerometers: Accelerometers are sensors that measure acceleration and can be used to detect movement and changes in motion [55]. They are often used in wearable devices such as fitness trackers and smartwatches to monitor physical activity.
2. Gyroscopes: Gyroscopes are sensors that measure rotational motion and can detect changes in orientation and movement [56]. They are often used with accelerometers to provide more accurate information about a person's movements.
3. Pressure sensors: Pressure sensors are used to detect changes in pressure and can be used to detect when a person is sitting, standing, or lying down [57]. They are often used in furniture, such as chairs and beds, to monitor a person's posture and activity.
4. Camera sensors: Camera sensors can detect human activity by analyzing visual information [58]. They can detect changes in posture, movement patterns, and facial expressions.
5. Microphone sensors: Microphone sensors can detect human activity by analyzing sound [59, 60]. They can detect changes in speech patterns, breathing, and other auditory cues.

Overall, the sensor's choice depends on the application's specific needs and the type of activities being monitored. Combining multiple types of sensors and using machine learning algorithms to classify activities makes creating an effective ADL monitoring system possible.

The use of ADL monitoring devices raises significant privacy concerns. These devices can collect a wealth of sensitive information about a person's daily activities, movements, and biometrics. This information could be used to infer personal information about a person's health, habits, and behavior, which could be used for various purposes, including targeted advertising, insurance underwriting, and law enforcement. The relationship between sensor granularity and user perception of privacy is important when designing ADL monitoring devices [61]. The more granular the data collected by the sensors, the more invasive the monitoring may be perceived by the user. For example, collecting data on a person's heart rate, blood pressure, and other biometrics may be perceived as more invasive than simply monitoring their physical activity.

It is important to design ADL monitoring devices with privacy in mind to address these privacy concerns. This may include implementing privacy-preserving technologies, such as differential privacy, which can help protect individual privacy while providing useful data for analysis. It may also involve implementing clear policies for data collection, storage, and use and allowing users to control their data. Overall, it is important to balance the benefits of ADL monitoring devices with the privacy concerns they raise. By designing devices with privacy in mind and providing users with transparency and control over their data, it may be possible to create effective ADL monitoring systems that respect individual privacy.

Video cameras that detect almost all human movement within their field of view can raise significant privacy concerns [62, 63]. While these cameras may be effective for ADL monitoring and classification, they can also capture sensitive information about a person's daily life and habits. In many cases, such cameras may be too invasive to be used in private spaces such as bedrooms or bathrooms, where people expect more privacy. Even in public spaces, such cameras can capture information about a person's physical characteristics, movements, and behavior, which could be used to identify or track individuals without their consent.

To address these privacy concerns, it may be necessary to implement more targeted and selective monitoring systems. This could involve using sensors with more limited fields of view or incorporating privacy-preserving technologies such as blurring or anonymization. It could also involve limiting data collection to specific times of the day or particular types of activities, such as monitoring only when a person performs a specific task rather than continuously monitoring all movements. Overall, the use of video cameras for ADL monitoring and classification must be balanced against the privacy concerns they raise. By implementing privacy-preserving technologies and limiting data collection to specific contexts, it may be possible to create effective monitoring systems while respecting individual privacy.

6.2   STATE OF THE ART IN ADL EXPERIMENTAL SETUPS

ADL experimental setups study and analyze human behavior during everyday activities. Significant research [64–66] has been conducted in this area, and several state-of-the-art experimental setups have been developed to assess and quantify human activity. One popular setup is a smart home environment with various sensors that monitor human activity, such as movement, temperature, and sound [67]. The data collected from these sensors can be used to understand how people interact with their surroundings and perform different tasks.

Another standard setup is wearable sensors that can be worn on the body to track physical activity, sleep patterns, and other parameters related to daily living [68–70]. These sensors can be embedded in clothing, jewelry, or other accessories, providing real-time data on the wearer's activity level. VR and AR setups also simulate ADL scenarios, allowing researchers to study human behavior in a controlled environment [71, 72]. These setups can provide a more immersive and interactive experience, making observing and analyzing specific behaviors easier. Overall, the state of the art in ADL experimental setups is continually evolving, with new technologies and methods being developed to understand human activity and behavior better.

A multi-camera system is another standard experimental setup used to study ADLs. This setup involves placing multiple cameras throughout a participant's home to capture visual information from different angles. The data collected from these cameras can be used to analyze the participant's behavior and activity patterns, including how they move around the house, interact with objects, and perform different tasks. This setup can provide a more comprehensive and detailed view of the participant's behavior compared with a single-camera setup.

One advantage of a multi-camera system is that it can capture data from different perspectives, which can help analyze complex activities. For example, suppose a participant is cooking in the kitchen. In that case, a multi-camera system can capture their movements from multiple angles, making it easier to analyze how they use different utensils and appliances. However, one potential limitation of this setup is that it can be challenging to manage and analyze large amounts of data generated by multiple cameras. To address this issue, researchers may use automated tracking algorithms to extract relevant information from the video data or employ human coders to annotate and analyze the footage manually. Overall, the multi-camera setup is a valuable tool for studying ADLs and can provide valuable insights into how people interact with their environment and perform everyday tasks.

Wearable sensors are a popular experimental setup for studying ADLs [30, 34]. These sensors can be worn on different body parts, such as the wrist, ankle, or chest. They can provide continuous data on physical activity, sleep patterns, and other health-related metrics. Wearable sensors, such as smartwatches and fitness trackers, often include a variety of sensors, such as accelerometers, heart rate monitors, and GPS, that can track movement and other physiological signals [73]. The data collected from these sensors can be used to monitor a participant's activity level, sleep quality, and other health-related metrics.

One advantage of using wearable sensors is that they are non-invasive and provide continuous real-time data [74]. Participants can wear the sensors throughout the day, and the data collected can provide insights into their activity level and behavior patterns over time. Another advantage is that wearable sensors can be used in various settings, including home, work, and outdoor environments, making them versatile tools for studying ADLs.

However, wearable sensors also have some limitations. For example, some participants may want to avoid wearing the sensors or forget to wear them, which can affect the data quality. Additionally, the data collected from wearable sensors may only be sometimes accurate, and researchers must be cautious when interpreting the results. Overall, wearable sensors are a valuable tool for studying ADLs, and they can provide valuable insights into how people move and behave in different settings.

Ambient sensors are another experimental setup used in ADL research [36, 75]. These sensors are designed to measure environmental factors such as temperature, humidity, light, and sound levels, providing contextual information that can be used to understand the conditions in which activities are performed. For example, ambient temperature sensors can measure the temperature of different rooms in a participant's home, providing information on how environmental factors may affect their behavior and activity patterns. Similarly, light sensors can measure the intensity and quality of light in a given space, providing insights into how lighting conditions may impact the performance of various activities.

One advantage of ambient sensors is that they provide a more comprehensive view of the environment where activities are performed. By collecting data on environmental factors, researchers can better understand how these factors may impact behavior and activity patterns. However, one potential limitation of using ambient sensors is that they only sometimes provide a complete picture of the environment. For example, while temperature sensors can measure the ambient temperature of a room, they may need help to capture localized temperature variations, such as those around heating or cooling vents. Overall, ambient sensors are a useful tool for studying ADLs, and they can provide valuable insights into how environmental factors may impact behavior and activity patterns.

VR and AR are emerging experimental setups used in ADL research [71, 72]. These technologies allow researchers to simulate ADL scenarios in a controlled environment, providing a standardized way to study and compare different methods for ADL recognition. VR involves creating a fully immersive, computer-generated environment that users can interact with using a VR headset and other input devices. Conversely, AR overlaps virtual objects with the real world, typically using a mobile device or headset. Both VR/AR can simulate various ADL scenarios, such as cooking, cleaning, and personal grooming, allowing researchers to control the conditions under which participants perform these activities. This can be useful for comparing different methods for ADL recognition, validating results, and understanding the underlying factors that influence ADL performance. One advantage of using VR and AR for ADL research is that they can provide a more controlled and standardized way to study ADLs. Researchers can control the variables influencing ADL performance by creating a simulated environment, such as lighting conditions, noise levels, and other environmental factors. This can help to ensure that the results are consistent and reliable.

However, one potential limitation of VR and AR is that they may only sometimes accurately represent real-world ADL scenarios. While these technologies can simulate many aspects of real-world environments, they may only partially capture the complexity and variability of real-world ADL scenarios. Overall, virtual and AR are promising experimental setups for studying ADLs, and they can provide valuable insights into the underlying factors that influence ADL performance.

State of the art in experimental setups for assessing ADLs often involves collecting data from participants in naturalistic settings using a variety of sensors to capture real-world ADLs. Researchers are constantly exploring new methods to improve the performance and robustness of these systems, and there are several emerging trends in this area. One direction is using multiple sensors to capture a more comprehensive view of ADL performance. By combining data from different types of sensors, such as accelerometers, gyroscopes, and ambient sensors, researchers can capture a complete picture of the activities and the environmental conditions in which they are performed [76].

Another trend is using VR/AR technologies to simulate ADL scenarios in a controlled environment. This can help to standardize the conditions under which ADLs are performed and make it easier to compare different methods for ADL recognition. Machine learning techniques are also increasingly being used to improve the performance and robustness of ADL recognition systems. These techniques can help to identify patterns in the data collected from sensors and enhance the accuracy of ADL recognition algorithms. Overall, state of the art in experimental setups for assessing ADLs is focused on improving the performance and robustness of these systems and increasing the realism and naturalness of the ADL scenarios being studied. As new technologies and techniques emerge, researchers will likely continue to explore new ways to improve the accuracy and reliability of ADL recognition systems.

The main goal of Ambient Assisted Living (AAL) is to use ambient intelligence to support and enhance the independence and quality of life of older adults living in their homes. One of the critical applications of AAL is in assessing ADLs, focusing on identifying any changes or abnormalities in the routines of older adults in their daily activities, such as eating, cooking, and bathing [77–79].

To achieve this goal, AAL researchers often use smart home technology to monitor the behavior of older adults in their homes. Smart home technology typically involves a range of sensors and devices installed throughout the house to gather data on the environment and the occupants' activities. These data can then be used to monitor the health and well-being of the occupants, identify any changes in behavior or routines, and alert caregivers or healthcare providers if any issues are detected.

A key advantage of AAL and smart home technology is that it allows older adults to continue living in their homes for longer while receiving the support and care they need. By using technology to monitor their behavior and provide timely interventions if needed, older adults can maintain their independence and quality of life while reducing the burden on caregivers and healthcare providers. Overall, AAL and smart home technology are important areas of research in the field of ambient intelligence, with the potential to improve the lives of older adults and support their continued independence and well-being.

The experimental conditions and requirements for smart home environments vary depending on the research goals and objectives. Some studies may use a natural home fitted with sensors to collect data on human behavior, while others may use a lab-based smart home environment where participants live temporarily. The kinds of sensors used in these smart home environments can also vary depending on the research objectives. For example, some studies may focus on energy efficiency and use sensors to monitor energy usage patterns in the home. In contrast, others may prioritize privacy concerns and use non-intrusive sensors to collect data on human behavior.

Additionally, the scenarios used in these studies can vary depending on the research objectives. Some studies may involve using carefully prepared scenarios to test activity detection algorithms, while others may focus on analyzing patterns of human behavior in a more naturalistic setting. Overall, the requirements for smart home environments in ambient intelligence research vary widely depending on the research goals and objectives. Researchers must carefully consider the experimental conditions and types of sensors used to ensure that the data collected are relevant and useful for their research.

Ambient intelligence research often involves lengthy, real-world studies in participants' homes or smart home environments. Smart homes are beneficial for testing activity identification algorithms because they provide a controlled environment that makes collecting and annotating accurate and balanced data easier. One of the key advantages of using smart home environments in ambient intelligence research is that they allow researchers to collect data on participants' behavior in a more naturalistic setting. This can provide valuable insights into how people interact with their environment and daily activities, which can be challenging to capture in a laboratory setting.

In addition, smart home environments can be used to test activity identification algorithms in a more controlled and standardized way. For example, by using cameras to capture video footage of participants carrying out specific activities, researchers can annotate the data and use it to train and test machine learning algorithms for activity identification. Overall, smart home environments are an important tool for ambient intelligence researchers, providing a valuable platform for collecting real-world data on human behavior and testing and refining activity identification algorithms.

Data gathered in real-world situations can be more representative of usual behavior and are thus more suited for testing algorithms for behavior modeling [80, 81]. Using ambient sensors such as door contact, motion, and float sensor in the bathroom can help to detect activity patterns and provide valuable insights into how people carry out their daily activities. For example, by analyzing data from a door contact sensor, researchers can determine when participants enter and exit different rooms in the house. By combining these data with information from a motion sensor, they can better understand the activities carried out in each room. Similarly, using a float sensor in the bathroom can help researchers detect when participants are taking a shower or a bath, providing valuable insights into their daily routines and behavior patterns. By using ambient sensors to collect data in real-world situations, researchers can develop more accurate models of human behavior and activity patterns, which can inform the design of smart home systems and other ambient intelligence technologies.

6.3   SUMMARY

Automated ADL classification is an important aspect of assisted living technology. ADLs are basic self-care tasks that individuals perform daily, such as bathing, dressing, grooming, feeding, and toileting. These tasks are essential for maintaining independence, and the ability to achieve them is often used as a measure of an individual's functional ability.

Automated ADL classification uses sensors and machine learning algorithms to monitor a senior's daily activities and determine their ability to perform ADLs independently. For example, a sensor in the bathroom can detect when a senior enters and leaves the shower. The machine learning algorithm can use this information to determine if the senior can bathe independently.

Automated ADL classification can provide valuable insights into a senior's functional ability and help caregivers and healthcare professionals make informed decisions about the senior's care. It can also alert caregivers if there is a decline in a senior's ability to perform ADLs, which can help prevent accidents and hospitalizations.

Early identification of dementia and Alzheimer's disease is crucial for effective treatment and management. ADL classification can play an important role in the early identification of these conditions by monitoring changes in a senior's daily activities and routines. ADL classification can be carried out using various sensors, including wearable and non-wearable sensors. Wearable sensors, such as smartwatches and fitness trackers, can monitor seniors' physical activity and detect any changes in their activity levels. Non-wearable motion and pressure sensors can be installed in elders' homes to monitor their movements and activities. The deployment of ADL classification can also vary depending on the senior's needs and circumstances. For example, sensors can be installed in specific home areas, such as the bathroom and kitchen, to monitor specific activities. Alternatively, a comprehensive sensor network can be established throughout the home to monitor continuously.

Signal processing and machine learning strategies are also important components of ADL classification. Signal processing techniques extract helpful information from the sensor data, such as identifying patterns in a senior's movements and activities. Machine learning algorithms can then be applied to the processed data to automatically classify the senior's activities and determine their ability to perform ADLs independently. Overall, ADL classification using wearable and non-wearable sensors, deployment options, signal processing, and machine-learning strategies can help identify early signs of dementia and Alzheimer's disease, enabling timely intervention and better management of the condition.

Eye-gaze methods involve eye-tracking technology to monitor a person's gaze and determine their focus of attention. This technology can assess a senior's ability to perform specific tasks, such as cooking or reading, by tracking their gaze as they interact with objects in the environment. Eye-gaze methods can be non-wearable, using cameras or other sensors to track the person's gaze, or wearable, using specialized glasses or head-mounted displays. Both eye-gaze techniques have advantages and disadvantages, depending on the use case. Signal processing and machine learning algorithms often analyze the data collected by eye-gaze methods and classify the senior's activities and abilities. These techniques can detect changes in gaze patterns over time, which may indicate cognitive decline or other health issues. Overall, the use of eye-gaze methods in ADL classification is an active area of research, and the effectiveness of non-wearable eye-gaze methods compared with wearable methods may depend on the specific use case and the quality of the data collected.

The ability to reuse sensors from smart home apps can help reduce the overall infrastructure and installation costs of ADL monitoring systems. Smart home devices, such as motion and door sensors, can be repurposed for ADL monitoring, eliminating the need for additional sensors to be installed. This can also make it easier to scale ADL monitoring systems to accommodate more seniors or expand to new locations. However, as you mentioned, legal data ownership and security issues must be addressed before ADL monitoring devices can be used. Seniors and their families may be concerned about who owns the data collected by ADL monitoring systems and how it is used. In addition, there may be legal requirements around data privacy and security that must be met.

To address these issues, ADL monitoring systems must be designed with data privacy and security in mind. This includes implementing robust security measures to protect the data collected by the sensors and providing clear and transparent information about data ownership and use.

In addition, it may be necessary to work with legal and regulatory experts to ensure that ADL monitoring systems comply with all relevant laws and regulations. This can help build trust with seniors and their families and ensure that the ADL monitoring systems are legally and ethically sound. Addressing legal issues related to data ownership and security is an important step in developing and adopting ADL monitoring systems. By prioritizing data privacy and security, ADL monitoring systems can help seniors maintain their independence and provide their families and caregivers peace of mind.

Involving seniors in the design and implementation of ADL monitoring systems is crucial for ensuring that the systems are user-friendly and meet the needs and preferences of the users. User-centered design principles, prioritizing the needs and perspectives of the end-users, can help ensure that ADL monitoring systems are intuitive, accessible, and acceptable to seniors.

Involving seniors in the design process can also help address privacy and technology acceptance concerns. By engaging seniors in data privacy and security discussions and providing clear and transparent information about how their data will be used, ADL monitoring systems can help build trust and improve seniors' comfort with using technology in their homes.

In addition to involving seniors in the design process, it is also important to provide ongoing support and training to ensure elders are comfortable and confident using ADL monitoring systems. This can help ensure that the systems are used correctly and can help seniors overcome any barriers or challenges they may encounter.

As sensor technology advances, it is important to keep seniors at the center of ADL monitoring system design and implementation. By prioritizing openness, user-centered design, and ongoing support and training, ADL monitoring systems can help seniors maintain their independence and improve their quality of life while addressing privacy and technology acceptance concerns.

Familiarity with sensor technology in other aspects of life can help increase consumer understanding and acceptance of vision sensor technology for ADL monitoring. As sensor technology becomes more prevalent in our daily lives, such as security cameras or smart home devices, consumers may become more comfortable using sensors for ADL monitoring in their homes. Familiarity with sensor technology can also help address privacy and data security concerns, as consumers may already be familiar with the types of data sensors can collect and how that data can be used. This can help build trust and improve acceptance of ADL monitoring systems that use vision sensors.

In addition, clear and transparent communication about how vision sensor technology is used for ADL monitoring can help improve consumer understanding and acceptance. Information about the data types being collected, how that data is being used, and what privacy and security measures are in place can help build trust and improve consumer confidence in ADL monitoring systems. As consumers become more familiar with sensor technology in other aspects of their lives, they may become more comfortable using vision sensors for ADL monitoring. Clear communication and transparency around data privacy and security can also help improve understanding and acceptance of ADL monitoring systems.

Investigating the human gaze as an effective and intuitive human–user interaction is an important area of research in HCI and related fields. Eye-tracking technology to monitor and analyze human gaze patterns can provide valuable insights into how people interact with computers and other digital devices and can inform the design of more effective and user-friendly interfaces.

This book focuses on the scientific investigation of the human gaze as a form of HCI. It may cover topics such as the physiological and cognitive factors that influence gaze behavior, the use of eye-tracking technology for interface design and evaluation, and the development of gaze-based interaction techniques for specific applications. Overall, this book may interest researchers and practitioners in HCI, usability engineering, and user experience design, as well as those interested in the broader implications of gaze-based interaction for human cognition and behavior.

The study described in this thesis focuses on developing a method for users to express intuitively what tasks they naturally concentrate on as the subject of their attention in a given situation. This may involve eye-tracking technology or other methods for monitoring and analyzing users' gaze behavior and attentional focus.

This study may improve the usability and effectiveness of digital interfaces and other interactive systems by allowing users to provide more natural and intuitive input based on their attentional focus. By enabling users to express their natural attentional priorities, designers and developers can create more personalized and user-friendly interfaces that better meet the needs and preferences of individual users. Overall, this study may interest researchers and practitioners in HCI, usability engineering, and user experience design, as well as those interested in the broader implications of attentional focus for human cognition and behavior.

The investigation described in **Chapters 2 and 3** involved a study of a specific two-dimensional (2D) eye-gaze estimation method and its practical implementation. The purpose of this investigation may have been to evaluate the accuracy and effectiveness of the technique and explore its potential applications in various contexts. Eye-gaze estimation methods are commonly used in HCI, VR, and medical research to monitor and analyze users' gaze behavior. 2D eye-gaze estimation refers to using cameras and image processing algorithms to track the position of the user's eyes and estimate their PoG on a 2D plane. The practical implementation of the 2D eye-gaze estimation method may have involved the development of software or hardware tools for capturing and analyzing users' gaze behavior in real-world settings. This may have included designing and constructing custom hardware, developing software algorithms for processing gaze data, and testing and validating the system in various contexts. Overall, the investigation and practical implementation of a 2D eye-gaze estimation method may interest researchers and practitioners in fields such as HCI, VR, and medical research, as well as those interested in the broader implications of eye-gaze behavior for human cognition and behavior.

Chapters 4 and 5 describe developing a method for analyzing user eye-gaze data to infer their visual attention during ADLs. This may involve using ANN classifiers to identify patterns in the gaze data and make predictions about the user's attentional focus. Also, analyze ADLs to understand better how users allocate their attention during these activities. This may include using observational methods or other monitoring and analyzing user behavior. Also, it describes the development of a webcam-based gaze-tracking system for capturing user eye-gaze data. This system may be designed to capture the upper body of subjects to capture the image of both eyes and improve the accuracy of gaze tracking. Finally, **Chapters 4 and 5** may interest researchers and practitioners in fields such as HCI, artificial intelligence, and assistive technology, as well as those interested in the broader implications of eye-gaze behavior and attentional focus for human cognition and behavior.

The experiments involved in **Chapters 4 and 5** were a calibration and gaze estimation procedure for the participant's left and right eyes. The calibration process may have involved asking participants to look at calibration points or targets. In contrast, the gaze estimation procedure may have involved tracking the movement of the eyes using specialized software or hardware. After the calibration and gaze estimation procedures were completed for both eyes, the final PoG was calculated by averaging the PoG values obtained for the left and right eyes. This approach may help improve the gaze estimation accuracy, as it considers any differences in calibration or tracking performance between the left and right eyes. Overall, the experiments described may interest researchers and practitioners in HCI, VR, and medical research, as accurate and reliable gaze estimation is crucial for many applications in these fields.

A study was conducted to investigate the use of 2D gaze as a means of commanding caregivers to perform various tasks. The study may have involved participants who were elderly or had disabilities and used gaze-based interfaces to communicate with their caregivers. The study's results may have shown that participants could use 2D gaze to command their caregivers to perform tasks effectively. This may suggest that gaze-based interfaces have the potential to be a valuable and practical means of communication for individuals who have difficulty with traditional forms of communication.

In addition, the study may have included subjective evaluations of the gaze-based interfaces, demonstrating that participants found the modality practical and easy to learn. This may suggest that gaze-based interfaces have the potential to be widely accepted and adopted by users, which could have important implications for the development of assistive technologies and other applications of gaze-based interaction. The study may interest researchers and practitioners in HCI, assistive technology, and healthcare. It demonstrates the potential of gaze-based interfaces to improve communication and enable greater independence for individuals with disabilities or other challenges.

6.4 OUTCOME OF THE RESEARCH

An ANN-based eye-gaze communication system can effectively help older people who are deaf and disabled to communicate with their caregivers and others around them. Developing such a system involves several steps, including collecting and processing eye-gaze data, training an ANN to recognize and interpret different patterns of eye-gaze movements, and designing a user interface that enables users to communicate effectively using their eyes. The primary three outcomes of the research are described in the following.

6.4.1 To Develop the Neural Network-Based Implicit Intention Algorithm

Developing a neural network-based implicit intention algorithm involves several key steps. Here is a general outline of the process:

1. Define the problem: Determine the specific task you want the neural network to perform, such as recognizing different patterns of eye-gaze movements or inferring the user's intention based on their eye movements.
2. Collect data: Gather a large dataset of eye-gaze data from individuals performing the task you want the neural network to function. Ensure that the dataset is diverse and representative of the population you are designing the system for.
3. Preprocess the data: Clean and preprocess the dataset to remove any noise or irrelevant data. This may involve filtering, segmentation, or normalization techniques.
4. Train the neural network: Choose a neural network architecture and train it on the preprocessed data using a supervised or unsupervised learning approach. This involves adjusting the weights and biases of the network through multiple iterations until it achieves high accuracy.
5. Evaluate the performance: Test the neural network on a separate dataset to evaluate its performance and identify any potential issues or areas for improvement.
6. Fine-tune the network: Adjust the network architecture or training parameters as needed to improve its performance.
7. Implement the algorithm: Once the algorithm has been developed and tested, integrate it into the eye-gaze communication system and test it in a real-world setting.
8. Monitor and update the system: Continuously monitor the system's performance and update the algorithm as needed to ensure optimal performance and accuracy.

These steps are general guidelines, and the specifics of each stage may vary depending on the particular task and dataset. Developing a neural network-based implicit intention algorithm requires expertise in machine learning, data processing, and software development, so working with a team of experts in these areas may be helpful. The development of the ANN-based gaze vector estimation system involved a few important steps:

1. Mapping calibration markers to gaze vector functions: To train the neural network to estimate gaze vectors, calibration markers were used to establish the relationship between the user's eye movements and the corresponding gaze vectors.
2. Organizing gaze point coordinates: The neural network's output was organized to represent the gaze point's horizontal and vertical coordinates.
3. Estimating gaze vectors before training: An initial estimate of the gaze vectors was made before training the neural network using the calibration data.

4. Exploring hidden layer configurations: To improve the accuracy of the gaze vector estimation, various hidden layer configurations were tested to identify the optimal architecture for the neural network. This included testing different types of hidden units and the number of nodes in each layer.
5. Final architecture: The final architecture of the neural network included an input layer with four nodes, an output layer with two nodes (representing the horizontal and vertical coordinates of the gaze point), and a hidden layer with five nodes.

This approach demonstrates the importance of careful calibration and model selection when developing a gaze vector estimation system using ANNs. By testing various hidden layer configurations, the researchers could identify a neural network architecture that achieved the desired level of accuracy.

6.4.2   To Develop a Person-Independent System for Gaze Direction Classification

Developing a person-independent system for gaze direction classification involves creating a machine learning algorithm that can accurately classify gaze direction without relying on individualized calibration data. Here are some general steps that could be followed to develop such a system:

1. Gather training data: Collect a large dataset of gaze direction data from multiple individuals, covering a range of gaze directions and head positions. Ensure that the dataset is diverse and representative of the population you are designing the system for.
2. Preprocess the data: Clean and preprocess the dataset to remove any noise or irrelevant data. This may involve filtering and segmentation normalization techniques.
3. Feature extraction: Extract relevant features from the preprocessed data. For example, you might use a CNN to extract features from images of the user's eyes or use an algorithm to detect changes in the user's gaze direction over time.
4. Train the model: Train a machine learning algorithm on the preprocessed data using a supervised learning approach. This may involve using various algorithms, such as decision trees, SVMs, or deep neural networks, to find the best-performing model.
5. Evaluate the model: Test the trained model on a separate dataset to evaluate its performance and identify any potential issues or areas for improvement.
6. Fine-tune the model: Adjust the model parameters or algorithm to improve its performance.
7. Validate the model: Test the final model on a more extensive dataset to validate its performance and ensure it can accurately classify gaze direction across various individuals and conditions.
8. Implement the system: Once the model has been developed and validated, integrate it into a gaze direction classification system and test it in a real-world setting.

Monitor and update the system: Continuously monitor the system's performance and update the algorithm as needed to ensure optimal performance and accuracy. Developing a person-independent system for gaze direction classification requires expertise in machine learning, data processing, and software development, so working with a team of experts in these areas may be helpful.

6.4.3   To Develop a Framework for User Intention Recognition Using Eye-Gaze Tracking

Recognizing user intention through eye-gaze tracking can create more natural and intuitive human–computer interfaces. Here's a framework that can be used for user intention recognition using eye-gaze tracking:

1. Eye-gaze data collection: The first step in the framework is to collect eye-gaze data. Eye-gaze data can be collected through eye-tracking devices such as Tobii Pro or EyeTribe. The data should be collected on user intention, such as selecting an item, scrolling through content, or navigating a menu.
2. Feature extraction: The next step is to extract features from the eye-gaze data. This can include information such as gaze dura, gaze position, and saccade velocity. Feature extraction is an important step because it creates more accurate machine-learning models.
3. Machine learning model: A machine learning model can recognize user intentions based on the extracted features. The model can be trained using various algorithms such as decision trees, random forests, or SVMs. The model's accuracy can be improved by tuning hyperparameters and cross-validation techniques.
4. Integration with user interface: Once the machine learning model has been developed and validated, it can be integrated with the user interface. This can be done by mapping eye-gaze data to specific actions within the interface. For example, if the user looks at a particular button for a certain amount of time, the machine learning models the user's intention user intends to select that button.
5. User testing and refinement: The final step is to test the system with users and refine the model based on feedback. User testing can help identify any usability issues or areas for improvement. The model can be refined by adding features or adjusting the algorithm to improve accuracy.

Above this framework, it is possible to develop an effective system for recognizing user intentions using eye-gaze tracking. This can help create more natural and intuitive user interfaces that improve the overall user experience.

6.5   CONTRIBUTIONS

The research described in the statement has contributed to three fundamental problems in designing and developing an ANN-based system for gaze-based communication:

1. Gaze point estimation: One of the primary challenges in developing an ANN-based system for gaze-based communication is accurately estimating the user's gaze point. The research has addressed this problem by developing a novel ANN for estimating gaze points. This is a significant contribution, as accurate gaze point estimation is critical for effective communication.
2. Implicit intention detection: Another challenge in gaze-based communication is detecting the user's intention. The research has addressed this problem by developing an implicit intention algorithm for gaze-based communication. This algorithm detects the user's intention based on their gaze behavior without requiring explicit commands or gestures. This is a significant contribution, making gaze-based communication more natural and intuitive.
3. Eldercare: The research has also contributed to applying gaze-based communication in elder care. This is an important study area, as elder care is a growing concern in many societies. Gaze-based communication can help improve the quality of life for elderly individuals by providing them with a more natural and intuitive way to communicate with caregivers and family members.

Overall, the research described in the statement has important contributions to developing an ANN-based system for gaze-based communication. These contributions have addressed critical challenges in the field and have the potential to improve the lives of individuals who rely on such systems.

The thesis aims to examine eye gazing as a natural and effective method of interaction with human users to develop a way for users to express their desires to caregivers naturally and intuitively. Specifically, the study focuses on developing a method for users to indicate which chores they want their caregivers to perform by looking at an object of interest in a manufactured kitchen environment.

By examining eye gazing as a method of interaction, the study is likely to contribute to the growing body of research on natural and intuitive HCI. Eye gazing has the potential to be a powerful tool for communication, particularly for individuals who have difficulty with other forms of communication, such as speech or gesture.

The focus on developing a method for users to indicate which chores they want their caregivers to perform is particularly relevant to elder care. As the elderly population grows, the need for effective and efficient caregiving solutions is increasing. By providing a natural and intuitive way for elderly individuals to communicate their needs and desires to their caregivers, the method developed in this study can potentially improve the quality of life for many elderly individuals.

Overall, the thesis is likely to contribute to our understanding of eye gazing as a method of interaction and has the potential to positively impact the lives of individuals in need of caregiving support.

In this context, a database of 6,000 photographs taken with a typical camera was used to evaluate the approach. The approach, presumably an image recognition or classification algorithm, was tested for accuracy using these photographs. The results showed an average accuracy of 90.83% for a four-way classification task. To further test the algorithm's robustness, the researchers exposed it to various modifications, including noise, adjustments to brightness and contrast, rotation, and blurring. The algorithm's performance was evaluated for each improvement to assess its qualitative robustness.

The results showed that introducing noise was the most critical component affecting the algorithm's performance. This finding suggests that the algorithm may be susceptible to noise in the images it processes. It also highlights the importance of considering the impact of image quality and modifications when developing image recognition or classification algorithms.

Overall, this research demonstrates the algorithm's effectiveness in classifying images, with a high level of accuracy achieved on a large dataset of typical photographs. The study also highlights the importance of evaluating an algorithm's robustness by exposing it to various modifications that may affect image quality, providing insights into potential weaknesses and areas for improvement.

In this study, an algorithm was assessed by 30 people using a webcam. The study aimed to explore how non-wearable technology can improve elder care. The participants were asked to rate a 2D eye-gaze system for daily life designed to assist elderly individuals in communicating their needs and desires. The survey results showed that 78.14% of respondents gave the system a favorable rating. However, more than 11.26% of respondents gave the system a bad rating. Additionally, 10.6% of those who needed clarification about the method provided further details.

The study suggests that using non-wearable technology, such as the 2D eye-gaze system, can improve the quality of life for older people by easing the strain of caregiving and lowering operating costs. The study used a kitchen environment with four items, as viewed from the perspective of an older adult, to demonstrate how technology can assist with daily tasks. Furthermore, the study suggests that the technology can benefit those with hearing loss. Individuals with hearing loss are more likely to experience developmental delays in language, knowledge, society, emotion, and behavior, which can substantially impact their cognitive health. Therefore, technology could be a valuable tool for improving communication and enhancing the quality of life for this population. Overall, the study demonstrates the potential of non-wearable technology in improving elder care and communication for individuals with hearing loss. However, the study also highlights the importance of considering user feedback to improve the usability and effectiveness of such systems.

In this study, a camera method was developed to calibrate and identify a user's gaze on a computer screen. The method was designed to enable older people to interact with machines using HCI and vision-based activity detection. The study aimed to fuse senior support programs with vision-based activity detection to provide an implicit intention strategy for ADL at home. The researchers found that the 2D gazing mode could be changed into an interactive mode to teach caregivers how to do common chores, making it easier for older people to use and understand. The researchers recorded and analyzed the user's eye-gaze motions to infer the user's aim. Based on their research on implicit intention communication for older citizens engaging in everyday activities, the study suggests that this approach can enhance user engagement. Overall, the study demonstrates the potential of using vision-based activity detection and HCI to improve elder care by providing a more natural and intuitive way for older people to interact with machines. Providing an implicit intention strategy for ADL at home can help ease the strain of caregiving and enhance the quality of life for older adults.

6.6 LIMITATIONS

The system will limit the limitations of the proposed eye-gaze tracking framework for user intention recognition.

1. The proposed eye-gaze tracking framework for user intention recognition may not work as effectively on smaller screens or objects. The experiment used a 15-inch laptop screen and a specific masking area to capture more efficiently gazes. If the object size is reduced, the masking area is also reduced, potentially making it more difficult for elderly users to focus on an object for more than five seconds. This may limit the system's usability for older people needing help focusing or requiring larger objects for visibility.
2. The proposed eye-gaze tracking framework may be limited to screen or object size. However, it may still be effective for specific applications or user groups, particularly for older people with limited resources. Considering the size and visibility of objects when designing the system, optimizing its performance and usability for specific users or contexts may be possible. For example, the system could be designed to use larger objects or screens to make it easier for elderly users to focus on and interact with the system. Overall, it is important to consider the potential limitations of the proposed framework and explore ways to address or work around those limitations to maximize its benefits for users.
3. Optimize the proposed eye-gaze tracking framework for user intention recognition in the kitchen scenario to maximize the utilization of objects within humans' 40-mm^2 eye-gaze working area. This could involve designing the system to prioritize objects that are most relevant or important for daily activities in the kitchen, such as appliances, utensils, and food items. Objects could be positioned within the working area to make them more easily accessible and visible to users, and the system could be programmed to recognize and respond to gaze movements toward these objects. By maximizing the utilization of objects within the eye-gaze working area, the system could improve its usability and effectiveness for elderly users who may have difficulty focusing on smaller objects or screens. It could also help to streamline and simplify everyday activities in the kitchen, reducing the strain on caregivers and improving the quality of life for elderly individuals.

This research has focused on elder caring in a home environment with low-cost and minimum facilities. The proposed eye-gaze tracking framework for user intention recognition was developed to improve the quality of life for elderly individuals and reduce the burden on caregivers. The system was designed to be easy to use and understand, even for individuals with limited resources and abilities. The goal was to provide a non-intrusive and affordable solution for elder care that could be implemented in a wide range of home environments.

6.7   RECOMMENDATIONS AND FUTURE WORK

The proposed eye-gaze tracking framework for user intention recognition has some limitations related to pupil detection and head position modification. A head posture adjustment algorithm is recommended to improve the system's accuracy. While the study has shown the potential of using 2D gaze as a natural and effective interaction modality, several issues still need to be addressed before the gaze-based interaction modality can be further developed. These issues may include improving pupil detection accuracy and reliability, reducing head movement impact on gaze tracking, and developing better calibration and calibration-free techniques for gaze estimation. Additionally, the size and visibility of objects may need to be considered when designing the system for specific users or contexts.

6.7.1   Multimodal Interaction

In summary, while the gaze modality has shown potential as a single interaction method in the workplace, multimodal interfaces are generally more versatile and reliable. Research has shown that combining multiple modalities can improve information processing and accuracy. The gaze interaction mode may also benefit from using other modes to increase effectiveness. However, it is important to consider the user's experience and avoid burdening them with excessive gaze contact. The optimal combination of interaction modes and how work should be distributed among them is an ongoing area of research.

Multimodal interaction with eye-gaze tracking involves integrating gaze tracking technology with other input and output modalities to provide a more natural and effective way for users to interact with devices. This approach can help overcome some limitations and challenges of using gaze tracking as a standalone modality and improve user experience and task performance. For instance, combining gaze tracking with voice commands or gesture recognition can provide users with additional ways to interact with devices and improve accessibility for users with different abilities and preferences.

Another example of HCI using eye-gaze tracking is gaze-based interaction to trigger actions, such as clicking a button or selecting an option, by fixating on the target for a certain amount of time. This technique is called dwell-based interaction and can also be helpful for users with mobility impairments or for hands-free operation in certain situations, such as in industrial or medical settings. Additionally, eye-gaze tracking can be combined with voice input for more efficient and natural interaction, such as in virtual assistants or in-car systems.

Gaze-based interaction can also be used with other modalities to create more versatile and efficient HCI systems. For example, a user might use gaze-based interaction to control the cursor while using a keyboard for text input and voice commands to control other system aspects. This multimodal approach can improve the overall user experience and accessibility of the system.

Eye gaze can also be used to scroll or zoom in and out on a screen by looking at specific areas, making it easier for users with limited mobility to navigate digital content. Additionally, eye gaze can select text or images on a screen, allowing users to copy, paste, or move content without physically manipulating the touchpad. Eye-gaze tracking combined with other modalities can enhance the usability and accessibility of various technologies. For example, in virtual and AR, eye-gaze tracking can be used to improve the realism and interactivity of the experience, allowing users to interact with objects in the virtual environment simply by looking at them. Moreover, combining eye-gaze tracking with voice commands or hand gestures can further enhance the usability and versatility of the system.

Combining eye-gaze tracking technology with other forms of input and output can result in more versatile and reliable interaction methods. It enables people with different abilities to interact with technology in a more accessible way. Additionally, combining multiple modalities can speed up information processing, improve comprehension accuracy, and create more immersive experiences. Overall, multimodal interaction using eye-gaze tracking technology can revolutionize how we interact with technology in various settings.

6.7.2 Validation of Users With Special Needs

One of the advantages of using eye-gaze tracking in HCI is its potential to improve accessibility for individuals with disabilities. Gaze-based interaction can be an effective and straightforward way for individuals with limited mobility or motor impairments to interact with computers and other devices. It is important to consider the specific needs of individuals with disabilities when designing and evaluating gaze-based interaction systems and to develop strategies for generalizing these systems to a wide range of users.

Eye-tracking technology has a lot of potential applications, but it is still a relatively new and evolving technology. As more research is done and the technology improves, we can expect to see even more innovative and valuable applications of eye tracking in various fields. There have been significant improvements in eye-tracking technology in recent years, including the development of more affordable, accurate, and user-friendly devices. Video-based eye-tracking systems are now widely available and offer a non-invasive and reliable method for tracking eye movements. Additionally, calibration procedures have become more streamlined and straightforward, making eye-tracking technology more accessible to researchers and practitioners. While cost can still be a barrier for some, the increasing availability of eye-tracking systems and their potential benefits for research and applications make them an increasingly valuable tool.

Another way to validate eye-gaze tracking technology for users with special needs is to collaborate with healthcare professionals, therapists, and other experts who work with the specific population. They can provide valuable feedback on the technology's usability and effectiveness for their clients/patients. This can help to identify any limitations or challenges with the technology and inform improvements or modifications to make it more accessible and effective for users with special needs. It is also essential to consider the ethical implications of using eye-gaze tracking technology with users with special needs. Privacy and informed consent are crucial considerations, as well as ensuring that the technology does not cause harm or discomfort to the users. Therefore, it is important to involve the users in the validation process and to consider their feedback and preferences when developing and refining the technology.

Controlled experiments can also validate eye-gaze tracking with special needs users. These experiments can involve comparing the performance of eye-gaze tracking with other input or eye-tracking technology and measuring factors such as accuracy, speed, and user satisfaction. By conducting these experiments, researchers can better understand the strengths and limitations of eye-gaze tracking for users with special needs and identify ways to improve the technology to meet their needs better.

It is important to ensure that technology is designed and developed with accessibility and inclusivity in mind and validated for diverse users, including those with special needs. This requires careful consideration of ethical and privacy concerns and providing appropriate documentation, training, and technical support to users with special needs. By taking these steps, we can ensure that eye-gaze tracking technology is a valuable tool for enhancing the lives of all users, regardless of their abilities or disabilities.

Interdisciplinary collaboration is crucial in eye-tracking research, as it involves a range of technical, methodological, and theoretical expertise. Collaborating across different fields can help ensure that the research is rigorous and comprehensive and that the findings are meaningful and applicable in real-world contexts. For example, in developing eye-tracking systems and software, engineering, computer science, and HCI, experts may need to work together to ensure that the technology is accurate, reliable, and user-friendly. Similarly, in designing and implementing eye-tracking studies, experts in psychology, neuroscience, and education may need to collaborate to ensure the research is theoretically grounded and relevant to the target population.

REFERENCES

1. Land, M. F. (2006). Eye movements and the control of actions in everyday life. Progress in Retinal and Eye Research, 25(3), 296–324.
2. Wang, P., & Smeaton, A. F. (2013). Using visual lifelogs to characterize everyday activities automatically. Information Sciences, 230, 147–161.
3. Nayak, A., & Dutta, K. (2017, June). Impacts of machine learning and artificial intelligence on mankind. In 2017 International Conference on Intelligent Computing and Control (I2C2) (pp. 1–3). Coimbatore: IEEE.
4. Wan, S., Qi, L., Xu, X., Tong, C., & Gu, Z. (2020). Deep learning models for real-time human activity recognition with smartphones. Mobile Networks and Applications, 25, 743–755.
5. Leo, M., Medioni, G., Trivedi, M., Kanade, T., & Farinella, G. M. (2017). Computer vision for assistive technologies. Computer Vision and Image Understanding, 154, 1–15.
6. Pirsiavash, H., & Ramanan, D. (2012, June). Detecting activities of daily living in first-person camera views. In 2012 IEEE Conference on Computer Vision and Pattern Recognition (pp. 2847–2854). Providence, RI: IEEE.
7. Yao, B., & Fei-Fei, L. (2010, June). Modeling mutual context of object and human pose in human-object interaction activities. In 2010 IEEE Computer Society Conference on Computer Vision and Pattern Recognition (pp. 17–24). San Francisco, CA: IEEE.
8. Murphy-Chutorian, E., & Trivedi, M. M. (2008). Head pose estimation in computer vision: A survey. IEEE Transactions on Pattern Analysis and Machine Intelligence, 31(4), 607–626.

9. Alzubaidi, L., Zhang, J., Humaidi, A. J., Al-Dujaili, A., Duan, Y., Al-Shamma, O.,. . . Farhan, L. (2021). Review of deep learning: Concepts, CNN architectures, challenges, applications, future directions. Journal of Big Data, 8, 1–74.

10. Rokni, S. A., Nourollahi, M., & Ghasemzadeh, H. (2018, April). Personalized human activity recognition using convolutional neural networks. In Proceedings of the AAAI Conference on Artificial Intelligence (Vol. 32, No. 1). New Orleans, LA: AAAI Press.

11. Madhusanka, B. G. D. A., Ramadass, S., Rajagopal, P., & Herath, H. M. K. K. M. B. (2022). Attention-aware recognition of activities of daily living based on eye gaze tracking. In Internet of Things for Human-Centered Design: Application to Elderly Healthcare (pp. 155–179). Singapore: Springer Nature.

12. Pettersson, R. (1993). Visual information. Educational Technology.

13. Juhel, J. (1991). Spatial abilities and individual differences in visual information processing. Intelligence, 15(1), 117–137.

14. Green, A. M., & Angelaki, D. E. (2003). Resolution of sensory ambiguities for gaze stabilization requires a second neural integrator. Journal of Neuroscience, 23(28), 9265–9275.

15. Madhusanka, B. G. D. A., Ramadass, S., Rajagopal, P., & Herath, H. M. K. K. M. B. (2022). Biofeedback method for human–computer interaction to improve elder caring: Eye-gaze tracking. In Predictive Modeling in Biomedical Data Mining and Analysis (pp. 137–156). Cambridge: Elsevier.

16. Kornmeier, J., & Bach, M. (2012). Ambiguous figures–what happens in the brain when perception changes but not the stimulus. Frontiers in Human Neuroscience, 6, 51.

17. Götschi, T., Garrard, J., & Giles-Corti, B. (2016). Cycling as a part of daily life: A review of health perspectives. Transport Reviews, 36(1), 45–71.

18. Mustafa, M. A., Konios, A., & Garcia-Constantino, M. (2021). IoT-based activities of daily living for abnormal behavior detection: Privacy issues and potential countermeasures. IEEE Internet of Things Magazine, 4(3), 90–95.

19. Klasnja, P., Consolvo, S., Choudhury, T., Beckwith, R., & Hightower, J. (2009, May). Exploring privacy concerns about personal sensing. In International Conference on Pervasive Computing (pp. 176–183). Berlin, Heidelberg: Springer.

20. AL-mawee, W. (2012). Privacy and security issues in IoT healthcare applications for the disabled users a survey (Thesis, Western Michigan University).

21. Lorenzen-Huber, L., Boutain, M., Camp, L. J., Shankar, K., & Connelly, K. H. (2011). Privacy, technology, and aging: A proposed framework. Ageing International, 36, 232–252.

22. Adams, R. J., Lichter, M. D., Krepkovich, E. T., Ellington, A., White, M., & Diamond, P. T. (2014). Assessing upper extremity motor function in practice of virtual activities of daily living. IEEE Transactions on Neural Systems and Rehabilitation Engineering, 23(2), 287–296.

23. Yoshida, H., Faust, A., Wilckens, J., Kitagawa, M., Fetto, J., & Chao, E. Y. S. (2006). Three-dimensional dynamic hip contact area and pressure distribution during activities of daily living. Journal of Biomechanics, 39(11), 1996–2004.

24. Fortin-Simard, D., Bilodeau, J. S., Bouchard, K., Gaboury, S., Bouchard, B., & Bouzouane, A. (2015). Exploiting passive RFID technology for activity recognition in smart homes. IEEE Intelligent Systems, 30(4), 7–15.

25. Qiu, S., Zhao, H., Jiang, N., Wang, Z., Liu, L., An, Y.,. . . Fortino, G. (2022). Multi-sensor information fusion based on machine learning for real applications in human activity recognition: State-of-the-art and research challenges. Information Fusion, 80, 241–265.

26. Bouchabou, D., Nguyen, S. M., Lohr, C., LeDuc, B., & Kanellos, I. (2021). A survey of human activity recognition in smart homes based on IoT sensors algorithms: Taxonomies, challenges, and opportunities with deep learning. Sensors, 21(18), 6037.

27. Diraco, G., Rescio, G., Siciliano, P., & Leone, A. (2023). Review on human action recognition in smart living: Sensing technology, multimodality, real-time processing, interoperability, and resource-constrained processing. Sensors, 23(11), 5281.

28. Bharucha, A. J., Anand, V., Forlizzi, J., Dew, M. A., Reynolds III, C. F., Stevens, S., & Wactlar, H. (2009). Intelligent assistive technology applications to dementia care: Current capabilities, limitations, and future challenges. The American Journal of Geriatric Psychiatry, 17(2), 88–104.

29. Gurbuz, S. Z., & Amin, M. G. (2019). Radar-based human-motion recognition with deep learning: Promising applications for indoor monitoring. IEEE Signal Processing Magazine, 36(4), 16–28.

30. Pantelopoulos, A., & Bourbakis, N. G. (2009). A survey on wearable sensor-based systems for health monitoring and prognosis. IEEE Transactions on Systems, Man, and Cybernetics, Part C (Applications and Reviews), 40(1), 1–12.

31. Thakur, N., & Han, C. Y. (2021). An ambient intelligence-based human behavior monitoring framework for ubiquitous environments. Information, 12(2), 81.

32. Mihailidis, A., Boger, J., Czarnuch, S., Jiancaro, T., & Hoey, J. (2012). Ambient assisted living technology to support older adults with dementia with activities of daily living: Key concepts and the state of the art. In Handbook of Ambient Assisted Living (pp. 304–330). Amsterdam: IOS Press.

33. Madhusanka, B. G. D. A., & Ramadass, S. (2021). Implicit intention communication for activities of daily living of elder/disabled people to improve well-being. IoT in Healthcare and Ambient Assisted Living, 325–342.

34. Liu, J., Sohn, J., & Kim, S. (2017). Classification of daily activities for the elderly using wearable sensors. Journal of Healthcare Engineering, 2017.

35. Bang, S., Kim, M., Song, S. K., & Park, S. J. (2008, August). Toward real time detection of the basic living activity in home using a wearable sensor and smart home sensors. In 2008 30th Annual International Conference of the IEEE Engineering in Medicine and Biology Society (pp. 5200–5203). Vancouver, BC: IEEE.

36. Roy, N., Misra, A., & Cook, D. (2016). Ambient and smartphone sensor assisted ADL recognition in multi-inhabitant smart environments. Journal of Ambient Intelligence and Humanized Computing, 7, 1–19.

37. Nef, T., Urwyler, P., Büchler, M., Tarnanas, I., Stucki, R., Cazzoli, D.,. . . Mosimann, U. (2012). Evaluation of three state-of-the-art classifiers for recognition of activities of daily living from smart home ambient data. Sensors, 15(5), 11725–11740.

38. Herath, H. M. K. K. M. B., & Mittal, M. (2022). Adoption of artificial intelligence in smart cities: A comprehensive review. International Journal of Information Management Data Insights, 2(1), 100076.

39. Herath, H. M. K. K. M. B., Karunasena, G. M. K. B., Madhusanka, B. G. D. A., & Priyankara, H. D. N. S. (2021). Internet of medical things (IoMT) enabled TeleCOVID system for diagnosis of COVID-19 patients. Sustainability measures for COVID-19 pandemic, 253–274.

40. Karunachandra, R. T. H. S. K., & Herath, H. M. K. K. M. B. (2021). Binocular vision-based intelligent 3-D perception for robotics application. International Journal of Scientific and Research Publications (IJSRP), 10(09), 689–696.

41. Sanjeewa, E. D. G., Herath, K. K. L., Madhusanka, B. G. D. A., Priyankara, H. D. N. S., & Herath, H. M. K. K. M. B. (2021). Understanding the hand gesture command to visual attention model for mobile robot navigation: Service robots in domestic environment. In Cognitive Computing for Human-Robot Interaction (pp. 287–310). Cambridge: Elsevier.

42. Nicolas-Alonso, L. F., & Gomez-Gil, J. (2012). Brain computer interfaces, a review. Sensors, 12(2), 1211–1279.

43. Shih, J. J., Krusienski, D. J., & Wolpaw, J. R. (2012, March). Brain-computer interfaces in medicine. In Mayo clinic proceedings (Vol. 87, No. 3, pp. 268–279). Elsevier.

44. Herath, H. M. K. K. M. B., & de Mel, W. R. (2021). Controlling an anatomical robot hand using the brain-computer interface based on motor imagery. Advances in Human-Computer Interaction, 2021, 1–15.

45. Herath, H. M. K. K. M. B., de Mel, W. R., & Mittal, M. (2023). Brain-computer inter-facing for flexion and extension of bio-inspired robot fingers. International Journal of Cognitive Computing in Engineering, 4, 89–99.
46. Baig, M. M., Afifi, S., GholamHosseini, H., & Mirza, F. (2019). A systematic review of wearable sensors and IoT-based monitoring applications for older adults–a focus on ageing population and independent living. Journal of Medical Systems, 43, 1–11.
47. Zhu, H., Samtani, S., Chen, H., & Nunamaker Jr, J. F. (2020). Human identification for activities of daily living: A deep transfer learning approach. Journal of Management Information Systems, 37(2), 457–483.
48. Herath, H. M. K. K. M. B., Prematilake, R. D. D., & Madhusanka, B. G. D. A. (2022). Integration of fog computing and IoT-based energy harvesting (EHIoT) model for wire-less sensor network. Energy Conservation Solutions for Fog-Edge Computing Para-digms, 215–231.
49. Irfan, M., Jawad, H., Felix, B. B., Abbasi, S. F., Nawaz, A., Akbarzadeh, S.,. . . Chen, W. (2021). Non-wearable IoT-based smart ambient behavior observation system. IEEE Sensors Journal, 21(18), 20857–20869.
50. Jalal, A., Kamal, S., & Kim, D. (2017). A depth video-based human detection and activ-ity recognition using multi-features and embedded hidden Markov models for health care monitoring systems. International Journal of Interactive Multimedia & Artificial Intelligence, 4(4), 54–62.
51. Debes, C., Merentitis, A., Sukhanov, S., Niessen, M., Frangiadakis, N., & Bauer, A. (2016). Monitoring activities of daily living in smart homes: Understanding human behavior. IEEE Signal Processing Magazine, 33(2), 81–94.
52. Pareek, P., & Thakkar, A. (2021). A survey on video-based human action recognition: Recent updates, datasets, challenges, and applications. Artificial Intelligence Review, 54, 2259–2322.
53. Henderson, M., & Phillips, M. (2015). Video-based feedback on student assessment: Scarily personal. Australasian Journal of Educational Technology, 31(1).
54. Gochoo, M., Tan, T. H., Huang, S. C., Batjargal, T., Hsieh, J. W., Alnajjar, F. S., & Chen, Y. F. (2019). Novel IoT-based privacy-preserving yoga posture recognition system using low-resolution infrared sensors and deep learning. IEEE Internet of Things Journal, 6(4), 7192–7200.
55. Stikic, M., Huynh, T., Van Laerhoven, K., & Schiele, B. (2008, January). ADL rec-ognition based on the combination of RFID and accelerometer sensing. In 2008 Sec-ond International Conference on Pervasive Computing Technologies for Healthcare (pp. 258–263). Tampere: IEEE.
56. Casilari, E., Álvarez-Marco, M., & García-Lagos, F. (2020). A study of the use of gyro-scope measurements in wearable fall detection systems. Symmetry, 12(4), 649.
57. Cepriá-Bernal, J., & Pérez-González, A. (2021). Dataset of tactile signatures of the human right hand in twenty-one activities of daily living using a high spatial resolution pressure sensor. Sensors, 21(8), 2594.
58. Nguyen, T. H. C., Nebel, J. C., & Florez-Revuelta, F. (2016). Recognition of activities of daily living with egocentric vision: A review. Sensors, 16(1), 72.
59. Medjahed, H., Istrate, D., Boudy, J., & Dorizzi, B. (2009, August). Human activities of daily living recognition using fuzzy logic for elderly home monitoring. In 2009 IEEE International Conference on Fuzzy Systems (pp. 2001–2006). Jeju: IEEE.
60. Fleury, A., Vacher, M., & Noury, N. (2009). SVM-based multimodal classification of activities of daily living in health smart homes: Sensors, algorithms, and first experimental results. IEEE Transactions on Information Technology in Biomedicine, 14(2), 274–283.
61. Woznowski, P., Fafoutis, X., Song, T., Hannuna, S., Camplani, M., Tao, L.,. . . Crad-dock, I. (2015, June). A multi-modal sensor infrastructure for healthcare in a residen-tial environment. In 2015 IEEE International Conference on Communication Workshop (ICCW) (pp. 271–277). London: IEEE.

62. Adams, A. A., & Ferryman, J. M. (2015). The future of video analytics for surveillance and its ethical implications. Security Journal, 28, 272–289.

63. Moeslund, T. B., Hilton, A., & Krüger, V. (2006). A survey of advances in vision-based human motion capture and analysis. Computer Vision and Image Understanding, 104(2–3), 90–126.

64. Andriluka, M., Pishchulin, L., Gehler, P., & Schiele, B. (2014). 2d human pose estimation: New benchmark and state of the art analysis. In Proceedings of the IEEE Conference on Computer Vision and Pattern Recognition (pp. 3686–3693). Columbus, OH: IEEE.

65. Nweke, H. F., Teh, Y. W., Al-Garadi, M. A., & Alo, U. R. (2018). Deep learning algorithms for human activity recognition using mobile and wearable sensor networks: State of the art and research challenges. Expert Systems with Applications, 105, 233–261.

66. Angerer, J., Ewers, U., & Wilhelm, M. (2007). Human biomonitoring: State of the art. International Journal of Hygiene and Environmental Health, 210(3–4), 201–228.

67. Bianchi, V., Bassoli, M., Lombardo, G., Fornacciari, P., Mordonini, M., & De Munari, I. (2019). IoT wearable sensor and deep learning: An integrated approach for personalized human activity recognition in a smart home environment. IEEE Internet of Things Journal, 6(5), 8553–8562.

68. Teixeira, E., Fonseca, H., Diniz-Sousa, F., Veras, L., Boppre, G., Oliveira, J.,. . . Marques-Aleixo, I. (2021). Wearable devices for physical activity and healthcare monitoring in elderly people: A critical review. Geriatrics, 6(2), 38.

69. Gokalp, H., & Clarke, M. (2013). Monitoring activities of daily living of the elderly and the potential for its use in telecare and telehealth: A review. Telemedicine and e-Health, 19(12), 910–923.

70. Herath, H. M. K. K. M. B., Karunasena, G. M. K. B., & Mittal, M. (2022). Monitoring the impact of stress on facial skin using affective computing. In Predictive Analytics of Psychological Disorders in Healthcare: Data Analytics on Psychological Disorders (pp. 55–85). Singapore: Springer Nature.

71. Fathima, S. J., Shankar, S., & Thajudeen, A. A. (2018). Activities of daily living rehab game play system with augmented reality based gamification therapy for automation of post stroke upper limb rehabilitation. Journal of Computational and Theoretical Nanoscience, 15(5), 1445–1451.

72. El Miedany, Y., & El Miedany, Y. (2019). Virtual reality and augmented reality. Rheumatology teaching: the art and science of medical education, 403–427.

73. Liao, L. D., Wang, Y., Tsao, Y. C., Wang, I. J., Jhang, D. F., Chuang, C. C., & Chen, S. F. (2020). Design and implementation of a multifunction wearable device to monitor sleep physiological signals. Micromachines, 11(7), 672.

74. Rofouei, M., Sinclair, M., Bittner, R., Blank, T., Saw, N., DeJean, G., & Heffron, J. (2011, May). A non-invasive wearable neck-cuff system for real-time sleep monitoring. In 2011 International Conference on Body Sensor Networks (pp. 156–161). Dallas, TX: IEEE.

75. Zhou, F., Jiao, J. R., Chen, S., & Zhang, D. (2010). A case-driven ambient intelligence system for elderly in-home assistance applications. IEEE Transactions on Systems, Man, and Cybernetics, Part C (Applications and Reviews), 41(2), 179–189.

76. Logan, B., & Healey, J. (2006, August). Sensors to detect the activities of daily living. In 2006 International Conference of the IEEE Engineering in Medicine and Biology Society (pp. 5362–5365). New York: IEEE.

77. Yared, R., & Abdulrazak, B. (2016). Ambient technology to assist elderly people in indoor risks. Computers, 5(4), 22.

78. Nehmer, J., Becker, M., Karshmer, A., & Lamm, R. (2006, May). Living assistance systems: An ambient intelligence approach. In Proceedings of the 28th International Conference on Software Engineering (pp. 43–50). New York: Association for Computing Machinery.

79. Cook, D. J., Augusto, J. C., & Jakkula, V. R. (2009). Ambient intelligence: Technologies, applications, and opportunities. Pervasive and Mobile Computing, 5(4), 277–298.
80. Cartas, A., Radeva, P., & Dimiccoli, M. (2020). Activities of daily living monitoring via a wearable camera: Toward real-world applications. IEEE Access, 8, 77344–77363.
81. Chung, S., Jeong, C. Y., Lim, J. M., Lim, J., Noh, K. J., Kim, G., & Jeong, H. (2022). Real-world multimodal lifelog dataset for human behavior study. ETRI Journal, 44(3), 426–437.

Index

Note: Page numbers in *italics* indicate a figure and page numbers in **bold** indicate a table on the corresponding page.